# Parental Involvement Across European Education Systems

This book addresses central questions regarding parental involvement across European educational systems; exploring the commonalities and differences across European countries and the extent to which current policy and practice pertaining to parental involvement is inclusive of diversity.

Adopting an interdisciplinary approach that draws from the fields of education, sociology and psychology, it presents a description of the policy context and empirical research on critical perspectives relating to parental involvement. Comprising a rich varied cross-section of national experiences from eleven European countries and the contexts surrounding them, case studies provide insights into parental involvement across Europe and identify challenges in the field.

This volume's in-depth approach and comprehensive interrogation of parental involvement across European education systems make it an ideal resource for parents, teachers and academics, researchers and post-graduate students in the fields of education policy and comparative education, as well as teacher educators and policy makers.

**Angelika Paseka** is Full Professor in Education at the University of Hamburg, Germany. She has expertise in teacher professionalism research, parental involvement and qualitative research methods.

**Delma Byrne** is a Sociology Lecturer at Maynooth University, Ireland. Her work focuses on comparative social stratification and the sociology of education.

# Routledge Research in International and Comparative Education

This is a series that offers a global platform to engage scholars in continuous academic debate on key challenges and the latest thinking on issues in the fast-growing field of International and Comparative Education.

Titles in the series include:

**Education and the Public Sphere**
Exploring the Structures of Mediation in Post-Colonial India
*Edited by Suresh Babu G. S.*

**Comparative Perspectives on Refugee Youth Education**
Dreams and Realities in Educational Systems Worldwide
*Edited by Alexander W. Wiseman, Lisa Damaschke-Deitrick, Ericka Galegher, and Maureen F. Park*

**50 Years of US Study Abroad Students**
Japan as the Gateway to Asia and Beyond
*Sarah R. Asada*

**Informal Learning and Literacy among Maasai Women**
Education, Emancipation and Empowerment
*Taeko Takayanagi*

**Parental Involvement Across European Education Systems**
Critical Perspectives
*Edited by Angelika Paseka and Delma Byrne*

For more information about this series, please visit: www.routledge.com/Routledge-Research-in-International-and-Comparative-Education/book-series/RRICE

# Parental Involvement Across European Education Systems
Critical Perspectives

Edited by Angelika Paseka and
Delma Byrne

LONDON AND NEW YORK

First published 2020
by Routledge
2 Park Square, Milton Park, Abingdon, Oxon OX14 4RN

and by Routledge
52 Vanderbilt Avenue, New York, NY 10017

*Routledge is an imprint of the Taylor & Francis Group, an informa business*

© 2020 selection and editorial matter, Angelika Paseka and Delma Byrne; individual chapters, the contributors

The right of Angelika Paseka and Delma Byrne to be identified as the authors of the editorial material, and of the authors for their individual chapters, has been asserted in accordance with sections 77 and 78 of the Copyright, Designs and Patents Act 1988.

All rights reserved. No part of this book may be reprinted or reproduced or utilised in any form or by any electronic, mechanical, or other means, now known or hereafter invented, including photocopying and recording, or in any information storage or retrieval system, without permission in writing from the publishers.

*Trademark notice*: Product or corporate names may be trademarks or registered trademarks, and are used only for identification and explanation without intent to infringe.

*British Library Cataloguing-in-Publication Data*
A catalogue record for this book is available from the British Library

*Library of Congress Cataloging-in-Publication Data*
A catalog record has been requested for this book

ISBN: 978-1-138-47919-7 (hbk)
ISBN: 978-1-351-06634-1 (ebk)

Typeset in Bembo
by Integra Software Services Pvt. Ltd.

# Contents

| | |
|---|---|
| *List of contributors* | vii |
| Introduction<br>ANGELIKA PASEKA AND DELMA BYRNE | 1 |
| 1 Cyprus<br>Depicting the landscape of school–family relationships and family–school involvement in Cyprus<br>LOIZOS SYMEOU | 8 |
| 2 Germany<br>Parental involvement in Germany<br>ANGELIKA PASEKA AND DAGMAR KILLUS | 21 |
| 3 Iceland<br>Home–school cooperation in Iceland: characteristics and values<br>KRISTÍN JÓNSDÓTTIR AND AMALÍA BJÖRNSDÓTTIR | 36 |
| 4 Ireland<br>Parental involvement in Ireland<br>DELMA BYRNE | 49 |
| 5 The Netherlands<br>Parental involvement in the Netherlands<br>EDDIE DENESSEN | 64 |
| 6 Norway<br>Parental involvement in Norway – ideals and realities<br>UNN-DORIS K. BÆCK | 77 |
| 7 Portugal<br>Family involvement and participation in schools in Portugal: the difficulty in sharing responsibilities<br>EVA GONÇALVES | 90 |

8 Slovenia
Overprotective parenthood: parental involvement in
the educational trajectories of their children in Slovenia 104
ANDREJA ŽIVODER AND MIRJANA ULE

9 Sweden
Parental involvement in Sweden exemplified through national policy
on homework support 120
MARIE KARLSSON, STINA HALLSÉN AND JOHANNA SVAHN

10 Switzerland
Parental involvement and career decision-making: the case of
Switzerland 133
MARKUS P. NEUENSCHWANDER

11 United Kingdom
Divided and United Kingdom: parents in education and the
common issue of inequality across the diversity
of four nations 149
SARAH CHRISTIE AND JOANNA APPS

12 United Kingdom
Parental involvement: a feminist critical review from a UK
perspective 162
MIRIAM E. DAVID

13 Home-based parental involvement and parental perception of schools
A cross-country analysis 175
PAULÍNA KORŠŇÁKOVÁ AND MIROSLAV ŠTEFÁNIK

14 Parental involvement across European education systems
A critical conclusion 191
DELMA BYRNE AND ANGELIKA PASEKA

*Index* 201

# Contributors

**Dr Loizos Symeou** is Professor in Sociology of Education and Vice-Rector of Academic Affairs at the European University Cyprus.

**Dr Angelika Paseka** is Full Professor in Education at the University of Hamburg, Faculty of Education.

**Dr Dagmar Killus** is Full Professor in Education at the University of Hamburg, Faculty of Education.

**Dr Kristín Jónsdóttir** is Assistant Professor in Pedagogy at the School of Education at the University of Iceland.

**Dr Amalía Björnsdóttir** is Professor in Research Methodology at the School of Education at the University of Iceland.

**Dr Delma Byrne** is Lecturer at Maynooth University Departments of Sociology and Education.

**Dr Eddie Denessen** is Professor in Socio-Cultural Diversity and Education at Leiden University and Associate Professor in the Department of Education at Radboud University, Nijmegen, the Netherlands.

**Dr Unn-Doris K. Bæck** is Professor at UiT The Arctic University of Norway, Department of Social Sciences.

**Dr Eva Gonçalves** is integrated researcher at CICS.NOVA and Lecturer at Nova University of Lisbon, Department of Sociology.

**Dr Andreja Živoder** is Assistant Professor at the Chair of Theoretical Sociology and researcher at the Centre for Social Psychology at the Faculty of Social Sciences, University of Ljubljana, Slovenia.

**Dr Mirjana Ule** is Professor and founder of a research centre, Centre for Social Psychology, at the Faculty of Social Sciences, University of Ljubljana, Slovenia.

**Dr Marie Karlsson** is Senior Lecturer at the Uppsala University Department of Education.

**Dr Stina Hallsén** is Lecturer at the Uppsala University Department of Education.

**Dr Johanna Svahn** is Lecturer at the Uppsala University Department of Education.

**Dr Markus P. Neuenschwander** is Professor and head of a research center at the University of Applied Sciences and Arts Northwestern Switzerland and at the University of Basel, Switzerland.

**Dr Sarah Christie** is Senior Research Fellow in the Research Centre for Children, Families and Communities at Canterbury Christ Church University, UK.

**Joanna Apps** is Senior Lecturer in the Research Centre for Children, Families and Communities at Canterbury Christ Church University, UK.

**Dr Miriam E. David** is Professor Emerita in Sociology of Education, University College London, Institute of Education.

**Dr Paulína Koršňáková** is Senior Research and Liaison Advisor to IEA, the International Association for Evaluation of Educational Achievement.

**Dr Miroslav Štefánik** is Researcher at the Institute of Economic Research of the Slovak Academy of Science.

# Introduction

*Angelika Paseka and Delma Byrne*

**Why this volume is necessary and innovative**

While both commonalities and differences exist with regard to parental involvement across European educational systems, there is a dearth of comparative and critical examination of the issue. This book aims to contribute to the research literature, and is unique in its treatment of parental involvement as a feature of *European* education systems. Here, we provide an in-depth examination of the European perspective on parental involvement in 11 countries, in a common broad analytical framework, with contributions from reputable academics working in this area in Cyprus, Germany, Iceland, Ireland, the Netherlands, Norway, Portugal, Slovenia, Sweden, Switzerland, and the United Kingdom (see Figure 0.1). Within the existing body of scholarly work on parental involvement in Europe, for the most part the comparative dimension has been neglected despite the fact that in many European countries legislation has given parents an increased role in both school choice and influencing school life. While it is acknowledged that the historical development of the recognition of parents in education differs across nations (see Crozier, 2018), a large-scale systematic analysis of commonalities and differences in policy, practice and research across European countries has not taken place. Instead, existing publications draw from specific institutional contexts typically beyond Europe (Carvalho, 2009; Christenson & Reschly, 2009; Jeynes, 2010; Epstein, 2016 in the US), or on specific issues such as the relationship between parental involvement and educational achievement (Deslandes, 2009; Punter, Glas & Meelissen, 2016). When the comparative dimension has been addressed, studies tend to be led by the Organisation for Economic Co-operation and Development (OECD) or the International Association for the Evaluation of Educational Achievement (IEA) with less critical examination of the issue of parental involvement. Furthermore, existing comparative studies tend to focus on a small number of country comparisons (see for example Schedel, Deslandes & Eshet, 2013).

The main endeavour of this book – and indeed in 11 of the 13 country case study chapters – is to present the stories of parental involvement policies, practices, research and challenges for each. The book seeks to communicate the richness of and variation in national experiences, largely adopting a uniform

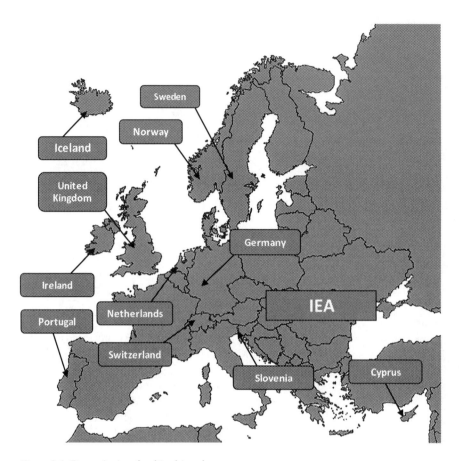

*Figure 0.1* Countries involved in this volume.
© kartoxjm(fotolia) europakarte.org (www.europakarte.org/leere-europakarte)

template in order to tell the story, so that each chapter can offer a contribution within itself. In the field of research on parental involvement, it is particularly distinctive to take this comparative approach and provide insights that are often overlooked at national level. In addressing this considerable research gap we examine 11 case study countries and parental involvement as a feature of *European* education systems. In our final chapter, we examine parental involvement across these diverse institutional contexts, paying attention to the political context, the extent of economic inequality, the degree of equity in the education system, and the role of the state in family matters.

We cover a variety of countries that can be grouped into a geographical classification, which roughly corresponds to the standard welfare regimes typology. The countries covered in this volume include:

- One Continental European welfare state (Germany), which has experienced a considerable increase in economic inequality between 1985 and 2007, and 2000 and 2005 (Tóth, 2014).
- Three Nordic countries (Iceland, Norway and Sweden) and the Netherlands represent a cluster of some of the least unequal countries in this volume. Yet, Tóth (2014) reports a gradual increase in economic inequality particularly in Sweden and the Netherlands.
- Two English-speaking liberal countries (Ireland and the UK) that show less influence from macroeconomic conditions on levels of inequality, but relatively high levels of inequality. Switzerland also fits into this liberal-market economy typology.
- Three Mediterranean countries (Cyprus, Portugal and Slovenia). Portugal represents the most unequal country in this volume, closely followed by Cyprus. Slovenia avoided a large inequality shock throughout the transition process, and is the least unequal country (alongside Iceland) in this volume. Tóth (2014) attributes this low level of inequality to efficient social and tax policies adopted in redistributing incomes.

The political context is of interest, as some European countries have been driven by political change and transformation processes in the last decades of the 20th century that have had an impact on the education system in general but also on the situation of parents, their children and visions of schooling and as consequence on parental involvement (Cyprus, Portugal and Slovenia). In other European countries, the political systems have been relatively stable over the last few decades.

The national background of parental involvement is also set against changes over time in the degree of equity in the education system. When estimating changes in the relationship between educational attainment and social background, OECD (2018) reports that few countries in our study have made significant progress in this area between the early 2000s and 2013–15. Across our country case studies, only Germany and Slovenia have improved in all three subject areas (reading literacy, mathematics and science), while equity in Ireland and Sweden (low and moderate economic inequality countries, respectively) did not improve in any of the subject domains assessed by PISA. Highlighting these macro patterns of educational inequality is especially significant when considering the extent to which current policy and practice pertaining to parental involvement is inclusive of a diverse range of parents and students.

Finally, a comparative study of parental involvement in education is also set against the backdrop of societal norms regarding children's well-being as a public responsibility. This draws our attention to the tensions and paradoxes along a continuum of familialism (family responsibility for caring) and de-familialism (public and state responsibility for caring). The Nordic countries (Iceland, Norway and Sweden) are classified as systems with high de-familialism through the provision of public childcare services. These countries represent a system where the individualisation of social rights reduces family responsibilities and dependencies, and family obligations for care are minimal. In contrast, the two Mediterranean countries (Cyprus and Portugal) represent the most economically unequal countries in this volume, and also Slovenia, where there is a high degree of familialism whereby care obligations are allocated to extended family in Portugal (Saraceno & Keck, 2010). Other European countries remain in the middle of the familialism and de-familialism continuum.

Looking at the European landscape specifically with regard to the development of parental involvement in education policy, some changes can be charged as fundamental for *all* European education systems and the situation of parents. Since the late 1960s, demands for establishing parental participation were guided by the call for greater democratisation in schools (Crozier, 2018). The later development of large-scale assessments that were promoted and carried out by the global player OECD in the 1990s provoked knowledge construction regarding the determinants of learning and academic achievement. Policy and research since this time has emphasised the role of parents and the home environment for academic achievement, and schools and the education system consistently call for more parental involvement. Currently, the pedagogical justification for parental involvement is emphasised by the rhetorics of 'shared responsibility', 'cooperation', 'partnership' and 'collaboration', with a view to improving learning outcomes. As a result, parents are increasingly expected to be active partners at the school-level as well as more generally in their children's educational and learning processes across a range of European education systems.

## The central questions addressed in this volume

This volume is unique in its research design that adopts a common broad analytical framework of the commonalities and differences in policy, practice and research across 11 European countries. It presents not only a description of the policy context and empirical research on parental involvement for each country, but also offers new research on critical perspectives relating to parental involvement. The point of departure for the country case studies was a common template, used by country experts to produce in-depth country reports for 11 countries. This common approach, applied across very different institutional settings, provides a unique opportunity to evaluate and cast new light on the following research questions:

(1) To what extent is the national background of parental involvement (legislation, national policy, rights and duties of parents) comparable across education systems?
(2) To what extent is current policy and practice pertaining to parental involvement inclusive of a diverse range of parents and students across education systems?
(3) What are the commonalities and differences in the research base and theoretical framing of parental involvement across education systems?
(4) What are the key policy challenges pertaining to parental involvement?

In seeking to answer these questions, this volume adopts an interdisciplinary approach that draws from the disciplinary fields of education, sociology and psychology. The final chapter will systematically address each of the four questions, and we will provide critical insights into parental involvement across a range of European countries, as well as identify the challenges in this field.

## How this book came to be

This book is a product of an extensive and fruitful collaboration across countries and disciplines, focused on the issue of parental involvement in education. It was greatly facilitated by our membership of the European Educational Research Association (EERA). The history of this book began at an annual European Conference on Educational Research (ECER) in Porto (Portugal) in 2014, when the first of four symposia took place on 'Parental Involvement in Schools in Different National Contexts: Future Challenges for Practice and Research'. This was a positive experience that brought together academics working on the topic of parental involvement from all over Europe. In 2015 (Budapest, Hungary) and in 2016 (Dublin, Ireland) two other symposia were organised with the aim of extending the body of researchers conducting research in the field of parental involvement. At this point, we were encouraged by Routledge to think about a European volume on this topic. As members of the EERA Network 'Communities, families, and schooling in educational research' in the European Educational Research Association (EERA), we found authors from a range of European countries with diverse political, social and economic institutional contexts to participate in this project.

## Key challenges

In addressing our central research questions, what became evident in the discussions and the exchange of research results while working across diverse institutional contexts were the many challenges we faced in planning and writing this European volume. A first challenge was the *terminology*: Sometimes we used the same expression, however, it was also evident that a term does not always carry the same meaning across education systems. Furthermore, given the range of national policies and legislation, diverse terms accentuate different aspects in our policy development discussions. That is, some countries use the term 'parents', while in other countries this term was critically assessed as it places a focus on biological fathers and mothers but does not refer to single-mothers, single-fathers, or same-sex families. Therefore, in some institutional contexts, the term was complemented by 'caregivers' or 'guardians'. The term 'family' is sometimes used synonymously for parents and/or home, while in other countries this term is only used to express the wider context of socialisation.

A second challenge was the *language*. We became aware that the translation of national terms into English sometimes can become very tricky as, especially in the field of parental involvement, multiple expressions exist. This prompted us to ask whether 'parental involvement' is quite a neutral term that can be accepted from all authors? Or is it better to use 'parental participation' or 'home–school cooperation' or the term 'family–school involvement'?

A third challenge was the fact that diverse *education systems* and their development have to be considered as a context for parental involvement. A closer look at each institutional background became necessary to understand the policy discourses in each country, but also to contextualise the type of research that is conducted on parental involvement which is framed by such discourses.

A fourth challenge was to differentiate between the *policy discourse* typical in the political discussions and civil movements to strengthen the right and options of parents, and the *empirical discourse* emanating from research on parental involvement in each institutional context.

A fifth challenge came from an examination of the *research fields* that exist across country contexts. Against this backdrop, the issue of parental involvement has been addressed from multiple research perspectives by using a range of analytical approaches and methods framed by diverse theoretical approaches and schools of thought. In some countries a considerable body of research has already been conducted on parental involvement, while in others the topic is gaining interest among researchers but remains marginal.

In 2017, at the ECER in Copenhagen, we brought together each of the country experts from across Europe who accepted our offer to write a chapter for this volume. The aim of this fourth symposium was to find a clear structure for this book, while keeping in mind the challenges described above, as well as the identification of blind spots. We decided that each country case study should adopt the following structure: (1) an overview of the education system, (2) a discussion of the terminology and national policy directions, (3) a review of existing empirical research on parental involvement including the dominant theoretical frameworks employed and research areas under investigation, and (4) new research carried out by the author(s). The result is a volume both evidence-based and theoretically driven. While many studies of parental involvement document the forms and nature of parental involvement, this book is underpinned from a critical theoretical perspective, which seeks to interrogate and critically assess parental involvement policies and practices across Europe. The majority of chapters are research-based, and the volume draws from a range of qualitative and quantitative research methodologies.

## Structure of the book

As we have described the focus and the aim of the volume, how the project came about and how the work was carried out, it is now helpful to set out the structure of the book. Each country chapter sets the scene in terms of key features of the local context. The book is organised alphabetically, so the country chapters progress as follows: Cyprus, Germany, Iceland, Ireland, the Netherlands, Norway, Portugal, Slovenia, Sweden, Switzerland, and the United Kingdom. Chapters 12 and 13 are distinct and intentionally follow a format different to each of the case study country chapters. Given the limited body of research that explores parental involvement from a feminist perspective, Chapter 12 draws on a feminist analysis of the development of policy and practice on parental involvement in the United Kingdom. In the absence of large-scale comparative European research on parental involvement, Chapter 13 draws from IEA data to consider the relationship between home-based parental involvement and educational achievement in mathematics. The final chapter of the book then brings together the key findings from across the 11 European country contexts.

## References

Carvalho, M.E.P. (2009) *Rethinking Family-School Relations. A Critique of Parental Involvement in Schooling.* New York and London: Routledge.

Christenson, S.L. and Reschly, A.L. (2009) *Handbook of School-Family Partnerships.* New York: Routledge.

Crozier, G. (2018) Editorial. *International Journal about Parents in Education*, 10(1), I-II.

Deslandes, R. (2009) *International Perspectives on Student Outcomes and Homework. Family-School-Community Partnerships.* London: Routledge.

Epstein, J.L. (2016) *School, Family, and Community Partnerships.* Boulder, CO: Westview Press.

Jeynes, W.H. (2010) *Parental Involvement and Academic Success.* London: Routledge.

OECD (2018) *Equity in Education: Breaking down Barriers to Social Mobility.* Paris: OECD.

Punter, R.A., Glas, C.A. W. and Meelissen, M.R.M. (2016) *Psychometric Framework for Modeling Parental Involvement and Reading Literacy.* IEA Research for Education. Amsterdam: Springer Open.

Saraceno, C. and Keck, W. (2010) Can We identify intergenerational policy regimes in Europe? *European Societies*, 12(5), 675–696.

Schedel, B., Deslandes, R. and Eshet, Y. (2013) Educational legislation and parental motivation for becoming involved in education: A comparative analysis between Israel and Quebec-Canada. *International Journal about Parents in Education*, 7(2), 107–122.

Tóth, I.G. (2014) Revisiting grand narratives of growing inequalities: Lessons from 30 country studies. In: Nolan, B., Salverda, W., Checchi, D., Marx, I., McKnight, A., Tóth, I.G. and van der Werfhorst, H., eds. *Changing Inequalities & Societal Impacts in Rich Countries.* Oxford: Oxford University Press. 11–48.

# 1 Cyprus

Depicting the landscape of school–family relationships and family–school involvement in Cyprus

*Loizos Symeou*

## 1 Introduction

Cyprus, an EU Member State since 2004, has had a relatively short post-independence period. The country has a population of 854,800, of whom around 20 percent are non-nationals (EU citizens and third country nationals) (Cyprus Statistical Service, 2016). The indigenous population consists of two constitutional communities: Greek-Cypriots, who form the majority, and Turkish-Cypriots. There are also Maronite, Armenian and Latin populations, who are defined in the constitution as religious groups. Following inter-communal violence between the two constitutional communities in 1963, and since Turkey's invasion in 1974, 37 percent of the country is occupied, leading to the division of the island. The discussion in this chapter pertains to the Greek-Cypriot education system under the jurisdiction of the Republic of Cyprus.

This chapter depicts school–family relationships and family–school involvement in the Greek-Cypriot education system and describes how they currently appear to be marginalised in policy, research and practice agendas. It focuses thereby on the legal provisions – which largely determine current school–family relations in the education system – and stresses the calls to strengthen the existing policy framework through relevant education reforms. It concludes by asserting that the existing policy and practice framework is indicative of the envisaged education policy as well as the low priority attributed to issues of equity and inclusion in the education system in Cyprus.

## 2 Overview of the education system in Cyprus

The education system in Cyprus has been strongly influenced by the historical and political developments on the island. As a result of political concerns, but also for economic purposes, the education administration and policy-making structures remain highly centralised (Karagiorgi & Symeou, 2006). After Cyprus gained independence in 1960, the centralisation of the education system was reinforced[1] (Persianis, 1981, 1998), with the Ministry of Education and Culture responsible for the enforcement of education laws and the preparation of new legislation. One indicator of this centralisation is the Education Commission, a five-member body responsible for teacher appointments, secondments, transfers and promotions. Inspectors play a dominant role in the Cypriot education system and are responsible for the guidance, supervision, evaluation and part of the in-service training of teachers as well as for the evaluation of schools. There is also a centrally planned, nationwide curriculum. The Ministry of Education and Culture provides textbooks for every subject and grade, so teaching content is likewise controlled.

Education is provided through pre-primary and primary schools, lower secondary schools (*gymnasia*), upper secondary schools (*lycea*), technical/vocational schools, special schools, institutions of tertiary education and non-formal institutions and centres. Education is mostly state-run, but there are also a number of private, self-funded institutions under the control of the Ministry of Education and Culture. Around 5 percent of primary school pupils and 12 percent of secondary school pupils attend such schools. In 1972, education became compulsory until the age of fifteen, and state-funded education became free at all school levels. More recently, free compulsory education was extended to include one year of pre-primary schooling.

Once a family decides to enrol its child in a state school, they have no choice regarding the actual school, as the child must be registered at the family's local state school unless the local school authorities (*Scholiki Eforia*) decide otherwise. This was recently challenged in court but still seems to be the rule.

State schools usually operate from early morning until 1:05 p.m. (primary schools) or 1:35 p.m. (secondary schools). However, there are also two forms of full-day schooling at the primary school level available. The optional form offers additional courses that can be taken in the afternoon for those pupils in the school that would like to do so. The compulsory form has a comprehensive full-day timetable and is obligatory for all pupils attending the specific school. Families whose local state primary school follows the compulsory full-day timetable have the option to move their child to another state primary school if they do not want their child to attend a full-time school timetable. Just over half (56 percent) of primary schools close by 1:05 p.m., 40 percent offer the optional full-day format and 4 percent provide compulsory full-day schooling. In both full-day options, lunch has to be paid for by the parents.

Given its small population and lack of natural resources, Cyprus has shown a collective determination to substitute these limitations with intellectual achievements (Persianis, 1981). Hence, Cyprus now ranks very highly in international comparisons for its number of tertiary/university students in relation to its population.

## 3 Parental involvement in schools in Cyprus

### 3a Terminology

Most studies in Cyprus as well as the rhetoric at both policy and practice level regarding the relationship between parents/family/home and the school refer to the relationships between parents and schools. Hence, most of the early literature in this field appeared under the heading of parental involvement or participation in school. However, the last decade has seen a shift in this rhetoric from parents to family, especially when referring to the actual relationships. Accordingly, 'family involvement' in schools is now the more commonly used term, and 'school–family relationship' is used to denote the links between the two. 'Family involvement' thus refers to any type of involvement of member(s) of a pupil's family in matters associated with a child's schooling that is undertaken to support the child. The term 'family' is used here in its broader sense and includes family members beyond the mother or father, i.e. also guardians, carers or other adult relations such as siblings, grandparents, aunts, uncles, etc. (Symeou et al., 2018). The involvement of families rather than just parents is now more widely accepted than before.

A key development in the discourse on school–family relationships in Cyprus is the recognition of parental diversity and intersectionality. This has also been highlighted in other education systems and varies in different countries and societies depending on their socio-political contexts (Crozier & Symeou, 2017).

This shift in terminology from 'parents' to 'family' could be claimed to be a more general one in the case of Cyprus. In a context of heightened child protection, and despite the use of different terms to define the adults who are responsible for children (e.g. parents, guardians, carers), it appears that the term 'family' is adopted in Cyprus when referring to issues pertaining to the rights of the child. This highlights a local shift to recognising is not only parents who are tasked with safeguarding children's rights. For instance, in the Commissioner for the Protection of Children's Rights Laws of 2007 and 2014, local Cypriot society is requested to 'safeguard in practice children's rights in the family'. The text does not make a single reference to 'parent(s)' and only uses the adjective 'parental' in one instance (Office of the Law Commissioner, 2014; Part II, Point 4).

### 3b National legislative and regulative context

Due in part to the context described above, school–family relationships in Cyprus are marginalised in the policy, research and practice agendas. Research in this field is limited and mainly focused on primary education. Studies conducted over the last few decades suggest that the relationship between schools and families is very confined (Georgiou, 1996;

Phtiaka, 1996; Symeou, 2001, 2002, 2010; Savva & Symeou, 2019). The lack of any recent legislative action in this regard is indicative of the lack of substantial relations between schools and families (Savva & Symeou, 2019).

Georgiou (1996) classified school–family relationships in Cyprus into two general types: formal and informal. Formal relationships are those established through legislation. These include the establishment and running of parents' associations, a 'weekly visiting period' for parents to meet their children's teachers and up to two evening events for families in each school year. Informal relationships are elaborated later in this chapter.

Parents' associations (PAs; formal designation: 'Parents' and Guardians' Association') at all education levels function on a three-tiered basis at the school, regional and national/Pancyprian levels (Parents' Associations Law of 1992, 105 (I)/1992). At the *school* level, PAs are voluntary associations elected at an annual general meeting of a school's parents and guardians. Each state school in Cyprus has its own PA. All parents or guardians of pupils attending a school are automatically deemed to be members of the school's PA if they pay an annual fee. Each association elects its board at the beginning of a school year. All parents have the right to vote in this election and stand for election if they have paid their annual fee. The overall aim of a PA is to cooperate with the school to provide the best possible education and environment for all pupils. It should encourage communication and collaboration between school and families and engage in activities, including fundraising, which support the school's infrastructure (e.g., for equipping the school with interactive boards, laptops, tablets, etc.). PAs also use the money they raise to fund school events and assist low-income pupils. They organise seminars for parents and voluntarily assist with school activities and events (Founding Association Statute). Each PA board has monthly meetings, to which the school principal is usually invited to inform parents about activities, programmes and other relevant issues at the school. A member of the board of each PA represents the school on its District Parents' Association (Parent's Associations Law of 1992, 105 (I)/1992).

At the *regional* level, there are separate District Parents' Associations (DPAs) for primary, secondary and vocational education schools, each representing one of the country's six geographical/administrative districts. All elected PAs are automatically members of their respective DPA. In turn, all DPAs are members of their corresponding Pancyprian Confederation of Primary/Secondary/Vocational Parents' Associations. Two representatives of each DPA are members of the General Secretariat of the Confederation (Parent's Associations Law of 1992, 105 (I)/1992). The main purpose of each DPA is to improve the education, safety, health and well-being of all schoolchildren in their particular district as well as to enable and coordinate cooperation between schools, local authorities, local committees and the District Education Office. Their primary activities include offering lectures and seminars for parents, organising fundraising events, attending meetings in which education matters are discussed, planning summer camps for pupils and offering 24-hour all-risk insurance to all pupils in the district.

At the *national* level, the Pancyprian Confederations of Parents' Associations represent all parents with children at their respective schools. In collaboration with the Ministry of Education and Culture, teachers' unions, local authorities and other organisations, they aim to contribute to the development of policies and decisions that promote the highest possible quality of education for all pupils in Cyprus. Their main goals are to support the advancement of effective educational development and to promote and advocate for the active involvement of parents as primary educators of their children. When issues related to education are discussed or improvement plans are made at the Ministry of Education and Culture, in the House of Representatives or other committees, parents are represented by members of the board of the Pancyprian Confederations of Parents' Associations. The Pancyprian Confederation of Primary School Parents' Associations, for instance, has been a full member of the European Parents' Association (EPA) for around two decades. Members of its board attend the two annual EPA meetings, where they represent all parents of primary school pupils in Cyprus.

Essentially, parents can participate on a voluntary basis after being elected to PAs at school, local and national level but do not participate in education-related decisions or policy-making. Nonetheless, parents' representatives at the national level constitute a significant power group and do manage to influence official education policy (Georgiou, 1996; Symeou, 2010) despite not having been officially accorded such a role in national legislation (Savva & Symeou, 2019).

Another formally legislated institution that frames school–family relationships in state schools in the Greek-Cypriot education system is the so-called parents' weekly visiting period introduced in the 1980s. Education regulations in Cyprus specify that teachers in all schools must assign one period in their weekly timetable when parents and guardians can visit them to find out about a child's school attainment and discuss any relevant issues. Parents are typically expected to go to the school for these 10–15-minute, one-to-one teacher-parent briefings where they receive information about their child's academic progress and behaviour, school activities in this regard and how they can support the work of the school (Symeou, 2002; Symeou et al., 2012).

Schools of all levels are obliged to offer at least two evening events for families in each academic year. At primary school level, these usually take the form of a Christmas party and end-of-year event, whereas in secondary schools they are the end-of-year graduation ceremony and a cultural (usually theatre) event. All families are invited to attend these free events.

Outside the legislative context, schools can also establish informal links with families. The extent and nature of these informal relationships depend on how inviting the school is, and how motivated families or individual family members are to get involved. Such activities establish and reinforce informal communication between parents and the school and can include parental participation in school events as well as opportunities for parents to volunteer in non-educational activities, e.g. providing breakfast for pupils, supervising them after lessons, repairing and maintaining school equipment, etc.

Overall, information exchange on children's academic progress and behaviour – either on a formal or informal level – seems to be the most widespread link between schools and families in the Greek-Cypriot educational system (Symeou, 2001; Zaoura & Aubrey, 2011).

## 4 Existing research on parental involvement in schools in Cyprus

Despite the large body of research on parental involvement in schools that is available worldwide, little research has been conducted in this regard in Cyprus. Most of the existing studies examine the beliefs and attitudes of teachers towards parental involvement (Phtiaka, 1996; Georgiou, 1998; Symeou, 2002). There has likewise been little research that explores the actual extent of parental involvement. A few short pilot programmes or action research case studies have investigated the impact of parental involvement practices on school staff, families and pupils (e.g. Georgiou et al., 1997; Symeou, 1997; Zachariou & Symeou, 2009). More recently, research has emerged that explores the education experiences of racial and ethnic minorities and how their resources and dispositions are utilised to achieve success at school (Theodorou & Symeou, 2013).

No dominant theoretical framing can be identified in studies on parental involvement in Cyprus. However, the starting points and underpinning rationales of most the studies cited in this chapter assert the benefits for schools and families of establishing strong, positive, communicative and collaborative relationships as well as the assumption that greater collaboration between the two can enhance children's success in school. When we bundle existing research in Cyprus in this field, three main areas emerge: research on parents and their involvement in schools, research on parental involvement and social inequality, and research on the schools' perspective on parental involvement.

### 4a Research on parents and their involvement in schools

Despite the limited relationships between parents and schools in Cyprus, there is evidence to suggest that Cypriot parents are willing to become more involved in schools, thus indicating a gap between family needs and school programmes and practices (Georgiou, 1996, 1998; Symeou, 2001, 2010; Zaoura & Aubrey, 2011). At the same time, parents do not seem to know or are confused about how this can be accomplished (Phtiaka, 1996). Despite having an encouraging attitude towards their children as far as their parenting roles are concerned, they lack advice and stimulation on how to support their children at home (Martínez-González et al., 2008; Zaoura & Aubrey, 2011). Existing studies also indicate that despite the differences in their socioeconomic or local backgrounds and the practical constraints and realities they face, all families seem to value their children's educational success and want them to do well in school (Symeou, 2007).

Interestingly, most parents appear to believe that education is a responsibility they share with the school and that they are in partnership with teachers in promoting their children's progress. Correspondingly, most parents feel that they support their children in this regard in one way or another (Symeou, 2007). However, their perspectives and evaluation of specific practices aimed at linking them with schools still point to mild modes of involvement (Symeou, 2001, 2002) in which family–school relationships depend upon teachers' initiatives and invitations (Zaoura & Aubrey, 2011). Cypriot families – to use Munn's (1993) distinction – are mainly interested in being 'involved' in practices that secure the well-being of their own child and not in engaging in 'participation' practices that also relate to the collective well-being of the whole school and to decision-making.

Phtiaka (1996) groups Cypriot parents by their attitudes to getting involved in their children's schools into three categories. (a) Parents who are 'close' to school and feel very confident with this contact. These parents appear to have no problem in acquiring all the information they seek or in resolving any problems relating to their child. (b) Parents who do not want to get involved or who react to the pressure and workload of such involvement. These parents often come into conflict with school because it demands either that they get involved more or makes excessive demands on their time. (c) Marginalised parents who feel estranged from school and do not participate in its events. They fear school due to their own negative experiences or regret their attitude but do not feel able to improve the situation.

There is some research evidence to support the notion that parents who actively participate in a school's PA fall into Phtiaka's (1996) first category, i.e. parents who are 'close' to school and feel very confident with this contact. They are also likely to gain an advantage from having more close contact with their child's teacher, having their voice heard and having more opportunities to get involved with the school (Symeou, 2001; Zaoura & Aubrey, 2011).

### 4b Research on parental involvement and social inequality

Research indicates that family cultural skills, social class and economic status in Cyprus become a form of cultural capital in the school setting and at home, and play a large role in facilitating and structuring family collaboration and communication with schools (Symeou, 2007). This is particularly evident in the ways that different families experience and cope with homework. Despite the fact that parents in Cyprus largely concur on the importance and purposes of homework and claim to support their children in meeting their homework requirements, most Greek-Cypriot families with a lower socioeconomic and/or working-class status (largely in rural areas) are found to dedicate more time and face more difficulties in assisting their children with homework than upper class and urban families (Symeou, 2009). This suggests that school practices in assigning homework might result in additional disadvantages for children from low socioeconomic, working-class and/or rural backgrounds, thus consolidating and exacerbating the existing stratification between privileged and underprivileged pupils.

### 4c Research on the school's perspective on parental involvement

Schools and teachers in Cyprus seem to have a conservative attitude towards family involvement in schools. Like their counterparts in other countries, they generally seem to encourage school–family relationships and recognise their theoretical benefits. Nonetheless, they also want to determine the nature and extent of family engagement in the school so as not to threaten their schoolwork and professional status (Georgiou, 1996; Symeou, 2002, 2010). Evidence also shows that teachers of lower grade or small classes seem to have a greater variety of relationships with their pupils' families (Symeou, 2001). Of the Cypriot primary schools that participated in the few studies available, those with smaller populations or in rural locations seem to have stronger links with families, enjoy significantly more teacher-family contacts and opportunities for exchanging information and extend more invitations to families to offer voluntary labour than their larger, urban counterparts (Georgiou, 1998; Symeou, 2001).

A new line of research that is emerging in Cyprus, and in other countries in Europe, is investigating family involvement in university undergraduate programmes (Lamprianou et al., 2018; Symeou et al., 2018). These studies indicate that family involvement in higher education does indeed exist and that while overly engaged parenting at this level of education is not particularly common, some universities in Cyprus have already adopted a few policies for families, such as the organisation of open days specifically targeted at prospective students and their families.

## 5 New research perspective: Teachers' representations of parents

To extend our understanding of teachers' conceptions of the families and types of parents they usually communicate and/or collaborate with, this chapter presents a new research study using an existing dataset. This study by Symeou and Stylianou investigates Greek-Cypriot teachers' representations of the parents they typically encounter in their daily professional practice. It aims to identify which parents typically communicate with school and explore their relationship with school from the perspective of the teachers involved.

The dataset used in the study includes the visual representations of 'typical' Cypriot parents gathered from 72 Greek-Cypriot teachers at different school levels and with different levels of teaching experience during a series of courses on school–family relations in 2010–2014. The sample of teachers, although opportunistic, can be considered representative of the teacher population in Cyprus in several key characteristics (level of teaching, gender, teaching experience, school district, private and state education sector).

The teachers who participated in these courses were asked to draw the 'typical' parent and add brief written descriptions of the parent's characteristics (e.g. outward appearance, gestures, age, gender, socioeconomic status, style, values, etc.). The drawings were used as a visual method for gathering data that offers an alternative to traditional interviews or observations.

We then analysed the drawings using visual methods. Initially, all drawings were closely inspected and analysed based on their similarities and common themes. The following categories emerged inductively using an open content and thematic analysis approach: gender; overall drawing of the parent; body language; facial expressions; context of the drawing; dress code based on elements showing wealth and religion; thoughts; relationship between the parent and the child; relationship between the parent and the teacher. These categories and observations were later considered in relation to the social landscape in which they emerged and to established literature in the field. This was important for identifying issues that could be confirmed or – more importantly – contradicted current literature and drawing preliminary conclusions about parent–teacher and parent–school relations in Cyprus.

The analysis of the data revealed a rather complex depiction of the relationship between teachers and parents. More specifically, our findings indicate that the 'typical' parent constructed by teachers belongs to the higher-income and middle-class strata of society and has more contacts with the school than other parents have. Indeed, the teachers' depictions of the 'typical' parent suggest that lower socioeconomic status families and working-class parents are less frequently involved in schools (Lareau, 2000; Reay, 1998; Symeou, 2010). In addition, the teachers who participated in our study confirm the distance between teachers/schools and parents/families that do not belong to the majority ethnic-cultural groups in Cyprus (Symeou, Karagiorgi, Roussounidou & Kaloyirou, 2009; Theodorou & Symeou, 2013) and other countries (Lareau, 2000; Crozier, 2007). Despite the increasing number of immigrant families in Cyprus and the growing number of pupils from these ethnic groups in schools, the typical parent for teachers seems to belong to the local ethnic-cultural dominant group (Greek-Cypriot). Moreover, the teachers confirm that mothers seem to get more involved than fathers do in matters relating to their child's schooling. Cooperating with school seems to be a female task, and men rarely featured in the scene. Our findings confirm what other research has documented: namely, that not all families have strong relationships with their children's schools.

One particularly interesting finding of our study is that teachers place a strong emphasis on the image presented by parents. The relationship between teachers and parents that emerged in the drawings included not only a position of defence and reservation towards the school and teacher but also a critical attitude and in some cases even an aggressive and slightly obnoxious stance towards teachers. This corresponds to previous findings demonstrating that parents appear critical of teachers for various reasons.

In addition, the implicit power relations in the drawings reveal that teachers are well aware of and slightly defensive regarding parents' criticisms, pointing to a level of insecurity and vulnerability. Thus, teachers appear to relate to their pupils' parents with hesitancy and maintain ambiguous attitudes towards them. As in other studies, the teachers in our study seem to fear family interaction because it questions their professional expertise and traditional authority and status. They thus establish a distance to families in order to safeguard their own positions (Lareau, 2000; Crozier, 2007).

## 6 Conclusions

The existing studies on school–family relationships in Cyprus demonstrate that despite family differences in socioeconomic status, local background, practical constraints and realities, all families value their children's educational success and want their children to do well in school. They thus transcend their personal and family constraints in their commitment to supporting their child. Nonetheless, the cultural capital of Cypriot families in the school setting and at home seem to play a large role in facilitating and structuring family–school relationships. These conclusions draw on Bourdieu's views of cultural capital (Bourdieu, 1977) and might offer a useful perspective for viewing school–family relationships and even children's success in school. The differences in the educational, cultural, economic and social resources available to Cypriot families might help explain the differences in their ability to monitor and make use of their contacts with school, particularly the reasons why some Cypriot parents feel that their educational skills might be inadequate, while others with superior educational resources feel more comfortable in helping their children.

The importance of school being an inviting and welcoming place for parents and families has also been highlighted in the Cypriot context as a factor in enhancing family involvement. Several studies on the education system in Cyprus (Georgiou, 1996; Symeou, 2002, 2010; Zaoura & Aubrey, 2011; Savva & Symeou, 2019) maintain that the extent and nature of school–family relationships in the country still depend heavily on how inviting schools are in initiating and promoting parental involvement and establishing a relevant ethos and culture. Hence, all relevant discourse and literature refers to 'school–family' and not 'family–school' relationships. Of particular concern is whether teachers treat parents and families as a homogeneous group with the same needs and roles and fail to recognise their diversity, thus leading to poor outcomes for those most in need, as indicated by the new study presented above. The outcomes of school–family relationships might also be linked with social stratification, i.e. with the consolidation or widening of existing stratification, in particular between pupils from educationally and culturally privileged versus disadvantaged backgrounds and between high achievers versus underachievers. It might be argued that this particular aspect of school–family relationships is a critical link in the process of educational, cultural and social reproduction.

If school–family relationships in Cyprus are to have pedagogical value, and their purpose is to ensure that all families have the information and guidance they need to successfully intervene in their children's schooling, there is an urgent need to address the 'de-homogenisation' of policies and approaches to collaboration with parents. However, no change can rely solely upon teachers' sensitivity and own initiatives. It will take more than good intentions and empathy on the part of the school and the teachers to provide meaningful support for parents and families. Thus, there is a need for professional development during pre- and in-service training or through generic professional development programmes (Symeou et al., 2012). This training should include information and guidelines on family involvement (Savva & Symeou, 2019).

The analysis of the current status of family–school relationships in Cyprus presented in this chapter demonstrates that parental involvement is a key factor to an effective education system and can lead to initiatives aimed at strengthening parental involvement in education as well as the development and implementation of policies that support such programmes in schools. Notably, this analysis indicates the lack of relevant local legislation, a situation that has persisted for several decades (see e.g. Georgiou, 1996; Symeou, 2010; Savva & Symeou, 2019), and how legislation could be improved in order to ensure parental involvement at all levels.

## Note

1 Constitutional responsibility for education was assigned to the Greek and Turkish Communal Assemblies, which exercised legislative power on religious, education and cultural matters in their respective communities. After the inter-communal conflict in 1963–1964, the Greek Communal Assembly was dissolved, and its legislative and administrative powers passed to a newly established Ministry of Education (now the Ministry of Education and Culture). The two education systems were left separate until 1974 and have functioned independently of one another since the Turkish invasion of Cyprus.

## References

Bourdieu, P. (1977) *Outline of a Theory of Practice*. Cambridge: Cambridge University Press.
Crozier, G. (2007) Hard to reach parents or hard to reach schools? A discussion of home–school relations, with particular reference to Bangladeshi and Pakistani parents. *British Educational Research Journal*, 33(3), 295–313.

Crozier, G. and Symeou, L. (2017) Editorial: Deconstructing the 'parent' in parent-school relationships: Addressing multiple identities and changing practice. *Gender and Education*, 29(5), 537–540.
Cyprus Statistical Service (2016) *Statistical abstract 2016*. Available at: www.cystat.gov.cy/mof/cystat/statistics.nsf/All/A6EB39CA3885F8ABC22582030022CF1F/$file/ABSTRACT-2016-EN-271217.pdf.
Georgiou, S., Tsouris, C., et al. (1997) Partnership in education: Luxury or necessity [Συνεταιρισμός στην εκπαίδευση: Πολυτέλεια ή αναγκαιότητα]. In: Pedagogical Association of Cyprus [Παιδαγωγική Εταιρεία Κύπρου], eds., *Cyprus Pedagogical Review [Παιδαγωγική Επιθεώρηση]*. Nicosia: University of Cyprus, 95–106.
Georgiou, S.N. (1996) Parental involvement in Cyprus. *International Journal of Educational Research*, 25(1), 33–43.
Georgiou, S.N. (1998) A study of two Cypriot school communities. *The School Community Journal*, 8(1), 73–91.
Karagiorgi, Y. and Symeou, L. (2006) Teacher professional development in Cyprus: Reflections on current trends and challenges in policy and practices. *Journal of In-Service Education*, 32(1), 47–61.
Lamprianou, I., Symeou, L. and Theodorou, E. (2018) All we need is love (and money): What do higher education students want from their families? *Research Papers in Education*. DOI: 10.1080/02671522.2018.1452957.
Lareau, A. (2000) *Home Advantage: Social Class and Parental Intervention in Elementary Education*. Lanham, MD: Rowman & Littlefield Publishers.
Martínez-González, R., Symeou, L., Álvarez-Blanco, L., Roussounidou, E., Iglesias-Muñiz, J. and Cao Fernández, M.A. (2008) Family involvement in the education of potential drop-out children: A comparative study between Spain and Cyprus. *Educational Psychology*, 28(5), 505–520.
Munn, P. (1993) *Parents and Schools: Customers, Managers or Partners*. London: Routledge.
Office of the Law Commissioner (2014) *The Commissioner for the Protection of Children's Rights Laws, 2007 and 2014*. Printing Office of the Republic of Cyprus. Available at: www.olc.gov.cy/olc/olc.nsf/all/7832D33FBC399522C2257D090032843F/$file/The%20Commissioner%20for%20the%20Protection%20of%20Childrennd Pakistan%20Laws,%202007%20and%202014.pdf?openelement.
Persianis, P. (1981) *The Political and Economical Factors as the Main Determinants of Educational Policy in Independent Cyprus (1960–1970)*. Nicosia: Pedagogical Institute of Cyprus.
Persianis, P. (1998) 'Compensatory Legitimation' in Greek educational policy: An explanation for the abortive educational reforms in Greece in comparison with those of France. *Comparative Education*, 34(1), 71–84.
Phtiaka, H. (1996) Each to his own? Home–school relations in Cyprus. *Forum of Education*, 51(1), 47–59.
Reay, D. (1998) *Class Work: Mothers' Involvement in their Children's Primary Schooling*. London: UCL Press.
Savva, M. and Symeou, L. (2019) Parental involvement in primary education schools in Cyprus: Looking into the stakeholders' perspective. *Aula Abierta*, 48(1), 105–112. DOI: 10.17811/rifie.48.1.2019.105-112.
Symeou, L. (1997) *Parental Involvement in Class E'1 of Aradippou B' Primary School During the School Year 1996–97*. Unpublished paper presented at: Conference of the Primary Schools of the district of Larnaca. Aradippou, Cyprus, 6 June 1997.
Symeou, L. (2001) Family–school liaisons in Cyprus: An investigation of families' perspectives and needs. In: Smit, F., van der Wolf, K. and Sleegers, P., eds. *A Bridge to*

the Future: Collaboration between Parents, Schools and Communities. Nijmegen, Netherlands: Institute for Applied Social Sciences, University Nijmegen, 33–43.

Symeou, L. (2002) Present and future home–school relations in Cyprus: An investigation of teachers' and parents' perspectives. *The School Community Journal*, 12(2), 7–34.

Symeou, L. (2007) Cultural capital and family involvement in children's education: Tales from two primary schools in Cyprus. *British Journal of Sociology of Education*, 28(4), 473–487.

Symeou, L. (2009) Mind the gap! Greek-Cypriot parents and their children's homework. In: Deslandes, R., ed. *International Perspectives on Student Outcomes and Homework: Family–School-Community Partnerships*. London: Taylor & Francis, 76–94.

Symeou, L. (2010) *Teacher-Family Communication in Cypriot Primary Schools*. Beau Bassin: VDM Publishing House.

Symeou, L., Karagiorgi, Y., Roussounidou, E. and Kaloyirou, C. (2009) Roma and their education in Cyprus: Reflections on INSETRom teacher training for Roma inclusion. *Intercultural Education*, 20(6), 511–521.

Symeou, L., Roussounidou, E. and Michaelides, M. (2012) 'I feel much more confident now to talk with parents': An evaluation of in-service training on teacher-parent communication. *School Community Journal*, 22(1), 65–88.

Symeou, L., Theodorou, E., Lamprianou, I., Rentzou, K. and Andreou, P. (2018) Has family involvement migrated into higher education? How the administrative staff documents the phenomenon in students' university experience in Cyprus. *International Studies in Sociology of Education*, 27(1), 78–99.

Theodorou, E. and Symeou, L. (2013) Experiencing the same but differently: Indigenous minority and immigrant children's experiences in Cyprus. *British Journal of Sociology of Education*, 34(3), 354–372.

The Parental Associations Law of 1992 (105 (I)/1992). Available at: www.cylaw.org

Zachariou, A. and Symeou, L. (2009) The local community as a means for promoting education for sustainable development. *Applied Environmental Education and Communication*, 7(4), 129–143.

Zaoura, A. and Aubrey, C. (2011) Home–school relationships in primary schools. Parents' perspectives. *International Journal about Parents in Education*, 5(2), 12–24.

# 2 Germany

## Parental involvement in Germany

*Angelika Paseka and Dagmar Killus*

## 1 Introduction

In recent decades, there have been two strands to the discussion on parents and parental involvement in schools in Germany: the first strand emphasised parents' importance as the experts on their children's assessment (especially after the publication of the PISA results in 2001, which were perceived as disastrous for Germany); the second strand enlarged the autonomy of schools and the need to involve parents as actors and partners in school development processes. Both strands are intertwined with the debate on social inequality: the first focuses on those parents who appear unable to effectively support their children in school, while the second looks at how to motivate 'hard-to-reach parents' to become more involved in school affairs.

In this chapter, we take a critical look at this social inequality discourse and examine the role of schools and how they involve parents. In Section 2, we begin with a brief description of the characteristics of the German education system. To explain the current challenges, we clarify the terminology used therein and the legislative and regulative context of parental involvement (Section 3). As the last 20 years have seen a rise in research on parents and parental involvement in Germany in the school context, we next summarise the empirical findings, theoretical approaches and underlying concepts behind this research and the political debate (Section 4). In Section 5, findings from the JAKO-O 2014 survey are presented, with a focus on parents, their involvement in home- and school-based activities, and how school and parent factors influence this engagement. We conclude by summarising the situation regarding parents and parental involvement in schools in Germany (Section 6).

## 2 Basic structure of the school system in Germany

Germany has a highly differentiated school system; the country has a long tradition of segregating school types and is made up of 16 federal states (*Länder*), each with their own – partly different – school regulations and school types. To coordinate and develop education across Germany, the Federal Government established The Standing Conference of the Ministers of Education and Cultural Affairs of the Länder in the Federal Republic of Germany (KMK, *Kultusministerkonferenz*, 2018). The following information applies to the whole country.

School is compulsory in Germany from age 6 to 15. Kindergartens are available for children up to the age of 6, whereby attendance is voluntary. Primary school usually lasts four years (grades 1 to 4) or six years in Berlin and Brandenburg (grades 1 to 6). Secondary school is split into a lower secondary level (*Sekundarstufe I*, grades 5/7 to 9/10) and an upper secondary level (*Sekundarstufe II*, grades 10 to 12/13). Secondary education is offered in several types of schools, which usually provide several school-leaving certificates: after nine years of schooling (basic certificate), after ten years of schooling (intermediate certificate) or an advanced leaving certificate as entrance qualification for higher education after 12 or 13 years of schooling (highest certificate, *Abitur*). After primary school, 43 percent of students go on to a *Gymnasium*, making it the preferred type of secondary school. In some *Länder*, the parents decide which type of secondary school their child will attend, while in others this decision is made by the primary school teachers. For demographic reasons, growing scepticism has increased over the past decade towards an early division of children within the highly divided school system and the educational aspirations of parents for their children, the number of school types and schools offering two or three types of secondary education under one roof have all increased over the past decade (Authoring Group Educational Reporting, 2016).

The types of secondary school available are determined by the different education laws and school systems in each *Länder*, which can differ significantly. Thus, only two types of school are common across Germany: the *Gymnasium* and the so-called special schools (*Sonderschule*) for children from grades 1 to 9/10. Although increasing numbers of students with and without disabilities now attend the same school, a broad range of special education institutions still persists (ibid., 73). The current tendency, however, is to make all schools more inclusive.

While most schools in Germany are state schools, there are now a small but growing number of private schools. In 2015/16 this was around 10 percent of primary and secondary schools. State schools are free of charge; parents only have to pay for materials such as exercise books, pencils or sportswear, class trips, theatre or concert visits and school lunches. School is generally attended on a half-day basis, but some schools also offer a full-day option with voluntary, semi-compulsory or compulsory lessons and courses in the afternoon.

## 3 Parental involvement in Germany

### 3a Terminology

In the legal documents that clarify the relationship between school and home, the term 'parents' is predominantly used to refer to those persons who primarily care for children. However, in light of changes in society, or if parents are not present or able to care for their child(ren), the term 'guardian' signals that various forms of 'parenthood' and families exist and that it is not only the biological parents who can be responsible for a child. The term 'family' refers more to the context in which a child grows up and emphasises the structural position, social inequality or larger group of people caring for a child.

## 3b National legislative and regulative context

The cooperation between parents and school in Germany is determined by three national regulations that are valid in all 16 *Länder*. (1) Article 6 (2) of the *Basic Law* (*Grundgesetz*) defines a clear responsibility for raising children: 'The care and upbringing of children is the natural right of parents and a duty primarily incumbent upon them.' The state can only intervene when parents are unable to care for their children properly. (2) Article 7 (1) of the *Basic Law* defines the supervisory role of the state with regard to the school system: 'The entire school system shall be under the supervision of the state.' As there is a statutory obligation for children to attend school, parents are obliged to place their child(ren)'s education at least partly in the hands of the school and the state education system (or private schools, which are regarded as equal). (3) As these laws did not fully clarify the relationship between the rights of parents and the state, in 1972 a *Decision of the Federal Constitutional Court* stated that the mandate of the state to educate children is not subordinate to the right of parents to raise and educate them; the goal of this shared responsibility is to ensure the personal development of a child; it cannot be broken down into individual competences and should be accomplished through meaningful cooperation between parents and the school (BVerfG, Bd. 34, 165).

More concrete specifications of the individual rights and duties of parents and their collective participation are formulated in various school-related regulations and decrees. For instance, parents have the right to elect representatives to participate on formal boards. However, the actual responsibilities of these representatives (obtaining information, being heard, giving advice, submitting request, voting) differ between the *Länder* (Witjes & Zimmermann, 2000; Schwanenberg, 2015). Accordingly, schools have considerable scope to define and interpret how they want to cooperate with parents – both on an individual and a collective basis.

## 3c Terminology: changing rhetoric

As the format of the cooperation between parents and schools is not explicitly regulated, different attitudes have emerged towards parents and their role in school. These are reflected in the various terms used to describe this relationship, such as cooperation, involvement, participation, information, advice, training, counselling or coaching. Of these, two central terms have prevailed: 'working with parents' (*Elternarbeit*) and 'educational partnership' (*Erziehungs- und Bildungspartnerschaft*). 'Working with parents' is used to describe activities that are initiated by schools. It is based on asymmetry, as it is the staff in the school who are responsible for establishing and maintaining the relationship. In recent years, this term has been mostly replaced by 'educational partnership'. The latter is a normative term insofar as the word 'partnership' has positive connotations. A partnership should be positive and equal, both partners should be active and communicate on equal terms, and both should feel responsible for providing students with the best possible education. The German term *Erziehungs- und Bildungspartnerschaft* refers not only to education in the school learning sense but also includes 'Bildung' as an aim of such a partnership.

This shift in thinking towards an educational partnership establishes a new imperative for parents – they must be more active and willing to support their children in their learning processes to ensure good learning. Given that children are a resource for the future, this support is both relevant and essential. To safeguard prosperity and the welfare state, we must invest in our children and it is parents who have to make this investment. Evidence of such a change in responsibility for children's success in school can be found in German government policy documents (Betz et al., 2017), where 'good' parents are expected not only to care for and rear children but also to accept and embrace these demands and tasks. Vandenbroeck et al. (2017) criticise this shift from 'child-rearing' to 'parenting' for its radicalisation of parental responsibility for the success of their children. Betz et al. (2017) refer to Bourdieu's concept of symbolic capital, Vandenbroeck et al. (2017) use Foucault's concept of power, and Ule et al. (2015) draw on the concept of individualisation and familialisation based on the neo-liberal discourse. Several other authors also address this trend, not only in Germany but also in other countries in Europe, however, they embed their analyses in different theoretical frameworks.

In a new shift in thinking, the idea of an educational partnership has been taken even further and broadened to involve children and the local/regional community as partners. The latter are expected to support parents and schools in improving learning results and contribute to the well-being of children by providing special programmes and initiatives. This shift is expressed by replacing the term 'parents' with 'family' (including parents and children) and/or 'community' (e.g. 'school–family-partnership' or 'school–family-community-partnership') (Sacher, 2008; Barge & Loges, 2011; Haase, 2012; Stange, 2012; Killus, 2017). From a critical perspective, it should, however, be noted that such strategies tend to be vague, diffuse and lacking in clarity with regard to responsibility. They also erode or weaken the tasks of all partners involved.

### 3d Stages of change

The programmatic shift goes hand-in-hand with different ways of treating parents. A historical-reconstruction analysis reveals several stages in this process, each of which includes its own normative vision of what constitutes 'good' parents (Killus & Paseka, 2016; Paseka, 2017).

The establishment of compulsory school education in the 19th century was by no means supported by all parents. This was particularly true for non-privileged parents (e.g. agricultural workers and craftsmen), who needed their children to work and earn money. Accordingly, working-class parents were seen as problematic by the government and treated as *opponents* of school education (stage 1). After World War II, all children attended school for at least eight years as a matter of course. However, schools at that time largely *ignored* parents. Parents and schools were seen as two separate spheres that – in the best-case scenario – did not come into contact with each other. Parents had to remain outside of school and were only granted entry for formal events (e.g. parent evenings) or if their child was behaving badly or not performing well, when they were 'invited' to come to the school by the teachers (stage 2). This stage was followed by the emergence of early models of parental participation, e.g. in the form of parents' councils. In the 1960s, the first activities were carried out to prepare parents for the task of educating children, treating them as *clients* who needed the support of experts to fulfil their primary tasks (stage 3). In the 1970s/1980s, two new approaches emerged (stage 4). First, parents were treated as *co-therapists* who were expected to continue the treatment started in school to help their children (especially when they had special needs). Second, the implementation of collective rights for parents emphasised their role as *actors*, e.g. with positions on school boards, and having the right to organise themselves in the community as well as at regional and national level (Eurydice, 1997; Witjes & Zimmermann, 2000). From the 1980s/1990s onwards, the importance of parents as actors was further extended, a development that was accompanied by the increasing autonomy of schools in Germany (stage 5). During this period, another change in governmental policy had striking consequences for the role of parents: options for choosing schools were extended, and private schools had the chance to grow. Parents became *consumers*, and schools endeavoured to become more attractive by enticing 'good' – i.e. socially attractive, well-educated – parents. Schools enlarged their education programmes, invited parents to open days and presented good results of external evaluations on their websites (see also Crozier, 2000, for the UK). The 1990s and post-1990s were shaped by the rhetoric of strong partnership and an emphasis on shared responsibility (stage 6). Since then, parents have been treated as *partners* and *experts*, who know a great deal about their children's abilities, needs and interests. It has become expected that parents and teachers share their knowledge to optimise every child's chances of obtaining good learning results. In more recent years (stage 7), parents have increasingly become *political actors*, especially those who are able to organise themselves within the options available. Examples here include the debate on inclusion and the pressure from parents to revoke school reforms.

One aspect that is rarely mentioned is the treatment of parents as *supporters*. Indeed, it would appear that parents are expected to assume this role as a matter of course. However, Tyrell had already criticised the role of families as the 'support system of school' in the 1980s, picking up issues which had been raised much earlier by feminists, e.g. the work done in the shadows by mothers for schools, including their emotional encouragement and ability to cope with school matters in the private realm of the family (Tyrell, 1987).

When we sum up these different ways of treating parents, the 'normative' construction of 'good' and 'bad' parents and different expectations of parents become obvious. When parents are treated as experts, actors or partners, schools expect 'good' parents to demonstrate active engagement by supporting their children and the school with their knowledge and expertise. 'Bad' parents are so-called 'hard-to-reach' parents: they are deemed to be not interested in engagement in school, weak and deficient in their expertise and have low aspirations for their children's education. Such parents are treated as clients, and special programmes (e.g. for non-privileged families in general and migrant/refugee families in particular) are required to remedy their deficiencies (see below; critically for the UK: Edwards & Villies, 2011). When we contrast the abilities of 'good' and 'bad' parents, it becomes evident that their assessment as such is linked to their social status. Well-educated parents with a good income are viewed positively, as they accept the school's dominant rules and expectations. Educationally deprived parents (in combination with a migrant/refugee status) attract negative connotations, as their ideas of school do not fit with expectations.

## 4 Research on parental involvement in Germany: theoretical framework, empirical results and dominant discourses

Two discourses on parental involvement currently dominate in Germany: (1) a normative discourse about concepts of parental involvement, and (2) an empirical discourse asking for evidence.

### 4a Normative discourse

The *normative* discourse is based mainly on Epstein's model of overlapping spheres (Epstein, 1986) and the standards developed by the Parent-Teacher Association in the USA (PTA, 2008). A German group of researchers funded by Vodafone (2012) revised these criteria and presented a paper for schools and practitioners, explaining the criteria and providing examples of how to achieve a high-quality home–school partnership by establishing a culture of welcome and well-being, respectful communication, collaboration in education and learning, and parental participation. The underlying assumption is that such a partnership is a win–win-situation for parents, teachers and students alike and plays a key-role in raising student achievement. The criteria are in line with the political goal to minimise social inequality and maximise inclusion and partnership. There is also some advisory literature for teachers that supports and instructs them how to realise such ideas, albeit without in-depth information on the theoretical and empirical background. In the meantime, this normative discourse has itself become a topic of research and critical analysis (Betz et al., 2017).

## 4b Empirical discourse

*Empirical* research on parental involvement in Germany is fairly heterogeneous in terms of its theoretical background, methodological approaches and research focus. However, there is one main topic that underlies this research: namely, the analysis of the different forms of social inequality (with a strong bias on migrants and 'hard-to-reach' parents). The summaries of current research indicate the following research areas (Sacher, 2012; Killus & Paseka, 2014; Betz et al., 2017):

a) *Expectations of parents concerning school, teachers and education policy.* While a few large surveys have been conducted, only the JAKO-O survey was carried out as trend analysis (2011, 2012, 2014, 2017). Its findings reveal that parents are very satisfied with teachers and the schools their children attend but much less satisfied with education policy. The differences between social classes and ethnic backgrounds are not as strong as expected. One result is remarkable and defies common thinking: non-privileged parents have high expectations, support their children (in some cases more than privileged parents) and are interested in cooperating with the school. In another survey funded by Vodafone (Walper, 2015), some 1,000 parents were interviewed. Their responses indicate a considerable level of uncertainty among parents, especially under-privileged parents. Wippermann et al. (2013) carried out 255 qualitative interviews with parents. Their data demonstrates that expectations, hopes and ways of supporting children and engaging in school are influenced both by socio-economic background and by the norms and values parents view as important. Nine milieus were identified in the German population, including similar milieus for parents with a migration background. The main conclusion of this study was that parents are more heterogeneous than had previously been assumed. A number of other quantitative studies have also included parents in the research, albeit from particular perspectives (e.g. parents of children attending full-day schools) (Züchner, 2011).

b) The *quantity and quality of home–school relationships* has mainly been assessed using questionnaires. These are usually based on various typologies that categorise where the involvement takes place (home- and school-based activities, OECD, 2012) or who is at the centre of the involvement (child-, class- and school-centred activities, Paseka, 2014, based on JAKO-O). A model of parental involvement tested by Schwanenberg (2015) differentiates between three foci of involvement: organisational, conceptual and learning affairs. The results indicate that a majority of parents support their child(ren)'s learning and become involved in organisational matters (e.g. concerning school events) but that only a minority participate in conceptual discussions (e.g. in school committees). Whereas parents with a migrant background are more involved in learning affairs, those without more frequently take on organisational tasks. Parents with a higher income support schools more in organisational and conceptual matters.

c) *Communication between school and parents.* Qualitative research dominates in this field, e.g. the analysis of interviews and authentic conversations (e.g. parent-teacher conferences) using linguistic and reconstructive methods. The main theme is the relationship between parents, teachers and (sometimes) pupils and how these relationships are created at the micro level. The data reveals mechanisms of reproducing social inequality that stem from the institutional setting, intermingled with power and trust, opposing expectations and the resulting opportunities to act (Bormann & Adamczyk, 2016). Non-privileged parents trust the school and teachers but do not have the power to present themselves as actors and 'lawyers' for their children and thus often feel helpless. In contrast, privileged parents have less trust but can present themselves more strongly (Hauser & Mundwiler, 2015).

d) *Correlation with learning results and further effects on pupils.* Such research combines data from large-scale assessments with data about parents. There is a clear correlation between learning results and the social/ethnic background of parents, not only in Germany but across Europe (e.g. for reading literacy, see Feld, 2017). Research on the effects of parental involvement on the assessment of students is rare. The few surveys that have been conducted indicate rather weak effects that only occur if the parental engagement is home-based (Sacher, 2012).

e) *Evaluation of programmes and projects.* In the last decade, many programmes have been developed across Germany to encourage more parents to be more involved. These have been financed in part by the government and in part by private sponsors and foundations. Most of them focus on 'hard-to-reach' parents (with a weak education and/or a migration background) and are aimed at making them 'good' parents who are able to support their children more effectively. Some seek to set up networks of 'school mentors' who are trained to help other parents, while others focus directly on parents by offering them special courses on 'How to support my child at home', or 'How to raise my child's reading or mathematics competencies', or 'How to cope with conflicts in the family'. While many of the programmes are also evaluated, in most cases this takes the form of self-assessments by participants, coordinators and initiators; only a few evaluations also consider the institutional background (e.g. Gerick & Feld, 2018). In general, the vast majority of those involved are quite satisfied and assess the programmes as successful. Only a few such programmes are/were planned as intervention studies with the children tested to determine the success (e.g. McElvany & Artelt, 2006). However, McElvany and Artelt are very critical of their results as the intervention only reached privileged families.

Overall, the results of the research on parental involvement in Germany indicate the following (in concurrence with Betz et al., 2017): (1) Expectations and hopes are fairly high and driven by the desire to decrease social inequality and support under-privileged parents and their children. (2) Programmes, initiatives and advisory literature are based on notions of how 'good' parents should act both in school and at home, notions which, in turn, are based on middle-class standards. (3) Parents are usually divided into two groups: privileged parents with good education and income, non-privileged parents with low education and low income in combination with a migrant background. (4) There is a lack of clarification of the underlying concepts of parental involvement. (5) There is a lack of testing of the effects of parental involvement. (6) There is a lack of analysis of the practices of parental involvement.

## 5 New research perspective: Further research on parental involvement in Germany

### 5a Introduction and research focus

While teachers (not only in Germany) complain that parents show little interest in school, they also complain when they get too involved. One of the aims of the JAKO-O surveys (2011–2017, see above) was to determine to what extent parents are really involved. Their activities were bundled into two categories: home- and school-based involvement (OECD, 2012). Home-based parental involvement includes activities relating to their own child, e.g. helping with homework, discussing school affairs with the child or meeting with teachers to discuss the child's academic achievements. From an analytical perspective, school-based involvement can be differentiated into class- and school-centred activities. The first focuses on parental activities that support their child's class, e.g. accompanying the class on excursions or to swimming lessons, supporting a teacher during a lesson, or serving as a parent representative. The second includes activities that involve the whole school, e.g. helping in the cafeteria, conducting sports or art courses, or serving as an elected representative on the school board. However, it is very difficult to differentiate these two kinds of school-based activities empirically as they are often intertwined (Killus & Paseka, 2014; Paseka, 2014).

The results of the JAKO-O study for *home-based* parental involvement reveal that a majority of parents support their children by checking their homework (73 percent), preparing them for tests and presentations (77 percent), or repeating subject material with them (66 percent) (Killus & Paseka, 2014). As far as *school-based* parental involvement is concerned, we would like to take a closer look at the responses to the following questions: (1) Which school-based parental involvement activities do parents prefer? 2) Are there different groups of parents who prefer different activities? 3) If so, which characteristics of the parents, children and school attract parents to these groups?

### 5b Data source and empirical results for school-based parental involvement

The data presented is taken from the 2014 JAKO-O survey in which 3,000 parents were interviewed via telephone about their opinion and expectations of education policy, schooling and teachers as well as their own support for their children and their school (Killus & Tillmann, 2014). The survey provided representative information on the views of parents across the whole of Germany.

Parents were asked about eight different school-based involvement activities. These were derived from theoretical considerations of informal and formal, occasional and regular, conceptual and practical options. The results (see Figure 2.1) indicated that two-thirds of the parents surveyed accompany class trips and excursions. Such activities only take place occasionally, do not require much commitment and give the parent an opportunity to gain a brief and interesting glimpse into school life. Around one-third of the parents provide more practical help (e.g. by helping to improve classrooms or the schoolyard, serving breakfast or lunch) or offer additional activities in which they are experts (e.g. through courses in the afternoon). One-third of parents also participate in conceptual activities such as discussing school issues in informal working groups or formal school committees. Parents are only rarely involved in classroom activities and help even less with homework at school.

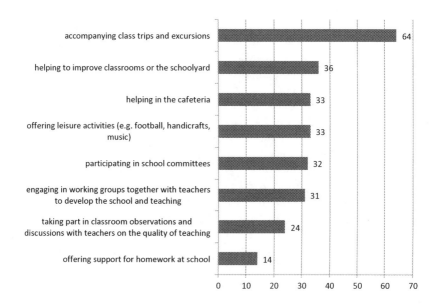

*Figure 2.1* Parental involvement activities (percentages)

*Question*: We would like to find out how parents are involved in several activities offered by the school. In which of the following activities have you/your partner already participated? In your answer, please refer to the school attended by your eldest child of school age. N=3,000 parents.

To determine whether there are indeed groups of parents who prefer certain activities, we carried out a latent class analysis (LCA). This probabilistic approach allowed the identification of subgroups of parents who share common patterns of response. The input variables were the eight parental involvement activities each with the values 0 (*no, not participated*) and 1 (*yes, participated*). Using the statistical programme *Mplus*, a model with four classes emerged (see Figure 2.2).

Class 1 comprised parents who refuse involvement as far as possible (31 percent of parents: hardly any parental involvement). Class 2 is the opposite and included parents who use diverse opportunities to become involved in their child's school (12 percent of parents: diverse range of parental involvement). Class 3 contained parents who accompany class trips and excursions but seldom get involved in other activities (36 percent of parents: class trips and excursions). Class 4 covered parents who not only accompany class trips and excursions but are also interested in more conceptual work, e.g. participating in formal and informal school development committees (21 percent of parents: accompanying activities and school development).

We then sought to determine which characteristics of parents, children and schools influenced their inclusion in one of the groups (educational and migration background of parents, willingness to get involved, type of school attended by the child and perceived willingness of teachers to work with parents). To determine these characteristics, we constructed a new variable with four values (one for each group). Cross tabulations led to the results described below.

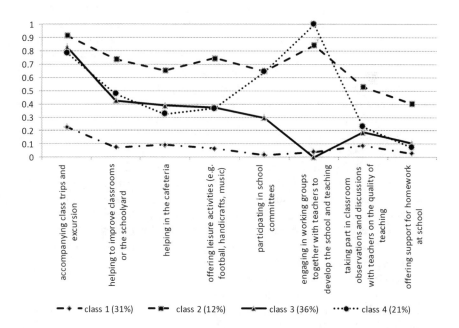

*Figure 2.2* Groups of parents who prefer different parental involvement activities (result of a latent class analysis, class-specific response probabilities)

Only one characteristic was significant and differed consistently for all four groups: the perceived willingness of teachers to work with parents. Those parents who essentially refuse to participate in any activities (class 1) are far less likely than the other classes of parents to experience that teachers are interested in them and signal a desire to cooperate. Parents who experience positive signals from teachers are found more often in classes 2 and 4. These results indicated that parental involvement can be shaped by schools and their staff. In contrast, personal characteristics of parents (such as educational and migration background), school type or child's age have hardly any effect on parental involvement.

In short, the most important factor for initiating and maintaining parental involvement is the school, which can do so by showing interest in parents and creating an atmosphere that supports their engagement for the school. This result is quite astonishing given the frequent complaints about 'hard-to-reach-parents' that are usually directed at migrant and low-educated parents.

## 6 Conclusions

The discussion about *parental involvement* in Germany is highly normative. The concept of 'good' and 'bad' parents is the common theme that underlies the ways parents are treated and leads to complaints about those parents who seem unable to meet the expectations of schools and teachers. However, these expectations themselves are only subjected to critical debate by reconstructing the norms and values that underlie them as 'white' and middle-class standards. The 'hard-to-reach' parents are seen as a less privileged group in terms of their education, financial and migrant background. Programmes are in place across Germany to empower these groups to become able to support their children more effectively and give them a voice in school.

The findings of *research* on parental involvement are partly inconsistent and also fragmentary. The reasons for this include the different concepts that underlie this research, e.g. concerning the term cooperation and its operationalisation, or the use of different criteria to measure success. For Germany, five research fields can be identified. Large assessment surveys provide evidence that good learning results differ along social class and migration status. However, research findings also indicate that parents are by no means a homogenous group – on the contrary, there are differences within a social class or within the migrants group that are not in line with the good/bad parents dichotomy. The results regarding the quantity and quality of home–school cooperation or communication between schools and parents have to be viewed critically insofar as the construction of 'hard-to-reach' only really focuses on the good/bad criterion in combination with social and migrant background. Qualitative studies that analyse such interactions on a micro level confirm this view. Based on the research available, no clear statements can be made concerning the effects of parental involvement.

A survey of parents reveals that their own characteristics are less important than expected by prior research and especially by schools and teachers. Instead, the results show that schools can influence parental involvement more than they think. However, they also indicate a lack of involvement in conceptual activities over all groups of parents. Around one-third of parents participate in such activities – either in informal working groups or more formal school committees. Furthermore, parents are seldom involved in classroom activities designed to develop teaching and even more rarely in supporting homework activities in the school.

While the topic of parents is still a marginal issue in the national political debate and programmatic papers (like those published by the KMK), it is somewhat gaining relevance. Various efforts and initiatives are being undertaken in the *Länder* to focus on parents or at least announce the intent to do so. Our results support the endeavours of the Parent-Teacher Association and the guidelines published for Germany to focus more on the quality of *schools* than on the deficits of parents.

## References

Authoring Group Educational Reporting (2016) *Education in Germany 2016. An Indicator-Based Report Including an Analysis of Education and Migration*. Bielefeld: Bertelsmann.

Barge, K. and Loges, W. (2011) Parent, student, and teacher perception of parental involvement. *Journal of Applied Communication Research*, 31(2), 140–163.

Betz, T., Bischoff, St., Eunicke, N., Kayser, L.B. and Zink, K. (2017) *Partner auf Augenhöhe?* Gütersloh: Verlag Bertelsmann Stiftung.

Bormann, I. and Adamczyk, J. (2016) Typen elterlichen Vertrauens gegenüber Schulen. *Zeitschrift für Bildungsforschung*, 6(2), 169–185.

Crozier, G. (2000) *Parents and Schools: Partners or Protagonists?* Oakhill: Trentham Books.

Edwards, R. and Villies, V. (2011) Clients or consumers, commonplace or pioneers? Navigating the contemporary class politics of family, parenting skills and education. *Ethics and Education*, 6(2), 141–154.

Epstein, J.L. (1986) *Toward an Integrated Theory of School and Family Connections*. Report No. 3. Baltimore: Center for Research on Elementary & Middles Schools.

Eurydice (1997) *The Role of Parents in the Education Systems of the European Union*. Brussels: European Unit of Eurydice.

Feld, I. (2017) Die Relevanz häuslicher Merkmale zur Erklärung von Leseleistung im Vergleich zwischen Kanada und Deutschland. *Tertium Comparationis*, 23(2), 192–216.

Gerick, J. and Feld, I. (2018) *Abschlussbericht der Evaluation des Projekts 'SchulMentoren – Hand in Hand für starke Schulen' in Hamburg*. Projektphase 2014–2017. Hamburg.

Haase, K. (2012) Erziehungs- und Bildungspartnerschaft von Familie, Schule und Kinder- und Jugendhilfe im Kontext der Schulentwicklung. Kooperation auf 'gleicher Augenhöhe' – realistische Leitvorstellung oder unerfüllbare Vision? *Pädagogische Rundschau*, 66(1), 29–44.

Hauser, St. and Mundwiler, V., eds. (2015) *Sprachliche Interaktion in schulischen Elterngesprächen*. Bern: hep Verlag.

Killus, D. (2017) Gemeinsam und auf Augenhöhe. *Friedrich Jahresheft*, XXXV, 5–6.

Killus, D. and Paseka, A. (2014) Elterliches Engagement für das schulische Lernen des eigenen Kindes. In: Killus, D. and Tillmann, K.-J., eds. *Eltern zwischen Erwartungen, Kritik und Engagement. Ein Trendbericht zu Schule und Bildungspolitik.* Münster u.a.: Waxmann. 131–148.

Killus, D. and Paseka, A. (2016) Eltern als Partner, Zulieferer oder Kunden von Schule? Empirische Befunde zum Verhältnis von Elternhaus und Schule. *Zeitschrift für Bildungsforschung,* 6(2), 151–168.

Killus, D. and Tillmann, K.-J., eds. (2014) *Eltern zwischen Erwartungen, Kritik und Engagement. Ein Trendbericht zu Schule und Bildungspolitik.* Münster u.a.: Waxmann.

KMK (Kultusministerkonferenz) (2018) *Information in English.* Available at: www.kmk.org/information-in-english.html (accessed 1 Aug. 2018).

McElvany, N. and Artelt, C. (2006) Das Berliner Eltern-Kind Leseprogramm. *Diskurs Kindheits- und Jugendforschung,* 1, 157–159.

OECD (2012) *Parental Involvement in Selected PISA-Countries and Economies.* OECD Education Working Paper number 73.

Paseka, A. (2014) Elternbeteiligung auf Klassen- und Schulebene. In: Killus, D. and Tillmann, K.-J., eds. *Eltern zwischen Erwartungen, Kritik und Engagement. Ein Trendbericht zu Schule und Bildungspolitik, 3. JAKO-O Bildungsstudie.* New York: Waxmann. 111–130.

Paseka, A. (2017) Gegner, Kunden oder Partner? *Friedrich Jahresheft,* XXXV, 29–31.

PTA (2008) *PTA National Standards for Family–school Partnerships.* USA. Available at: www.heartlandaea.org/media/documents/National_Standards_Assessment_Guide_5B9F37E771CD5.pdf (accessed 16 Apr. 2018).

Sacher, W. (2008) *Elternarbeit. Gestaltungsmöglichkeiten und Grundlagen für alle Schularten.* Bad Heilbrunn: Klinkhardt.

Sacher, W. (2012) Erziehungs- und Bildungspartnerschaften in der Schule: zum Forschungsstand. In: Stange, W. et al., eds. *Erziehungs- und Bildungspartnerschaften. Grundlagen und Strukturen von Elternarbeit.* Wiesbaden: Springer. 232–243.

Schwanenberg, J. (2015) *Elterliches Engagement im schulischen Kontext. Analyse der Formen und Motive.* Münster: Waxmann.

Stange, W. (2012) Erziehungs- und Bildungspartnerschaften. Grundlagen, Strukturen, Begründungen. In: Stange, W. et al., eds. *Erziehungs- und Bildungspartnerschaften. Grundlagen und Strukturen von Elternarbeit.* Wiesbaden: Springer. 12–39.

Tyrell, H. (1987) Die 'Anpassung' der Familie an die Schule. In: Oelkers, J. and Tenorth, H.-E., eds. *Pädagogik. Erziehungswissenschaft und Systemtheorie.* Weinheim: Beltz. 102–125.

Ule, M., Živoder, A. and Bois-Reymond, M.du. (2015) 'Simply the best for my children': Patterns of parental involvement in education. *International Journal of Qualitative Studies in Education,* 28(3), 329–348.

Vandenbroeck, M., Geens, N., Geinger, F., Schiettecat, T., Van Haute, D. and Roets, G. (2017) Parenting newspeak. *Journal of Family Research,* Special Issue 11, 23–40.

Vodafone-Stiftung, ed. (2012) *Qualitätsmerkmale schulischer Elternarbeit.* Available at: www.vodafone-stiftung.de/pages/presse/publikationen/subpages/qualitaetsmerkmale_schulischer_elternarbeit/index.html (accessed 12 Jun. 2018).

Walper, S. (2015) *Was Eltern wollen: Informations- und Unterstützungswünsche zu Bildung und Erziehung. Eine Befragung des Instituts für Demoskopie Allensbach.* Vodafone Stiftung Deutschland. Available at: www.vodafone-stiftung.de/uploads/tx_newsjson/Vodafone_Stiftung_Was_Eltern_wollen_2015_02.pdf (accessed 12 Jun. 2018).

Wippermann, K., Wippermann, C. and Kirchner, A. (2013) *Eltern – Lehrer – Schulerfolg. Wahrnehmungen und Erfahrungen im Schulalltag von Eltern und Lehrern.* Stuttgart: Lucius & Lucius.
Witjes, W. and Zimmermann, P. (2000) Elternmitwirkung in der Schule. Eine Bestandsaufnahme in fünf BundesLändern. In: Rolff, H.-G. et al., eds. *Jahrbuch der Schulentwicklung.* Weinheim & München: Juventa. 221–256.
Züchner, I. (2011) Ganztagsschulen und Familienleben. In: Fischer, N. et al., eds. *Ganztagsschule: Entwicklung, Qualität, Wirkungen.* Weinheim & Basel: Beltz. 291–311.

# 3 Iceland

Home–school cooperation in Iceland: characteristics and values

*Kristín Jónsdóttir and Amalía Björnsdóttir*

## 1 Introduction

In this chapter, we examine the organisation of the home–school relationship in Iceland, with reference to how it is described in Icelandic laws on compulsory schooling from 2008, and in the national curriculum. Furthermore, we discuss findings on home–school cooperation in light of educational policy that seeks to uphold the values of equity and quality. Parental involvement is a young research field in Iceland with few published research papers. However, even if research is limited, there is still a long tradition of home–school relationships both in pre-primary and compulsory schools. A positive relationship is considered an important part of school culture, and teachers hold a key position in developing the home–school relationship, just as in many other areas of school development (Jónsdóttir, 2005).

## 2 Overview of educational system in Iceland

Pre-primary (*leikskóli*) and compulsory education (*grunnskóli*) is the responsibility of municipalities in Iceland, and in a sense is somewhat decentralised. However, the system itself is largely centralised as the parliament determines the basic objectives and administrative framework of the educational system. The implementation of legislation is in the hands of the Ministry of Education, Science, and Culture, administrating at all four levels of education in the country, from pre-primary to higher education.

Pre-primary education is the first level of the educational system, providing education for children below compulsory school age (The Preschool Act No. 90, 2008). Pre-primary education is not mandatory, but the vast majority of Icelandic children attend pre-school and the fees are heavily subsidised. Over 80 percent of the children attending pre-schools stay in school for eight hours a day. In 2016, the total number of pre-schools in Iceland was 254, and the municipalities ran 213 of those (Statistics Iceland, 2017a).

The second level of the educational system is compulsory education for children aged 6–16 years old. Compulsory education is mandatory, which may be provided by municipalities or privately (The Compulsory School Act

No. 91, 2008). Most schools are single structured, with integrated primary and lower secondary levels. The municipalities are responsible for compulsory education and run most schools. There are just a few compulsory schools that are operated by private companies, mostly in the Reykjavík area. Parents choose such schools because of the pedagogical concepts offered there, and sometimes have to pay small fees. In 2016, the total number of compulsory schools in Iceland was 170, and the municipalities run 157 of them. Thirteen schools were operated by educational organisations but mainly funded by municipalities (Statistics Iceland, 2017b).

The third level is secondary education for students age 16 years and older, with a diversity of programmes for two, three, or four years. Upper secondary schools are run by the state (The Upper Secondary Education Act, No. 92, 2008). The fourth level is higher education and adult education (The Higher Education Act, No. 63, 2006). Higher education is provided at universities, either by the state or by private organisations. Institutions, companies, and organisations also provide adult education.

Both pre-primary and compulsory schools are single shift schools (Statistics Iceland, 2017c), meaning that all classes start at the same time. Children up to the age of 10 years can be in the care of the school for up to nine hours a day. Whole-day school is available, but parents pay for after-school programmes (i.e., from 2–5 pm) in compulsory schools if they choose to use that service. Parents pay for their child's education in pre-school according to the length of stay.

Policymakers in Iceland take pride in stating that Icelandic schools are inclusive and, according to the law, provide appropriate and quality education for all students according to their needs. According to Statistics Iceland (2017d), only 0.38 percent of students in compulsory schools in Iceland attend special schools. Special schools are intended for students with severe learning or behavioural difficulties, but children with physical handicaps attend their neighbourhood schools. Despite several obstacles, the schools have succeeded quite well in being inclusive, and international studies have shown high levels of equity amongst compulsory schools (Sigurðardóttir, Guðjónsdóttir, & Karlsdóttir, 2014). Lack of funding in recent years, after the economic downfall in 2008, has made it harder for schools to fulfil the demands of the official inclusion policy.

## 3 Parental involvement in Iceland

The terms regarding parental involvement in Iceland are not clearly defined in The Compulsory School Act of 2008 or The National Curriculum Guide for Compulsory Schools. It is assumed that stakeholders have a similar understanding or the same ideas of what the home–school relationship might mean, but a lack of clear definitions opens the way for misunderstandings in discussions. Another challenge, or perhaps a consequence, are the widely different translations of Icelandic terms into other languages.

## 3a Terminology

The term used in this chapter is 'home–school relationship' (*tengsl heimila og skóla; samstarf heimila og skóla*) and refers to the connection between the two important institutions in every child's life: school and home. 'Parent–teacher relation' (*samband foreldra og kennara*) is another broad term often used to comprise home–school relations. Parents and teachers are key persons in the home–school relationship concerning children's education in Iceland. Therefore, it is sometimes more appropriate to refer to parent–teacher relations instead of home–school relations, since the core is the connection between individuals (Christiansen, 2010). A distinction should be made between communication and cooperation whenever possible, but these terms are often used interchangeably in discussions and writings, in both Icelandic and other languages, when referring to parent–teacher relations. The idea that communication or any contact between home and school automatically includes cooperation is often taken for granted, but that is not necessarily true (Dannesboe et al., 2012; Jónsdóttir, Björnsdóttir & Bæck, 2017).

'Parental involvement' (*hlutdeild foreldra*) is the broadest term used in Icelandic research in the field, and it includes communication, cooperation, and participation (Jónsdóttir, 2018). The term is equivalent to the home–school relationship and parent–teacher relations. It also refers to opportunities for parents to be involved in policymaking and management of compulsory schools (Kristoffersson, 2009).

In Icelandic documents, the term 'parents' (*foreldrar*) is used to refer to parents and other adults who have legal custody of children. 'Parents' participation' (*þátttaka foreldra*) describes parents who attend social school events or take part in other school activities. Parents can also participate by assisting their children with homework, and in policymaking and management (Guðmundsson, 2003). Parental participation can therefore refer to an inactive role as passive attendants at social events, as well as to active participation regarding the child and the child's school.

The 'supervisory teacher' (*umsjónarkennari*) has special obligations regarding parental involvement in Icelandic compulsory schools. Each class is assigned a supervisory teacher at the beginning of the school year, but it is common for classes to have the same supervisory teacher for three or four school years. Supervisory teachers monitor their students' studies, personal development and general welfare. They guide students in their studies and school work, and provide assistance and advice regarding personal matters, thus strengthening the cooperation between school and home (The Compulsory School Act No. 91, 2008). The special role of the supervisory teacher as a link between school and home, and as the students' special guardian and adviser, is well known and acknowledged in different ways in Icelandic society. The Office of The Ombudsman for Children (2017) affirms this status; the Ombudsman is an official national protector of children´s rights. This office states that the supervisory teacher should always be the first person consulted when students encounter a problem that affects their studies and well-being at school.

## 3b National legislative and regulative context

Comprehensive legislation regarding children's education first appeared with the Compulsory School Act No. 63/1974. Before that, laws from 1946 regarding children´s schooling were in force, but home–school cooperation was not mentioned. Research shows, however, that some principals introduced meetings with parents much earlier: the first was mentioned in 1910, and a journal called *The Parents Paper* was first published in 1930 (Guttormsson, 2008).

In the Compulsory School Act 1974, Article 21, parents' rights to influence regarding their children's schooling are described as follows: 'If a principal, teachers' assembly or parents, having children at school, wish for a Parents Council to support the school and promote relations between schools and parents, then the school leader is obliged to establish a Parents Council'. Furthermore, the Article states that a Parents Council forms its own operating procedures, and its representative can participate in teachers' assembly but without voting rights.

After almost half a century, parental rights have grown and are clearly defined by laws. Now, Article 2 of Compulsory School Act No. 91/2008 addresses the legal rights of parents and the home–school relationship: 'The compulsory school shall encourage good cooperation between the school and the home, with the objective of ensuring successful school operation, general welfare and safety for pupils.' The policy on shared responsibility of home and school in the upbringing and education of children is reinforced in The Icelandic National Curriculum Guide for Compulsory Schools General Section from 2011. According to the Compulsory School Act and the National Curriculum, parents have the formal right to choose a compulsory school for their children in accordance with the regulation of the municipality, and to have the special needs of their children met at that school. However, there is a long tradition that children attend school in their local area.

Every school district has a School Board for all compulsory schools in the municipality; this arrangement of communal governance over the schools has been in effect for two decades. The School Board is the official authority and makes all major decisions on policy issues. Headmasters, teachers, and parents (or parents´ associations in bigger municipalities) elect one representative, each to take part in the School Board meetings, with the right to speak and propose a motion (The Compulsory School Act, No. 91, 2008). Parents' representatives and parents' organisations participate in school boards policy development but have no formal influence at the national level.

Parents' opportunities to influence school practices increased with the Compulsory School Act in 2008, as Article 8 states that every compulsory school in Iceland is also required to have its own School Council with two parent representatives. The School Council participates in policymaking for the school and discusses the school curriculum guide and annual operational schedule, amongst other things. The School Council has a say regarding any plans for major changes to school operations and activities before a final decision is made (The Compulsory School Act, No. 91, 2008). Every compulsory school also has a Parents Council, an organisation for the parents of all students. The role of the Parents Council is defined in Article 9, as 'to support school activities, encourage pupils' welfare and promote the relations between school and home'.

Articles 6, 8 and 9 grant parents' significant possibilities to influence their children's schools. New legislation and associated regulations are indicative of the educational policy, which aims to increase the impact and responsibility of parents. Both political and pedagogical arguments support this emphasis on the role of parents and their influence within Icelandic compulsory schools (Finnbogason, 2009), but parent representatives face a difficult task when representing all parents. This is also the situation in neighbouring countries; a Norwegian study showed that parent representatives on school boards and school councils face complicated tasks because parents are never a homogenous group (Bæck, 2009). In a Swedish study about parental involvement through local school boards, Kristoffersson (2009) found that parental influence has increased in recent years, but questions whether or not this really has a positive effect on local democracy as intended.

Parents are entitled to have detailed information about their child school and about their child's schooling. According to compulsory school law and the national curriculum, every school must publish a school curriculum and a plan for the school year, containing information on school values, important events and daily practices. Parents have the right to access all information about their child collected by the school. That includes everything registered by school staff regarding the child's education, behaviour and well-being. One of the challenges that compulsory schools in Iceland now face is how to comply with the *General Data Protection Regulation* and the extensive use of school information systems.

## 4 Existing research on parental involvement in Iceland

Parental involvement is a young research field in Iceland, with few published research papers. Most of the available writings regarding home–school relationships, e.g. in articles for teachers, have mainly focused on giving teachers good advice on how to handle home–school relations in a professional manner, referring to some research and to the writer's own experience. Parent organisations have not published research papers but have published informative articles on home–school relations, advising parents and explaining their rights. In recent years, there has been some new interest in the field of parental involvement, with a more critical approach in research taking a closer look at how social factors influence education.

Nevertheless, even if research is limited, there is still a long tradition of home–school relationships, both in pre-primary and compulsory schools. Cooperation is considered an important part of school culture, and teachers hold a key position in developing home–school relations, just as in many other aspects of school development (Jónsdóttir, 2005). A study on school discipline in compulsory schools in Reykjavík showed that in schools where teachers had positive attitudes towards parental involvement the disciplinary problems were fewer than in schools where home–school relations were weaker (Sigurgeirsson & Kaldalóns, 2006). There were frequent invitations encouraging parents to get involved, and great emphasis was put on informing parents with newsletters and emails, focusing on communicating positive results, successes, and victories. Even though causality is questionable, the findings reveal that the school staff in the 'problem-free' schools managed to blend kindness into their organised relations with parents, and this correlated with fewer disciplinary problems.

The options for parents to become involved in their child's education have been strengthened during the last 50 years. At the same time, developments towards inclusive schooling have been ongoing and it is apparent that parents, or at least some parents, feel more confident now in requesting support and services for their children. There are several blind spots in Icelandic research in the field even though the research project described below maps out the characteristics of home–school relations and brings forth a social critical perspective on the topic. A better understanding of social factors and power structures within the Icelandic educational system seems necessary. Nordic or international cooperative studies would be useful, comparing organisation and preferences and discovering barriers in home–school relations. A broader perspective is needed in Iceland on how to develop competencies amongst school staff as well as strategies of cooperation according to different situations in diverse schools and municipalities.

## 5 New research perspective: parental involvement in compulsory schools

A research project called *Teaching and learning in Icelandic compulsory schools* started in Iceland in 2009. The aim was to provide an overview of school practices at the beginning of the 21st century, with special emphasis on exploring the development towards individualised learning (Björnsdóttir & Jónsdóttir, 2014; Jónsdóttir & Björnsdóttir, 2014; Óskarsdóttir, 2014; Óskarsdóttir et al., 2014a, 2014b). This project contributed to the research base in many areas of educational research in Iceland, including parental involvement.

The project *Parental involvement in compulsory schools in Iceland* (Jónsdóttir, 2013, 2015b, 2018; Jónsdóttir & Björnsdóttir, 2012; Jónsdóttir, Björnsdóttir & Bæck, 2017) uses data that was collected as part of the project *Teaching and learning in Icelandic compulsory schools*. The data was gathered in

2009–2011, from questionnaires to all school staff and the parents of first to tenth grade students in 20 compulsory schools, as well as from a questionnaire for seventh to tenth grade students in 14 schools; six of the 20 participating schools did not have students at the lower secondary level. The schools were situated in four municipalities; 17 schools were selected randomly and three schools were selected because of their emphasis on individualised learning. The sample was large; for example, the students in those 20 schools were 17 percent of all students in compulsory schools in Iceland. The response rate was 67 percent (n=3,481) for the parents, around 82 percent (n=823) for staff, and 86 percent (n=1,821) for the students.

The project *Parental involvement in compulsory schools in Iceland* (Jónsdóttir, 2018) was guided by the overall research question: What role does parental involvement play in compulsory schools in Iceland? Three underpinning questions were addressed. 1) What characterises the home–school relationship and the cooperation between parents and teachers? 2) What do teenagers prefer regarding parents' participation and how could their wishes affect cooperation? 3) Which factors influence parents' satisfaction with schools and how do they affect the home–school relationship? The main findings are presented briefly in the following sections.

## 5a Characteristics of home–school relationship

The organisation of the home–school relationship in Iceland seems similar to that in other Nordic countries, and the supervisory teacher plays a leading role. There are two or three 15–20 minute parent–teacher conferences per year, in addition to communication via emails, letters, and phone calls. Parents also attend various social events. The organisation of communication seems to be systematic and regular, which is considered important for empowering parents and keeping them involved in schools.

There was little parental initiative in contacting teachers, and the results indicate that many Icelandic parents are rather distant from schools. Over half of Icelandic parents said they contacted teachers less than annually regarding their child's behaviour or student interactions, and less than 28 percent contacted teachers annually about their child´s learning. However, 90 percent of parents found communication with supervisory teachers to be easy, and much easier than with other teachers or principals and heads of departments (Jónsdóttir & Björnsdóttir, 2012).

Cooperating with parents was slightly more difficult for the supervisory teachers: 77 percent indicated that the communication with parents was easy, 16 percent were neutral, and 7 percent found that communicating with parents was difficult. The youngest teachers, aged 29 years or younger, found contact with parents more difficult than older teachers, indicating a need for supporting young teachers in parent–teacher cooperation (Jónsdóttir & Björnsdóttir, 2014).

Teachers spend considerable time on the home–school relationship: two-thirds said this amounted to two to four hours per week. A major part of the cooperation concerns individual students, and the reason for contacting parents most often regards a student's behavioural problems in class (Jónsdóttir & Björnsdóttir, 2012). Apparently, Icelandic teachers spend more time communicating with parents about bad behaviour or learning difficulties than on growing a positive relationship with the parent group. Given these results, it is worth considering whether supervisory teachers' time on home–school relations is sensibly spent.

According to Jónsdóttir (2013), most adults (parents and school staff) favour the more traditional kind of parental participation, which primarily involves social activities. The strongest opinions appeared in the answers from school staff, as 98 percent found it to be rather or very desirable to have parents attend extracurricular activities, such as social events in school, and 85 percent wanted parents to participate in organising these activities. Parents who are satisfied with the cooperation may feel little need for stepping out of secure grounds and adding new roles more related to their child's studies to their traditional social support role. Teachers may also feel little need for opening their field of practice (Jónsdóttir, 2013; Jónsdóttir & Björnsdóttir, 2014). The result is that supervisory teachers alone continue to carry the main responsibility for students' education and well-being in school.

## 5b Teenagers' opinions on their parents' participation

Students' voices in research on parental involvement in schools are rather weak as many studies report only the opinions of parents and school staff. Results on teenage students' wishes regarding parental involvement (Jónsdóttir, 2015b) revealed that the students in the seventh to tenth grades have preferences differing from adults. The teenagers really showed an interest in relating parental participation to their academic activities, not just social events. Students wanted their parents to engage, and gender, grade, and student confidence in their learning ability explained some of the variance in students' wishes. Girls were more positive towards parents' participation than boys were, and as they grew older, student interest in parents involvment diminished. Students' positive opinion and experiences in school went hand-in-hand with positive opinions about parental participation. Those variables explained 18 percent of the variability in teenagers' wishes for parental participation.

The supervisory teachers' importance in this matter was also reflected in the analysis of the data. If student estimates on the quality of teaching and on relations with teachers rose, they were also more positive towards parental participation. Furthermore, students who were pleased to be in school and took an interest in their learning tasks and homework found parental participation more desirable than those who reported poor contact with their teachers or found their tasks boring. The belief that parental support as well as discipline and a peaceful class environment affect the students' achievement were the two most influential variables in explaining teenagers' opinions (Jónsdóttir, 2015b).

Implications for the supervisory teachers are that they should direct home–school cooperation more into activities related to the academic side of school life, act to improve the relations between students and themselves, and focus on the quality of teaching. The result would be increased student interest for parental participation, which in turn would positively contribute to academic achievement.

### 5c Pressure on the parent–teacher relationship

Parents and school professionals in Iceland completely agreed that working together is important for the education of children (Jónsdóttir & Björnsdóttir, 2012). Overall, 99 percent of parents and school professionals considered parental support rather or very important for academic achievement. Furthermore, 95 percent of teachers considered cooperation with parents vital to ensure proper behaviour in schools. At a first glance, the findings portray parents as a rather homogenous group, all in a happy relationship with their children's schools; around 85 percent of parents were totally, very or rather satisfied with the schools, and only around 6 percent were unsatisfied.

When further explored, a distinctive group of parents could be revealed: those whose children have some problems in school due to educational and/or behavioural difficulties (Jónsdóttir, 2015a). Around one-quarter of the parents said that their child needed special support, assistance, or teaching. Interestingly, more than half of those children did not get any or not enough support from the school. When parents of children with learning or behavioural problems feel that schools do not meet their needs, they perceive the communication with supervisory teachers as difficult and are dissatisfied with the school in general. Surprisingly, if parents feel that schools meet the special needs of their child, they are more satisfied and find the communication even easier than parents who have children with no special needs (Jónsdóttir & Björnsdóttir, 2012). One can assume that the discontented and disappointed parents are those who take up most of the supervisory teachers' time and put pressure on the parent–teacher relationship.

### 5d Parents' education and marital status matters

The feeling of being able to influence the school's decisions and future vision is important to parents (Jónsdóttir, Björnsdóttir & Bæck, 2017). This result supports findings from studies that failing to include parents in important decisions in school settings indicates they are not treated as equals (Bæck, 2009). International research has shown that parental participation in school-related activities contributes to children's success in school (Desforges & Abouchaar, 2003; Hattie, 2009, 2012; Jeynes, 2005, 2011). Parents experience pressure to participate because they believe it is in their child's best interest (Böök & Perälä-Littunen, 2014). The results in this Icelandic study echo these findings: both parents and school professionals believe that parental support is essential for the academic achievement of children.

Parents with more formal education are more likely to participate in home–school cooperation and acknowledge the importance of parental support in education (Bæck, 2009). Researchers claim that schools are more likely to match middle-class parents' values and involvement styles than those of the working class (Bæck, 2005; Lareau, 2000). This may affect the extent to which parents' voices are heard when arguing for their child's needs for special support in school. Even though parental assessment of whether their child needs special support in school is not the basis for schools' decisions to provide such support, parental confidence in speaking on behalf of their child may play a role in the decision. Worryingly, according to our results, single mothers are overrepresented in the group of parents who view their children in need of special support in school but who do not get any or not enough.

The educational level amongst single mothers was lower compared to the other parent groups in this study, and the findings revealed that the parents' educational background influenced aspects such as receiving special support in school (Jónsdóttir, Björnsdóttir & Bæck, 2017). Results also showed that it was somewhat harder for schools to please the more educated parents. Single mothers felt powerless compared to other parents, but were also more willing than others to participate in social activities at school. Perhaps school staff tended to listen more carefully when two parents spoke on behalf of a child, or when those with higher levels of education voiced their concerns. Bearing in mind that the majority of teachers in Icelandic compulsory schools are women, just like the single mothers, these findings also call for critical discussions about respect and power structures within the school system.

## 6 Conclusion

It is a common belief that Iceland is a society of educational equity. The present findings concerning different levels of access to special support, the influence of parents' educational level, and the importance of feeling that the school appreciates parents' opinions, all contest the idea of equity as a major value in the relationship between schools and student families. A major issue that needs to be addressed is probably the *illusion* of equity, since it is not necessarily a leading value in practice. It is necessary to acknowledge that the social status, gender, educational level, and cultural values of parents have, indeed, an impact on the rationale and practice of parental involvement in Icelandic schools, just as in schools in other countries (Bæck, 2009, 2010; Pepe & Addimando, 2014).

The Icelandic educational system is presented as upholding the values of equity and quality. Perhaps that is why the downplaying of equity in practice remains rather unnoticed, but it is displayed in parents' dissatisfaction in this study. Quality and equity are often promoted as values generally emphasised in Nordic countries (Sahlberg, 2014), but the findings discussed here signal the importance of bringing these values forth when working with home–school relations and including them in discussions about school development, where school professionals, parents, and students should all have a respected voice.

## References

Bæck, U.-D.K. (2005) School as an Arena for Activating Cultural Capital: Understanding Differences in Parental Involvement in School. *Nordisk Pedagogik*, 25(3), 217–228.

Bæck, U.-D.K. (2009) From a distance. How Norwegian parents experience their encounters with school. *International Journal of Educational Research*, 48(5), 342–351.

Bæck, U.-D.K. (2010) Parental involvement practices in formalized home–school cooperation. *Scandinavian Journal of Educational Research*, 54(6), 549–563.

Björnsdóttir, A. and Jónsdóttir, K. (2014) Viðhorf nemenda, foreldra og starfsmanna skóla. In: Óskarsdóttir, G.G., ed. *Starfshættir í grunnskólum við upphaf 21. aldar*. Reykjavík: Háskólaútgáfan. 29–56.

Böök, M. and Perälä-Littunen, S. (2014) Responsibility in home–school relations. Finnish parents' views. *Children & Society*, 29(6), 615–625.

Christiansen, N.K. (2010) *Skóli og skólaforeldrar: Ný sýn á samstarfið um nemandann*. Reykjavík: Author.

The Compulsory School Act No. 63. 1974.

The Compulsory School Act No. 91. 2008. Available at: http://eng.menntamalaraduneyti.is/Acts (accessed 13 Mar. 2018).

Dannesboe, K.I., Kryger, N., Palludan, C. and Ravn, B. (2012) En hverdaglivsstudie af skole-hjem-relationer. In: Dannesboe, K.I., Kryger, N., Palludan, C. and Ravn, B., eds. *Hvem sagde samarbejde? et hverdagslivsstudie af skole-hjem-relationer*. Aarhus: Aarhus universitetsforlag. 9–20.

Desforges, C. and Abouchaar, A. (2003) *The impact of parental involvement, parental support and family education on pupil achievement and adjustment*. Annesley, Nottingham: DfES Publications.

Finnbogason, G.E. (2009) Nútímaskóli – ný grunnskólalög. *Uppeldi og menntun*, 18(1), 105–109.

Guðmundsson, K.B. (2003) Samskipti heimilis og skóla: Forsendur, umfang og leiðir. In: Hansen, B., Jóhannsson, Ó.H. and Lárusdóttir, S.H., eds. *Fagmennska og forysta*. Reykjavík: Rannsóknastofnun Kennaraháskóla Íslands. 137–155.

Guttormsson, L. (2008) *Almenningsfræðsla á Íslandi 1880–2007*. Reykjavík: Háskólaútgáfan.

Hattie, J. (2009) *Visible learning: a synthesis of over 800 meta-analyses relating to achievement*. New York: Routledge.

Hattie, J. (2012) *Visible Learning for Teachers: Maximizing Impact on Learning*. London: Routledge.

The Higher Education Act No. 63. 2006. Available at: https://eng.menntamalaraduneyti.is/media/frettir2015/Thyding-log-um-haskola-oktober-2015.pdf (accessed 13 Mar. 2018).

Jeynes, W. (2005) A meta-analysis of the relation of parental involvement to urban elementary school student academic achievement. *Urban Education*, 40(3), 237–269.

Jeynes, W. (2011) *Parental Involvement and Academic Success*. New York: Routledge.

Jónsdóttir, K. (2005) Er unglingakennslan einstaklingsmiðuð? Rannsókn á kennsluháttum og viðhorfum kennara á unglingastigi grunnskóla í Reykjavík. *Uppeldi og menntun*, 14(2), 33–55.
Jónsdóttir, K. (2013) Desirable parental participation in activities in compulsory schools. *BARN*, 4, 29–44.
Jónsdóttir, K. (2015a) *A Happy Relationship Between Parents and Compulsory Schools. Symposium, Part 2: Positive Parenting: Assessment, Programmes and Evaluation.* Paper presented at the ECER, 10th of September 2015, Budapest.
Jónsdóttir, K. (2015b) Teenagers opinions on parental involvement in compulsory schools in Iceland. *International Journal about Parents in Education*, 9(1), 24–36.
Jónsdóttir, K. (2018) *Parental Involvement in Compulsory Schools in Iceland*. PhD. University of Iceland.
Jónsdóttir, K. and Björnsdóttir, A. (2012) Home–school relationships and cooperation between parents and supervisory teachers. *BARN*, 4, 109–127.
Jónsdóttir, K. and Björnsdóttir, A. (2014) Foreldrasamstarf. In: Óskarsdóttir, G.G., ed. *Starfshættir í grunnskólum við upphaf 21. aldar.* Reykjavík: Háskólaútgáfan. 197–216.
Jónsdóttir, K., Björnsdóttir, A. and Bæck, U. (2017) Influential factors behind parents' general satisfaction with compulsory schools in Iceland. *Nordic Journal of Studies in Educational Policy*, 3(2), 155–164.
Kristoffersson, M. (2009) Parental involvement all the way through local school boards. *International Journal about Parents in Education*, 3(1), 37–41.
Lareau, A. (2000) *Home Advantage: Social Class and Parental Intervention in Elementary Education*. Second edition. Lanham: Rowman & Littlefield.
Ombudsman for Children (Umboðsmaður barna) (2017) Available at: www.barn.is/um-embaettid/upplysingar-a-erlendum-tungumalum/enska/ (accessed 13 Mar. 2018).
Óskarsdóttir G.G. (2014) *Starfshættir í grunnskólum við upphaf 21. aldar*. Reykjavík: Háskólaútgáfan.
Óskarsdóttir, G.G., Björnsdóttir, A., Sigurðardóttir, A.K., Hansen, B., Sigurgeirsson, I., Jónsdóttir, K., Sigþórsson, R. and Jakobsdóttir, S. (2014a) Framkvæmd rannsóknar. In: Óskarsdóttir, G.G., ed. *Starfshættir í grunnskólum við upphaf 21. aldar*. Reykjavík: Háskólaútgáfan, 17–27.
Óskarsdóttir, G.G., Björnsdóttir, A., Sigurðardóttir, A.K., Hansen, B., Sigurgeirsson, I., Jónsdóttir, K., Sigþórsson, R. and Jakobsdóttir, S. (2014b) Starfshættir í grunnskólum: meginniðurstöður og umræða. In: Óskarsdóttir, G.G., ed. *Starfshættir í grunnskólum við upphaf 21. aldar*. Reykjavík: Háskólaútgáfan. 323–347.
Pepe, A. and Addimando, L. (2014) Teacher-parent relationships: Influence of gender and education on organizational parents' counterproductive behaviors. *European Journal of Psychology of Education*, 29(3), 503–519. DOI:10.1007/s10212-014-0210-0
The Preschool Act No. 90. 2008. Available at: https://eng.menntamalaraduneyti.is/media/MRN-pdf_Annad/Preschool_Act.pdf (accessed 13 Mar. 2018).
Sahlberg, P. (2014) *True Facts and Tales about Teachers and Teaching: A Nordic Point of View*. Paper presented at the Future teachers: A profession at Crossroads: 14th of August 2014, Reykjavík: Iceland. Available at: http://starfsthrounkennara.is/future-teachers-a-profession-at-crossroads (accessed 13 Mar. 2018).
Sigurðardóttir, A.K., Guðjónsdóttir, H. and Karlsdóttir, J. (2014) The development of a school for all in Iceland: Equality, threats and political conditions. In: Blossing, U. et al., eds. *The Nordic education model: 'A School for All' encounters neo-liberal policy*. Dordrecht: Springer. 95–113. Available at: https://link.springer.com/content/pdf/10.1007%2F978-94-007-7125-3.pdf (accessed 13 Mar. 2018).

Sigurgeirsson, I. and Kaldalóns, I. (2006) *Gullkista við enda regnbogans: rannsókn á hegðunarvanda í grunnskólum Reykjavíkur skólaárið 2005-2006*. Reykjavík: Rannsóknarstofnun Kennaraháskóla Íslands.

Statistics Iceland (2017a) *Pre-Primary Schools*. Available at: www.statice.is/statistics/society/education/pre-primary-schools/ (accessed 13 Mar. 2018).

Statistics Iceland (2017b) *Compulsory Schools*. Available at: https://hagstofa.is/utgafur/frettasafn/menntun/nemendur-og-starfsfolk-i-grunnskolum-haustid-2016// (accessed 13 Mar. 2018).

Statistics Iceland (2017c) *Single Shift System in Schools 1998-2016*. Available at: http://px.hagstofa.is/pxen/pxweb/en/Samfelag/Samfelag__skolamal__2_grunnskolastig__2_gsSkolahald/SKO02201.px/table/tableViewLayout1/?rxid=10c917dd-9c59-461a-8ec7-5c8c3f957904 (accessed 13 Mar. 2018).

Statistics Iceland (2017d) *Private, Public and Special Compulsory Schools 1998–2016*. Available at: http://px.hagstofa.is/pxen/pxweb/en/Samfelag/Samfelag__skolamal__2_grunnskolastig__2_gsSkolahald/SKO02202.px/table/tableViewLayout1/?rxid=f9ca4d9a-9453-4590-8f5b-b4dfa27eeffb (accessed 13 Mar. 2018).

The Upper Secondary Education Act No. 92 (2008) Available at: https://eng.menntamalaraduneyti.is/media/frettatengt2016/Thyding-log-um-framhaldsskola-juli-2016.pdf (accessed 13 Mar. 2018).

# 4 Ireland

Parental involvement in Ireland

*Delma Byrne*

## 1 Introduction

Since the mid-1970s, Ireland has experienced considerable change in the relationship between parents, schools and the State. Over the period of the 1970s–1990s, the discourse of parents as partners in education spread beyond contexts defined as 'educationally disadvantaged' and into the mainstream. Thus, in the Irish context, the policy interest in parental involvement has always been strongly linked to the concept of social inequality. As both parental demand for voice in education has expanded, and the individual and collective rights of parents have grown, the education system and schools are increasingly accountable to parents.

This chapter examines how policy and discourse has changed over the past 40 years with regard to parental involvement. The chapter begins with a brief description of the characteristics of the Irish education system. It then moves on to describe the legislative and regulative context of parental involvement. A review of empirical findings and theoretical approaches to existing research on parental involvement is presented in Section 4. The chapter also presents new research that explores the determinants of home-based parental involvement, using nationally representative longitudinal data from the Growing up in Ireland study, given that parents are increasingly positioned in policy as being accountable for the learning of their children. The chapter ends with a summary and suggested areas for future research.

## 2 Overview of the education system in Ireland

Lagging behind many of our European counterparts, it is only since 2000 that the pre-school sector in Ireland began to receive significant State funding, and in 2010 universal free pre-school childcare was introduced. Since 2018, this has been extended, so that parents of young children can avail of two years of the Early Childhood Care and Education Scheme (ECCE).

Primary education lasts eight years from the ages of approximately 6 to 13 years, and is a form of whole-day schooling, however the school day is shorter for the first two years. While children as young as age 4 can enter primary school, increasingly this trend is in decline, from 39.2 percent in 2010/11 to

23.1 percent in 2017/18. Thus, in 2017/18, the vast majority of children (over 75 percent) attending the first year of primary school were aged 5. A majority of primary school-aged children attend publicly funded schools (97.8 percent in 2017/18), while just 0.7 percent attend private primary schools (Department of Education & Skills, 2018). Approximately 1.4 percent of children at primary level attend special schools – schools for children with special educational needs and other schools which cater for children who are not included in mainstream primary schools – that are a mix of public, religious, and private. In addition to special schools, approximately 330 mainstream primary and 300 second level schools also include special classes that cater exclusively for students with specific categories of need (McCoy et al., 2014a).

The vast majority of primary schools are privately owned by religious orders but are State funded and managed locally by Boards of Management representing teacher, parent, community and patron (owner) interests. Since 2010, attempts have been made by the State to encourage a diversification of owners in the name of parental choice, however, there has been little change in the historical role of the State as funder of schools managed by private patrons/owners. The financing of education is centralised, and the Department of Education and Skills (DES) has responsibility for policy, provision, funding and regulation. Private (independent) primary schools do not receive any State funding. While the curriculum is standardised at primary and second level, private primary schools are not obliged to deliver the curriculum.

Second level education in Ireland is a form of whole-day schooling and lasts either five or six years, to include a three-year lower second level programme, and either two or three years of upper second level. The sector comprises 711 schools, including secondary, vocational, community, comprehensive and Educate Together schools, each of which have different management structures and historical orientations. An additional 55 schools are fee-paying, and are privately owned and managed but their staffing costs are funded by the State.

## 3 Parental involvement in Ireland: policy and terminology

### 3a Terminology

The legislative definition of a 'parent' according to the Education Act (1988) includes foster parents or official guardians appointed under the Guardianship of Children Acts, 1964 to 1997. Most communication between parents and schools address parents as 'parents/guardians'. While there is no single term used in legislation to describe the relationship between parents/guardians and the school, the terms 'parental involvement' and 'home–school links' are most commonly used.

### 3b National legislative and regulation context and dominant discourses

The following sections outline the dominant discourses that have emerged alongside policy developments.

The Irish context represents an interesting case study to explore parental involvement given that, since the foundation of the Irish Free State in 1922, the family is recognised as the primary and natural educator of the child in Article 42 of the Constitution of Ireland (Government of Ireland, 1937). That is, under the Constitution of Ireland, *Bunreacht na hÉireann*, parents are responsible for ensuring that their child receives an education, meaning that they have a right to provide education in their home, or to send their children to a private- or State-recognised school.

Despite the centrality of parents in the education of their children as highlighted in the Constitution, neither Church nor State made much effort to include parents in policy-making between the late 1930s and 1950s. The 1960s saw the emergence of some greater interest in and tolerance of parental input into education (Byrne & Smyth, 2010). In 1969, before any legislation was enacted for parental involvement, a booklet titled *All Our Children* was distributed to the parents of primary school children, which indicated that the principal teacher was responsible for fostering a 'proper liaison' between home and school. However, at this time the required resources for schools to support this intention were not readily available (INTO, 1997; Mac Giolla Phádraig, 2010).

### 3c Parents as learners: parenting and family literacy

Since the 1960s, the State has placed onus on parents, particularly working-class and unemployed parents, to parent differently regarding education matters – much more in line with middle-class tendencies. The emergence of targeted early intervention (childhood care and education) and parental involvement programmes in areas of educational disadvantage around this time promoted parental involvement as a remedy for working-class educational underachievement. Such programmes aimed to develop stronger links between the home and the school by encouraging parents to participate in classroom activities, improve their understanding of the teaching and learning methods used in schools, and to participate in parenting programmes. State intervention focused on families, and in particular on disadvantaged families, continues as a core component of targeted educational policy. Yet, as outlined by Smyth and McCoy (2009) such home–school interventions were not immune to funding cuts during the recession of the late 2000s.

### 3d Parent as choosers and consumers: school choice

Over time, parental demand for voice in education has expanded, and the individual and collective rights of parents have been enlarged to some degree. Yet, Irish education policy has been slow to reflect the interests of an increasingly diverse population of parents, as Catholic schools still account for 90 percent of primary schools across the State. At both primary and second level, since the

1970s parents have gained increasing voice around school choice, with the multi-denominational (Educate Together) and Gaelscoil (Irish medium schools) movement network of schools. Both movements arose from the bottom-up, supported by parents, and are indicative of the central role that parents could play in the Irish education system. In doing so, parents have played a key role in challenging the traditional Church/State dominance of educational ownership and management, and the relatively conservative approach to educational change (Coolahan, 1981; Hyland, 1989). The first multi-denominational school that was both co-educational and under democratic management opened in Dublin in 1978. Parents have also challenged the prevalence of single-sex schooling, which can be attributed to the historic role of the Catholic Church. This is evidenced by an increase in the proportion of children educated in co-educational classes from 65 percent in 1985 to 82 percent in 2017/18 (Department of Education & Skills, 2018). While in theory parents in Ireland have free school choice, it is further constrained by processes of social and cultural reproduction, as well as geographic disparities in the types of schools on offer (Byrne & Smyth, 2010).

### 3e Parents as partners: partnerships and charters

Formal recognition of the role of parents in educational matters by the State came over 40 years ago in 1975, with the introduction of parents on Boards of Management in primary schools. It was not until the Education Act (1988) that the rights of parents to establish a parents' association (PA) was firmly established. Parental representation on the Board of Management was strengthened in the late 1990s; first, through equal representation alongside patron/owner, teacher and other community bodies, and later through increased orientation of the Board towards students in terms of providing them with information regarding the activities of the school, and encouraging the establishment of student councils in second level schools. It was through these mechanisms that parents as a collective body became formally involved in decision-making concerning the education of their children.

This discourse largely influences the ways in which the education system and schools perceive parents and their role in education. In the Irish context, the first explicit positioning of parents as 'partners' came in 1990, in a review of the primary education system (Primary Education Review Body, 1990). Here, the role of parents was clearly outlined. Firstly, the review body recommended that parents should not be seen merely as 'consumers' who demand a service but rather as 'interested partners' in the education process. Secondly, they recommended that parents should be consulted in educational matters, and should have a significant influence on national educational policy as well as its local implementation. Finally, they highlighted the role of schools and the continued importance of home–school linkages, recommending that every school should have an explicit, clearly defined policy and programme for 'productive parental involvement'.

In official policy terms, the positioning of parents as partners came into effect in 1991 when the Department of Education (1991) published a circular titled *Parents as Partners in Education*. In this document, partnership for parents and the promotion of parental involvement in the education of children was articulated as a policy aim. This partnership discourse continued in a number of education policy documents, requiring that schools recognise the collective rights of parents to be active participants in the education system at school, regional and national levels. Further parental involvement provisions require that schools share information with parents (and students) on access to student progress records, information and consultation regarding school plans, and the objectives of the school. Recent policy also places emphasis on school principals to encourage the involvement of parents, and greater onus on the education system to be accountable to students, their parents and the State for the education provided. Schools now have an obligation to produce academic report cards to inform parents of their child's achievement, subject choices and progress; and the Department of Education and Skills has the task of the online publication of Inspectorate reports. A more recent development in how schools attempt to partner with parents is through the use of 'Parent–Student Charters', which outline how parents, school staff and students will share responsibility for improved educational success. Every school is required to consult with parents and students and publish a Charter, placing increasing responsibility on schools to consult with parents on many aspects of schooling (Department of Education and Skills, 2016a). Yet, less successful have been the advances in parental individual and collective rights around inclusion and the education of children with special educational needs in particular (SEN) as well as the patronage/ownership question.

### 3f Parents as accountable

Despite the gains that parents have made as a partner in education, there also exists an accountability discourse regarding parental involvement in education policy documents. For example, the recent *Action Plan for Education (2016–19)* published by the Department of Education and Skills (2016b) places considerable emphasis on parents and their role in improving the learning experience and their role in the success of learners. Reminiscent of the discourse of 'parents as learners', a recent insistence on parental responsibility and self-sufficiency is specifically focused on parenting quality through the provision of behavioural programmes and anti-bullying materials for parents.

## 4 Research on parental involvement in Ireland: theoretical framework, empirical research

Research in the Irish context has explored parental involvement in some depth, and three key areas are discussed here: (i) research on parental involvement more generally, (ii) forms of parental involvement – both formal and informal; and (iii) parents and processes of social reproduction.

Early research highlighted the limited voice that parents have in educational matters. Parental involvement was constructed by parents as being mainly about fundraising and approving decisions that have already been made in the school, with parents feeling excluded from substantive policy decisions that may have significant financial implications for them (Hanafin & Lynch, 2002). Limited parental involvement in policy formation has also been reported in the Irish context, as parents indicated that they had too little influence on the education system (Kellaghan et al., 2004; Mac Giolla Phádraig, 2010).

Despite increasing emphasis in policy over time on providing information to parents, Eivers and Creaven's (2013) analyses showed that parents in Ireland had less access to information about their child's academic performance than parents in other countries, although they were more likely to receive frequent updates about non-academic issues (e.g. sports or fundraising). That is, Irish primary schools were less likely on average than other schools internationally to give parents regular updates on their child's behaviour and well-being, to discuss parental concerns, or to give parents regular updates on their child's learning progress or overall school academic achievement. Nonetheless, Irish parents were more likely than average to feel included in their children's education and less likely to agree that the school should do better at keeping them informed about their child's progress. Clear gaps were also evident in terms of the information that schools distribute to parents via their websites (Gilleece & Eivers, 2018).

More recently, research has shown that Irish schools, generally, are characterised by high levels of informal parental involvement and parental satisfaction, but low levels of formal involvement and parental information/feedback (Bleach, 2010; Byrne & Smyth, 2010; Cosgrove & Gilleece, 2012; Eivers & Creaven, 2013). Yet, Eivers and Creaven's (2013) analyses show that relative to other countries, principals and teachers in Ireland report high levels of parental involvement in primary school activities, as parents are highly involved in homework activities, and levels of attendance at parent–teacher meetings are high.

However, a closer look at *informal parental involvement* suggests that involvement in student learning at primary level continues to be largely limited to helping with homework and receiving general updates about school accomplishments (Eivers & Creaven, 2013). At second level, informal parental involvement largely centres around parent–child discussions about programme and subject options (Byrne & Smyth, 2010), and often, parent–teacher meetings are the only way that parents interact with the school (Cosgrove & Gilleece, 2012).

The range of *formal parental* involvement activities is much more limited in Ireland. All schools are expected to have a PA, but research has indicated that less than half of primary schools in Ireland are affiliated with the National Parents Council (National Parents Council, 2010). At second level, although parents are represented on the Board of Management, few play an active role in either the Board or the PA (Byrne & Smyth, 2010) and relatively few principals reported widespread parental attendance at PA meetings (Cosgrove & Gilleece, 2012). In 2015, just 5 percent of sixth class pupils had parents who had ever served on their school's Board of Management and 25 percent had a parent who had ever been a member of the PA committee (Kavanagh et al., 2015).

As in other institutional contexts, forms of parental involvement appear to be stratified. That is, levels of parental involvement are associated with family characteristics such as socioeconomic status, educational background, and family structure. Hall et al. (2008) reported that working-class parents were less comfortable than middle-class parents with the type of language used in primary school reports, and were less likely to question teachers than their middle-class counterparts, while Eivers et al. (2010) found that many parents – especially those whose children were performing at the lower end of the achievement spectrum – did not have a clear understanding of the progress their child was making in school. Among parents of children attending second level education, informal involvement (helping with homework, communication about school matters between parents and children, and making post-school plans) is somewhat more frequent among highly educated and middle-class parents (Byrne & Smyth, 2010).

Much of the theoretical orientation of studies of parental involvement in the Irish context have been framed in structuralist or post-structuralist schools of thought, and are largely sociological. Previous research tends to be framed in the work of Vygotsky and socio-cultural theories: Bourdieu, habitus and the role of capitals, but also rational choice approaches (Goldthorpe, Boudon) which emphasise the role of parents in decision-making. Studies have also adopted a Critical Discourse Analysis of policies pertaining to parental involvement, and highlighted the neoliberal and conservative logics of Irish education policy and reform. More recently, parental involvement has been framed in the work of post-structuralists such as Foucault and Deluze (Kitching, 2017).

## 5 New research on parental involvement in Ireland: determinants of home-based parental involvement at age 17

Given the increasing accountability that is expected of parents in the Irish context, this study sought to examine the role of individual, family and school characteristics on home-based parental involvement. While home-based parental involvement is argued to have a weaker association with student educational outcomes than school-based parental involvement, it has the advantage of getting beyond individualistic and school-centric forms of parental involvement (i.e. clear directives of how parents can help schools to promote students' education) to better understand how parents support their children in ways that are less understood or ignored by schools (Allen & White-Smith, 2018: 19). Thus, it is particularly of interest in the Irish context, whereby on the one hand there is increasing accountability expected of parents by the State, yet on the other home-based parental involvement and commitment tends to be perceived as less valuable and receives little recognition by schools (Crozier, 2005; Rollock et al., 2014). Decision-making by young people is largely informed by parents, and parental support is a key factor in encouraging working-class young people to aspire to higher education (McCoy et al., 2014b).

## 5a Data and measures

This research draws on longitudinal data gathered from the first three waves of the Growing up in Ireland study (GUI), a nationally representative study of nine-year-old children living in Ireland. In 2007/08, the GUI team interviewed 8,578 nine-year-old children, their parents, teachers and principals on a wide range of topics, and children were followed up again when they were aged 13 and age 17 (2015/16). The total number of children that participated in all three waves was 6,039. By wave 3, the majority of young people (83 percent) were still in school, thus, the 12 percent that were in full-time further education or training, and the 5 percent that were in the labour market are removed from this analysis.

The dependent variable that is used in this analysis captures a form of academically related home-based, child-centred parental involvement at age 17 (OECD, 2012). A composite scale (Cronbach's Alpha .830) was derived from parental reports of the frequency that they were involved in a discussion regarding school life with their child (discussions about subjects, workload, relationships with teachers, plans about the future, getting on with friends at school, performance in tests and examinations).

In terms of independent variables, a number of variables from wave one measured at the individual and at the school level are included in the model, as each had a significant association with parental involvement at age 17. These include the gender of the child, citizenship status and standardised reading score at age 9. In terms of family characteristics, the model captures forms of economic (household income), cultural (parental education, parental educational expectation of child, number of books in the home) and social capital in the home. The latter includes a measure of school-based parental involvement at age 9 and age 13, and an indicator of whether the parent was involved in community networks when the child was age 9. Key school level variables include an indicator of the importance of parents in the ethos of the school, and of whether the school buildings were accessible to the community after school hours. Other school level variables include the percentage of children living locally that the school admits; an indicator of whether the school has a high concentration of children from disadvantaged areas (referred to in the Irish context as having Delivering Equality of Opportunity in Schools (DEIS) status); and school size. The final sample size was 5,191 17 year olds in 898 schools.

## 5b Results

The descriptive findings (Figure 4.1) reveal that parents are typically involved in home-based parental involvement at age 17. Only a minority of parents indicate that they are 'never or hardly ever' involved.

The model presented in Table 4.1 is a random intercept multilevel model of home-based parental involvement at age 17. Analyses of the variance in parental involvement that the model explains suggests that there was some significant variation both within and between individual schools. That is, while the majority of the variation in parental involvement was within schools, there was also some variation between schools.

The multivariate findings show that home-based parental involvement is associated with a range of individual, family and school characteristics. In terms of individual characteristics, higher levels of home-based parental involvement are associated with the parents of females, while lower levels are associated with the parents of children who do not hold Irish citizenship.

In terms of family characteristics, the model captures forms of economic, cultural and social capital in the home. There appears to be a significant association between household income (economic capital) and home-based parental involvement, as parents in very low-income households are more likely to have lower levels of involvement than parents in high-income households. These findings mirror previous work of Lareau (2003), who found that low-income and/or minority groups may experience economic constraints as well as time poverty, thus limiting their ability to engage with their children in discussions around schoolwork or future planning.

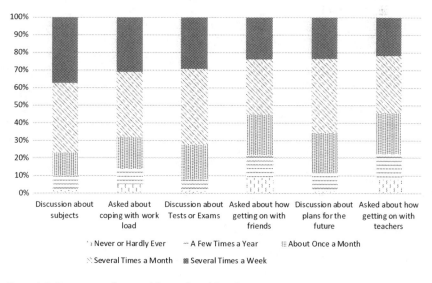

*Figure 4.1* Frequency of parental home-based involvement

Table 4.1 Multilevel random intercept model of home-based parental involvement.

| | Coefficient | Standard error | Significance |
|---|---|---|---|
| Intercept | 3.702 | 0.057 | 0.000 |
| Female | 0.153 | 0.025 | **0.000** |
| Ref: Male | | | |
| Standardised reading score | 0.008 | 0.013 | 0.527 |
| Child a citizen of a country other than Ireland | -0.122 | 0.058 | **0.035** |
| Ref: Child citizen of Ireland | | | |
| High-income household (quartile 5) | 0.011 | 0.038 | 0.774 |
| High-income household (quartile 4) | -0.028 | 0.035 | 0.431 |
| Low-income household (quartile 2) | -0.050 | 0.037 | 0.170 |
| Low-income household (quartile 1) | -0.086 | 0.041 | **0.038** |
| Household income unknown | -0.044 | 0.051 | 0.387 |
| Ref: Middle income household (quartile 3) | | | |
| Primary care giver (PCG) expects child to attend higher education | 0.129 | 0.029 | **0.000** |
| Ref: Other educational expectation | | | |
| PCG lower secondary or less | -0.022 | 0.031 | 0.469 |
| PCG third level non-degree | -0.045 | 0.033 | 0.174 |
| PCG higher education | -0.105 | 0.035 | **0.003** |
| Ref: PCG upper secondary/vocational | | | |
| Less than ten books in the home | -0.075 | 0.044 | 0.088 |
| 10–20 books in the home | -0.077 | 0.031 | **0.012** |
| Ref: 30+ books in the home | | | |
| PCG did not previously attend PT meetings | -0.038 | 0.033 | 0.250 |
| Ref: PCG did attend PT meetings previously | | | |
| PCG networks locally | 0.076 | 0.024 | **0.002** |
| Ref: No PCG networking | | | |
| Lone-parent family | 0.008 | 0.034 | 0.806 |
| Ref: Two-parent family | | | |
| **School level variables** | | | |
| DEIS status | 0.109 | 0.038 | **0.004** |
| Ref: Non-DEIS | | | |
| Little emphasis on parents in school ethos | -0.015 | 0.049 | 0.757 |
| Ref: Parents very important to the school ethos | | | |
| School building not open to public after school hours | -0.109 | 0.035 | **0.002** |
| Ref: School building open to the public after school hours | | | |
| < 30 percent of intake from local area | 0.023 | 0.048 | 0.636 |

(*Continued*)

Table 4.1 (Cont.)

|  | Coefficient | Standard error | Significance |
|---|---|---|---|
| 31–70 percent of intake from local area | -0.078 | 0.048 | 0.108 |
| 71–90 percent of intake from local area | 0.063 | 0.044 | 0.152 |
| Ref: 91–100 percent of school intake from local area | | | |
| Small school (80 or less) | -0.023 | 0.058 | 0.693 |
| Medium school (81–399) | -0.075 | 0.042 | 0.074^ |
| Ref: Large school (400+) | | | |

Standard errors in parentheses
^ p Approached significance, N=5,191 students in 898 schools.

Home-based parental involvement is also associated with measures of cultural capital in the home (educational expectations, parental education levels, number of books in the home). Parents who aspire for their child to progress to higher education (HE), and those with a greater number of books in the home, are more likely to have higher levels of involvement, yet those who hold the highest level of educational qualification themselves (HE) are likely to have lower levels of involvement than less well educated parents. One explanation of this might be that better educated parents may have more knowledge of their children's schooling and achievement, and can rely more heavily on their own educational experiences.

The model also includes measures of social capital in the home – an indicator of whether the parent was involved in local community networks, as well as an indicator of previous attendance at parent–teacher meetings when the child was both age 9 and age 13. Interestingly, the results show that parental networking – rather than previous school-based parental involvement – has a significant and positive influence on home-based parental involvement. That is, parental networking in the local community when children are young is associated with higher levels of home-based parental involvement at age 17. This is consistent with previous studies in the US that link parental networks to parental involvement when children are young (Li & Fischer, 2017). Contrary to expectations, previous school-based involvement is not a predictor of home-based parental involvement.

Importantly, the results also show that the characteristics of the primary school that children attend at age 9 have long-term influences on home-based parental involvement by age 17. The findings support and extend previous Irish and international research, which suggests that some school contexts are more successful than others in encouraging parental involvement (Becker & Epstein, 1982; Bleach, 2010; Gilleece et al., 2012). Results in Table 4.1 show that the parents of children who attended schools with a high concentration of children from disadvantaged backgrounds (a DEIS school) have higher levels of home-based parental involvement at age 17 than those attending schools with more advantaged intakes. This is contrary to the patterns of school-based involvement found by Eivers and Creaven (2013) using Progress in International Reading Literacy Study (PIRLS) and Trends in International Mathematics and Science Study (TIMSS) data.

Furthermore, physical access to a school when children are young matters for later home-based parental involvement. This physical access to school buildings outside of school hours is a stronger predictor of home-based parental involvement than a measure of the importance attached to parents in the ethos of the school. That is, those who attended a school that was not open outside school hours had significantly lower parental involvement scores at age 17, while the emphasis on parents in the ethos of the school could not distinguish those with different levels of home-based parental involvement.

These findings orientate us towards the diverse ways in which parents support the education of their children. Do these findings lead us to conclude that some parents are less accountable than others? Despite the fact that policy places expectations on parents (in particular working-class parents) to be accountable and responsible when it comes to their children's education, the findings presented here suggest that the vast majority of parents are involved in forms of academically related home-based parental involvement. Moreover, the parents of children attending disadvantaged school contexts demonstrate a stronger propensity to be involved in this way than the parents of children attending more advantaged school contexts. Furthermore, parents who hold a higher education qualification themselves are likely to have lower levels of involvement than parents with lower levels of education. These findings raise important questions about the normative construction of disadvantaged parents in the Irish context, in both schools and in education policy.

Do these findings demonstrate a causal effect on parental involvement at age 17? The findings indicate that parental involvement at age 17 is shaped by gender and citizenship of the child and the resources that families hold (economic, social and cultural capital) when children are young, as well as school characteristics, all else being equal. Each influence the development of parental involvement up to the end of second level education. Thus, it would appear that these factors have long-term effects on parental involvement. However, it is also important to note that limitations in the available data mean that the results here fall short of identifying a causal effect with certainty. However, because longitudinal data is used, some advances can be made compared to using cross-sectional data.

## 6 Conclusions

This chapter has sought to document changes in the relationship between parents, schools and the State since the formal recognition of parents in education over 40 years ago. From a critical perspective, the chapter problematises the existing policy response to increasing parental demand for voice in education, and three key points are made. Firstly, while the idea of parental involvement has always been strongly linked to the concept of social inequality, the development of parental involvement has also been viewed as a remedy by the State, resulting in the early deficit framing of working-class and unemployed parents. Secondly, as parental demand for voice in education has expanded and the individual and collective rights of parents have also expanded to some degree, Irish education policy has been slow to reflect the interests of an increasingly diverse population of parents. This is also an area that warrants considerable attention in future research. Finally, increasingly, there is an accountability rhetoric regarding parental involvement, as parents are accountable for the learning experience and success of learners.

The chapter also presents new research that explores the determinants of home-based parental involvement at age 17. The findings presented here orientate us towards the diverse ways in which parents support the education of their children, and reveal that parents are typically involved in home-based parental involvement at age 17. Moreover, the parents of children in disadvantaged school and home contexts demonstrate a stronger propensity to be involved in this way than the parents of children in more advantaged school and home contexts. These findings raise important questions about the normative construction of disadvantaged parents in the Irish context, in both schools and in education policy. This research also extends our understanding of the ways in which schools matter for inducing higher levels of parental involvement. Based on these findings, Irish education policy should consider the positive influence that physical access to a school outside of school hours has on promoting parental involvement during the student life-cycle.

## References

Allen, Q. and White-Smith, K. (2018) "That's why I stay in school": Black mothers' parental involvement, cultural wealth, and exclusion in their son's schooling. *Urban Education*, 53(3), 409–435.
Becker, H.J. and Epstein, J.L. (1982) Parent involvement: A survey of teachers practices. *Elementary School Journal*, 83, 85–102.
Bleach, M.J. (2010) *Parental Involvement in Primary Education in Ireland*. Dublin: The Liffey Press.
Byrne, D. and Smyth, E. (2010) *Behind the Scenes? A Study of Parental Involvement in Post-Primary Education*. Dublin: The Liffey Press in association with The Economic and Social Research Institute.
Coolahan, J. (1981) *Irish Education. History and Structure*. Dublin: Institute of Public Administration.
Cosgrove, J. and Gilleece, L. (2012) An international perspective on civic participation in Irish post-primary schools: Results from ICCS. *Irish Educational Studies*, 31(4), 377–395.

Crozier, G. (2005) Beyond the call of duty: The impact of racism on black parents' involvement in their children's education. In: Crozier, G. and Reay, D., eds. *Activating Participation: Parents and Teachers Working towards Partnership*. Stoke-on-Trent: Trentham Books. 39–55.

Department of Education (1991) *Parents as Partners in Education. Circular 24/91*. Dublin: Department of Education.

Department of Education and Skills (2016a) *Students, Parents and Schools*. Available at: www.education.ie/en/Parents/Information/Parent-and-Student-Charter/Charter-Briefing-Note.pdf (accessed 10 May 2017).

Department of Education and Skills (2016b) *An Action Plan for Education (2016–2019)*. Available at: www.education.ie/en/The-Department/Action-Plan-for-Education-2016-2019/2016.html (accessed 10 May 2017).

Department of Education and Skills (2018) *Department of Education and Skills Annual Statistical Report 2017/18*. Available at: www.education.ie/en/Publications/Statistics/Statistical-Reports/(accessed 1 Oct. 2018).

Eivers, E., Close, S., Shiel, G., Millar, D., Clerkin, A., Gilleece, L. and Kiniry, J. (2010) *The 2009 National Assessments of Mathematics and English Reading*. Dublin: Department of Education and Skills.

Eivers, E. and Creaven, A.M. (2013) Home–school interaction. In: Eivers, E. and Clerkin, A., eds. *National Schools, International Contexts: Beyond the PIRLS and TIMMS Test Results*. Dublin: Educational Research Centre. 105–128.

Gilleece, L. and Eivers, E. (2018) Primary school websites in Ireland: How are they used to inform and involve parents? *Irish Educational Studies*, 37(4), 1–20.

Gilleece, L., Shiel, G., Clerkin, A. and Millar, D. (2012) *The 2010 National Assessments of English Reading and Mathematics in Irish-Medium Schools*. Dublin: Educational Research Centre.

Government of Ireland (1937) *Bunreacht na hÉireann*. Dublin: Government Publications.

Hall, K., Conway, P.F., Rath, A., Murphy, R. and McKeon, J. (2008) *Reporting to Parents in Primary School: Communication, Meaning and Learning*. Dublin: NCCA.

Hanafin, J. and Lynch, A. (2002) Peripheral voices. Parental involvement, social class, and educational disadvantage. *British Journal of Sociology of Education*, 23, 35–49.

Hyland, A. (1989) The multi-denominational experience in the national school system in Ireland. *Irish Educational Studies*, 8(1), 89–114.

INTO (Irish National Teachers Organisation) (1997) *Parental Involvement. Possibilities for Partnership*. Dublin: INTO.

Kavanagh, L., Shiel, G., Gilleece, L. and Kiniry, J. (2015) *The 2014 National Assessments of English Reading and Mathematics*. Dublin: Educational Research Centre.

Kellaghan, T., McGee, P., Millar, D. and Perkins, R. (2004) *Views of the Irish Public on Education: 2004 Survey*. Dublin: Educational Research Centre.

Kitching, K. (2017) Parents navigating the moral norms of schooling: Education (re)production and alternative futures. Unpublished paper presented at: European Conference on Educational Research (ECER). Copenhagen, 24 August 2017.

Lareau, A. (2003) *Unequal Childhoods: Class, Race, and Family Life*. Berkeley: University of California Press.

Li, A. and Fischer, M.J. (2017) Advantaged/disadvantaged school neighbourhoods, parental networks, and parental involvement at elementary school. *Sociology of Education*, 90(4), 355–377.

Mac Giolla Phádraig, B. (2010) Towards partnership: The development of parental involvement in Irish primary education since 1970. *The Irish Journal of Education*, 38, 73–93.

McCoy, S., Banks, J., Frawley, D., Watson, D., Shevlin, M. and Smyth, F. (2014a) *Understanding Special Class Provision in Ireland*. Dublin: The Economic and Social Research Institute/NCSE.

McCoy, S., Smyth, E., Watson, D. and Darmody, M. (2014b) *Leaving School in Ireland: A Longitudinal Study of Post-School Transitions*. Dublin: The Economic and Social Research Institute.

National Parents' Council (2010) *Annual Report*. Dublin: NPC.

OECD (2012) *Parental Involvement in Selected PISA-Countries and Economies*. OECD Education Working Paper number 73.

Primary Education Review Body (1990) *Report*. Dublin: Government Publications.

Rollock, N., Gillborn, D., Vincent, C. and Ball, S. (2014) *The Colour of Class: The Educational Strategies of the Black Middle Classes*. London: Routledge.

Smyth, E. and McCoy, S. (2009) *Investing in Education: Combating Educational Disadvantage*. Dublin: The Economic and Social Research Institute.

# 5 The Netherlands

## Parental involvement in the Netherlands

*Eddie Denessen*

## 1 Introduction

The Dutch education system can be characterised by two significant features: its freedom to establish government-funded schools and the presence of early tracking after primary school. Both features are relevant to the debate regarding the involvement of parents in education. As is the case elsewhere, parental involvement is promoted in education policies as a means to support the school careers of children. Numerous interventions have been implemented to support parental involvement, especially aimed at the prevention of literacy gaps at entry to primary schools. More recently, parental involvement in a broader sense has been promoted to support children's learning. In addition, teacher education programmes have been developed to support teachers in their competencies to communicate with parents and to support parental involvement. In current educational debates, a controversy regarding parental involvement can be seen: on the one hand, parental involvement enhances the school outcomes of children from disadvantaged backgrounds; however, on the other hand, parental involvement is considered to increase educational inequalities, because highly effective involvement of highly educated parents leads to increased levels of inequality.

This chapter begins by presenting an overview of the education system of the Netherlands and will proceed with a discussion of the history of policy and research regarding parental involvement in the country. The chapter concludes with a reflection on the value of research evidence, which seeks to promote effective parental involvement practices, and on the divergent effects of involvement of parents with different socioeconomic backgrounds.

## 2 Overview of the education system in the Netherlands

### 2a Freedom of education

The year 1917 was a landmark in the history of Dutch education. The so-called 'school struggle' ended and freedom of education was realised and formally included in the Dutch constitution. The freedom of education implies that, apart from public government-established schools, religious groups have the right to establish schools and have them funded by the Dutch government. This freedom of education resulted in two prominent features of the Dutch school system, setting it apart from school systems in other countries.

Firstly, the number of expensive private schools is small, at approximately 3 percent. Because the Dutch government finances all schools, including those with a religious affiliation (denominational schools), it limits the need for private parties to establish schools for which parents have to pay. Whereas the distribution of public versus religious schools before 1917 was 70:30 percent, this distribution changed to 30:70 percent after the 1917 constitution. This 30:70 percent division of cost-free, public schools and cost-free, government-funded denominational schools has remained relatively stable.

Secondly, the freedom of education resulted in free school choice for all parents. Unlike most other countries, Dutch parents are not allocated a local school when their child reaches school age. All parents are expected to choose a school for their child. This means that school choice in the Netherlands is a system of forced choice – that is, parents have to choose. This freedom of choice also implies that parents possess the required cultural and social capital to make an informed choice. Especially in densely populated areas, the system of school choice leads to school segregation because white middle-class parents tend to choose schools with lower numbers of minority and at-risk children. Also, cultural-ethnic-minority parents, in particular those with a Muslim background, may choose Islamic schools and contribute to school segregation by choice (Denessen, Driessen & Sleegers, 2005). This process of self-segregation is visible in schools that attract students from orthodox religious groups.

For Dutch children, school is formally compulsory from age 5 to 16. However, almost every child starts primary school (*Groep 1*) at age 4 and finishes around age 12 (*Groep 8*). The first two years are comparable with kindergarten and formal instruction usually starts at age 6 (*Groep 3*). For children with special needs there are schools for special education. National education policy, however, is aimed at decreasing the number of referrals to special education and promoting inclusive regular education (*passend onderwijs*).

## 2b A system of early tracking

Another typical feature of the Dutch education system is its early tracking. After eight years of primary education, children move to secondary schools when they are about 12 years old. They enrol in secondary schools that provide education in seven tracks, ranging from lower vocational education (*vmbo*) to pre-university education (*vwo*), although approximately 40 percent of the first-year programmes in Dutch secondary education is provided in mixed tracks (*vmbo-havo* or *havo-vwo* tracks). Some schools provide more years of mixed tracks, although the number of schools providing mixed track-classes is decreasing (Inspectie van het Onderwijs, 2016), which is partly because of the demand of highly educated parents to send their children to a single pre-university track. There is no national curriculum in the Netherlands, but the standardisation of the education system is quite high, because of nationally standardised exams. The nation-wide exam requirements strongly steer the content of the curriculum in the distinct tracks of secondary school.

The transition from primary to secondary school is based on track recommendations provided by the primary schools. Secondary schools use this recommendation to place children in tracks. To validate the recommendation, students are required to take a standardised achievement test. When the outcomes of this test exceed the level of the recommended track, primary schools are obliged to reconsider the recommendation.

In the Netherlands there are approximately 6,350 primary schools that provide education for 1.5 million pupils. The number of secondary schools is much smaller, at around 640. In 2016, 46.9 percent of the third-year secondary school students (around 15 years old; 168,700 students in total) were enrolled in lower vocational education tracks (*vmbo*), 26.6 percent were enrolled in the lower general secondary education track (*havo*) and 26.4 percent in the pre-university track (*vwo*).

## 3 Parental involvement in the Netherlands

### 3a Terminology

In the Netherlands, parental involvement refers to the involvement of parents who are the primary caretakers of their children. In exceptional cases where parents are not present or capable of taking care of their children, the parental responsibilities are taken over by so-called 'caregivers'. Letters that schools send to children's homes are usually addressed to the parents/caregivers of the child. The use of 'father and mother' has become complicated, because of the increasing numbers of non-traditional families, especially one-parent households, reconstituted families, and same-sex parents.

Parental involvement is translated in Dutch as *ouderbetrokkenheid*. This concept relates to parental dispositions and behaviours that directly or indirectly influence children's cognitive development and school achievement (Fantuzzo, Davis & Ginsberg, 1995). However, the Dutch vocabulary regarding parental involvement has developed in congruence with the international literature, where the concepts of 'school–family partnerships' and 'school–family–community partnerships' are used to focus less exclusively on parents' involvement, but on a shared responsibility for children by family, school and the community. In Dutch, the equivalent term *educatief partnerschap* was introduced by Cees de Wit (2005).

### 3b National legislative and policy context

Parental involvement in the Netherlands is typically linked to the freedom of education within the Dutch education system. Two natural forms of involvement were the result of the constitutional right that religious groups gained to establish non-public-government-funded schools. First, it gave way to many groups of parents to establish their own schools that were governed by foundations or associations led by parents or in which parents were represented. Second, because of the obligation for parents to choose a primary school for their children, parents are involved in their child's school as active choosers.

Besides these two types of involvement that are direct consequences of the history of the Dutch education system, several developments led to increased parental involvement in schools. These developments were mostly related to educational policies aimed to counter inequalities of educational opportunities. Since the 1970s, parental involvement as a means to promote equal educational opportunities gained increasing attention in education policy and research. First, it became widely acknowledged that children's experience with language in their early years were strongly predictive of their literacy development at school (Heath, 1983). To overcome language deficits of children from less advantaged socioeconomic families and children from language minority immigrant families, interventions to support early literacy development in the home were developed and implemented. These programmes were aimed at promoting parental early socialisation practices, such as dialogic reading (de la Rie et al., 2016).

Second, parental involvement has been promoted to build bridges between families and schools and to connect school and family cultures to create stronger 'overlapping spheres of influence' (Epstein, 1995). Strongly based on Epstein's theory, policies to promote equality of educational opportunities were aimed at diverse types of parental involvement, ranging from parenting to collaboration with the community. Although legislation is restricted to formal parent participation (schools are required to provide seats for parents on school councils), schools are offered support from school advisers to strengthen all types of parental involvement (see for example de Vries, 2010).

In 2008, the Dutch Education Council (Onderwijsraad, 2008) published a report on parents as partners in educational outcomes. In this report, parents are addressed as important agents for school improvement. The council pointed to the opportunities that parents have to increase the quality of the school (in terms of student achievement). It was suggested that parents should be more proactive in holding the school accountable for the academic achievement of their children by making more effort to be informed about school outcomes. This advice seems to root in an educational effectiveness paradigm, triggered by neoliberalism and consumerism (Tienken, 2013).

Two years later, in 2010, the Dutch Education Council (Onderwijsraad, 2010) published a new report on parents as partners. In this report, the Education Council advised that school quality frameworks should be developed in which parents are included: a good quality agenda focuses on parental involvement and on schools and teachers that are able to work together with parents, with a focus on stimulating academic achievement and social skills of pupils and to reduce dropout and truancy. In addition, it advised that the scope of parental involvement should be broadened to parents of secondary and higher education students and that teachers should be educated to promote their competences for working with parents.

As the research on parental involvement progressed and evidence for the positive effects of parental involvement on children's learning grew, parents were increasingly advised to provide optimal support for learning, as a means to improve high school outcomes. Based on a large body of empirical studies showing that parent involvement adds to the academic achievements of children (e.g., Bakker et al., 2013; Carter, 2002; Desforges & Abouchaar, 2003), education policies have been designed to contribute to parental involvement both at school and at home. School programmes focused on promoting parent participation at school, as well as supporting home involvement with children's learning (e.g., helping with homework, reading with the child).

### 3c Parental involvement and educational inequality: the 'dark side' of parental involvement

In 2016, the Dutch Inspectorate of Education announced that educational inequalities were increasing. The Inspectorate reported that children from highly educated families had more successful school careers than their counterparts from lower educated families, and that the divide between both groups was growing. Apart from explanations that can be found in the education system (for example tracking students or the effects of implicit teacher biases), parents are suggested to play a significant role in this development. Over the past decades it can be observed that highly educated parents put various forms of capital in play to maximise their children's educational opportunities. The highly educated parents, in particular, appear to demand that the school optimally prepares their children for future life – putting pressure on primary schools to obtain a recommendation for a higher secondary school track, and enrolling their children in selective programmes (for example bilingual programmes; see Sieben & van Ginderen, 2014). Moreover, highly educated parents can – and do – pay more than lower educated parents do for additional homework support and exam preparation for their children. The commercial out-of-school support industry is rapidly growing in the Netherlands, as national expenditure on after-school tutoring, exam preparation and homework support has increased substantially between 1995 and 2015. With their involvement practices, highly educated parents contribute to increasing divergent school careers of children and to increasing inequality of educational opportunities. These parents engage in what Lareau (2002) calls 'concerted cultivation' of their children's talents.

It is a major challenge for the Dutch education system to counter the trend of increasing inequalities. In a context of neoliberalism, with high pressure on parents and children to get the most out of their education and where competition, selection, and accountability characterise the system of education, it is not easy to contribute to equal educational opportunities. In the case of parental involvement, with a division of powerful highly educated parents and less powerful lower educated and ethnic-minority parents, strong empowerment strategies that discriminate in favour of children from disadvantaged backgrounds are needed to counter the trend of divergence of school careers of advantaged and disadvantaged students.

## 4 Existing research on parental involvement in the Netherlands

As stated above, the theoretical framing of parental involvement in the Netherlands was largely connected with sociology of education. Cultural capital theory (Bourdieu, 1973) and social capital theory (Coleman, 1988) underpinned increased attention among academics with regard to parental involvement. During the 1990s and 2000s, a significant increase in research on parental involvement has been observed (Castelli & Pepe, 2008). Three main topics in research can be distinguished.

*(1) Parental involvement and academic achievement of students*

As research evidence grew on the effects of parental involvement on children's academic achievement (see for example Kloosterman et al., 2011), the topic gained a broader basis and was adopted by education psychologists and researchers of educational effectiveness. In the early 2000s, several reviews were published about the effects of parental involvement that provided input for school improvement programmes to promote effectiveness (Carter, 2002; Desforges & Abouchaar, 2003).

In 2011, the Dutch Education Research Council sent out a call for a review study on the effects of parental involvement and the contribution of teachers to effective parental involvement practices. The purpose of this review was to make an inventory of effective practices and to provide input for teacher education and school improvement programmes with which effective practices could be enhanced. This review study was published in 2013 (Bakker et al., 2013). The authors first reviewed the empirical evidence on the effects of parents' involvement on cognitive and non-cognitive outcomes (e.g., motivation, well-being, self-concept) of children from 6 to 18 years old. Next, the empirical research regarding the contribution of teachers to parents' involvement was reviewed. The findings of the first part of the review study were consistent with previous findings. For three age groups – pre-school and kindergarten, primary school pupils and secondary school pupils – parents' involvement was effective. For the youngest children, the effects were great for the home literacy environment, stressing the importance of parental cultural capital for children's literacy development. For the older children, the effects of parental socio-emotional support were relatively strong, indicating that for the school careers of older children parental social capital was of increasing importance. In addition to these findings, it was found that the effects of parental participation at school and formal school involvement were weak or absent.

The second part of Bakker et al.'s review study (2013) found that teachers were indeed able to promote effective forms of involvement. In line with the theoretical model of parents' involvement developed by Hoover-Dempsey and colleagues (see, for example, Green et al., 2007), teachers' competences to invite parents and to connect with parents' motivation to become involved were stressed as important predictors of parental involvement. Additionally, positive teacher attitudes towards parents and parental involvement were found to be relevant conditions for the development of teacher competences to build effective relationships with parents. That teacher attitudes are highly relevant for building positive relations with parents is supported by a large body of empirical research on teacher perceptions of parents and their involvement.

*(2) Teacher attitudes towards parents*

Research on teacher attitudes has shown that teachers overall have positive attitudes towards parents and their involvement (Bakker et al., 2013). However, not all is positive as some challenges have been observed. First, it appeared that teachers tend to be negative about too much involvement of parents (e.g., demanding, overprotective, or aggressive ways of involvement). These negative experiences with parents affect teachers' job satisfaction and induce stress (van der Wolf & Everaert, 2005). As stated by Hujala et al. (2009), teachers tend to value a relationship with parents that can be described as 'educational professionalism with a respectful distance'.

Second, teachers tend to underestimate parents' involvement in general, and the involvement of low socioeconomic status parents and ethnic minorities in particular. Dutch researchers have done some work in trying to identify different types of parents, with the aim of supporting teachers and schools in their understanding of parents and their approach to parents with different involvement profiles. Both van der Wolf and Everaert (2005) and Smit and Driessen (2009) developed typologies of parents based on ratings of typical parental involvement practice, which included overprotective parents, supportive parents, aggressive parents, and uninvolved parents. Although such typologies might be helpful for teachers to reflect on their relationship with parents, they give rise to stigmatisation and stereotyping. Research on teachers' perceptions of parents' involvement has shown that teachers tend to overestimate middle-class parents' involvement and to underestimate the involvement of lower-class parents and those of cultural-ethnic-minority backgrounds (Bakker, Denessen & Brus-Laeven, 2007). These misperceptions of parents' involvement can lead to self-fulfilling prophecy effects when teachers translate perceptions of parents into stereotypical expectations of their pupils (Bakker et al., 2013).

*(3) Teacher education and school reform*

Not only should positive teacher attitudes towards parents and unbiased perceptions of parents' involvement target teacher education programmes, but also their competences to work with parents, such as communication skills and the skills to invite all parents to become involved in their child's education. A Dutch review on teacher competences has resulted in a short list of teacher competences for school–family partnerships (Kassenberg, Petri & Doornenbal, 2016). Kassenberg et al. distinguished four types of *knowledge* (about the benefits of collaboration with parents, about diverse ways of communicating, about the community and family backgrounds, and being knowledgeable to answer questions of parents), three *attitudes* (a positive attitude towards parents and parental involvement, valuing parents as partners, being sincerely committed to parents), and five *skills* (building an open relationship with parents, rhetoric skills, making tasks and activities visible for parents, being able to deal with diversity, and being able to invite parents to become involved in their child's learning).

Research on Dutch teacher education programmes has shown that teachers feel ill prepared when they finish their initial teacher training (de Bruïne et al., 2014), as it concentrates more on communication skills and very little time is allocated for theory and practice regarding parental involvement and school–family partnerships. Teacher education for school–family-partnerships is on the agenda of teacher education institutes, although innovations in teacher education programmes seem strongly dependent on committed individual teacher educators (de Bruïne et al., 2014).

Besides a focus of research and intervention on teachers and teacher education, there is also a focus on schools and school improvement. In Rotterdam, Lusse (2013) was very successful in supporting school–family partnerships in schools for secondary education. Based on research at fifteen schools for secondary education, she developed a framework with ten factors for success, broadly focusing on contact between schools and parents; cooperation between schools, parents and pupils; and supporting student learning. These factors can be taken as design principles for school improvement and in-service teacher education. In line with previous research, especially the promotion of the conversation between parents and their children at home seems beneficial for students' learning.

### 4a Reflection on research informed education policies

As research has shown that parents' home involvement is related to cognitive and non-cognitive outcomes and that teachers and schools indeed can contribute to effective forms of parental involvement, it seems quite logical that policy makers focus on strengthening those effective forms of parental involvement. However, from a critical theory perspective, this approach can be considered problematic (Green, 2017; Lareau, 2002; Posey-Maddox & Haley-Lock, 2016). The problems with such a research evidence approach are as follows:

(a) Middle-class normativity of parental involvement

The main findings of parental involvement research show that typical middle-class types of involvement relate to positive school outcomes. These types of involvement are practices by parents with high amounts of cultural and social capital. When these practices are taken as the norm for all parents, educational interventions are likely to focus on cultural homogenisation and to promote a one-size-fits-all approach to moulding parents in a singular frame of the effective parent.

(b) Neglect of alternative ways of involvement

In contrast to quantitative, large-scale survey studies on which most of the reviews studies are based, qualitative research has opened up the conceptualisation of parental involvement beyond the focus of the researchers. For example, López (2001) and Posey-Maddox and Haley-Lock (2016) identified types of involvement that are different from mainstream notions of parental involvement, such as the transmission of a work ethos or staying away from schools as a way to show large amounts of trust in teachers and schools.

(c) Blaming, stigmatisation and exclusion of uninvolved parents

A risk of defining effective parental involvement practices is that parents who do not follow these practices are blamed for not being effective. Research has shown that teachers get frustrated, angry and disappointed when parents are uninvolved (Denessen & Raket, 2016). As a result, these parents are at risk of becoming marginalised by the school.

(d) Prescribing teacher practices with a one-size-fits-all approach

A focus on research evidence to improve education might lead to the development of context-free guidelines and scripts to promote parents' involvement, in which education is guided not by values but by standards (Biesta, 2010). The development of such practices enables the objectification of teachers and their de-professionalisation. When teacher professionalism is taken seriously, and it is acknowledged that the specific context of a school has to be considered when designing local policies for school–family partnerships, standardisation of teachers' work is not the correct route to follow.

(e) Accountability pressures that create tensions between schools and parents

Evidenced effective parental involvement practices may be translated into standards for high-quality education. For example, parental home involvement can be considered an indicator of quality of education, because it adds to positive school outcomes. When parents do not show these evidenced practices, tensions may arise between parents and schools, especially when schools are held accountable for student outcomes. There is then a high risk that teachers hold parents responsible for the quality of the school (i.e. educational outcomes of their children).

## 5 New directions: what can research tell us about the way forward?

To overcome the above mentioned problems, a different approach is needed, following suggestions that have been provided by critical scholars (Green, 2017; Lareau, 2002; Posey-Maddox & Haley-Lock, 2016). In particular, a localised approach of school improvement is needed to refrain from a one-size-fits-all approach of parental involvement. Local governments, schools and teachers should critically review the existing evidence and interpret these research findings in the light of their specific local context. In terms of Green (2017), we should move away from positivist assumptions that 'schools can function independent of their surrounding community, but realise the importance of collaboration between school, home, and community' and that there is 'one best model for school-community relations' (ibid., 374). We can move to interpretivist assumptions that 'schools and communities function independently', that there is 'no one best school-community model', and that 'school-community works best through dialogue, collaboration and understanding' (ibid., 377).

Taking a critical theory perspective, we should even move towards the assumptions that 'without a focus on justice and equity, schools operate as sites of social reproduction', that 'schools exist to interrupt inequity, oppression and inequality', and that 'schools can be critical sites for social change for traditionally underserved groups' (Freire, 1970; Green, 2017; 379). Recent developments in educational opportunities in the Netherlands indeed call for a more critical perspective on school–family partnerships.

In this light, new research should focus on existing parental involvement practices that add to diverging educational pathways for children. In the Dutch context, emerging research themes are the design, implementation, and evaluation of national and local policies that aim to support equal educational opportunities for all children. These policies in particular should include building resilience of schools and teachers towards the advantages that children from highly educated parents have because of the financial, social and cultural support that parents invest in their children's schooling. On the other hand, these policies should target teacher expectations and their responsiveness to the needs of children from disadvantaged backgrounds as well as their competences and willingness to build enduring positive relations with families.

## 6 Conclusion

This chapter presents the case of parental involvement in the Netherlands. Parental involvement is rooted in the Dutch education system, because of the freedom of education. Parents' roles have shifted from the founders of education to advocates of their children's careers. Recently, consumerism has put pressure on parents to promote the academic achievements of their children and also to hold schools accountable for the academic careers of their children. In line with these shifts, policy and research in the Netherlands is strongly inspired by a positivist perspective of providing effective education. In 2017, the Dutch government launched its government coalition agreement in which it proposed to strengthen relations between schools and parents in order to overcome educational inequalities, to improve schools, and to yield higher academic outcomes.

The Dutch government should be aware of disrupting parental involvement practices when highly educated parents persist in providing more and effective support to their children compared to their lower educated counterparts. This mechanism is very difficult to compensate for. Governments, schools and teachers will need to call for solidarity from highly educated parents, to put their capital to the best of the collective instead of placing only their own children at an advantage. Policy makers, schools and teachers should reflect on alternative ways to benefit from strong links between schools, families and communities if they really want to work towards a more equal and just education system. For educational researchers it is important to monitor the effects of parental involvement policies on the educational opportunities of children with different backgrounds and to provide empirical evidence for the effects of programmes that focus on inclusionary parent involvement policies and practices of schools and teachers.

# References

Bakker, J. and Denessen, E. (2007) The concept of parent involvement: Some theoretical and empirical considerations. *International Journal about Parents in Education*, 1, 188–199.

Bakker, J. and Denessen, E. (2011) Reflections on international perspectives on countering school segregation. In: Walraven, G., Peters, D., Denessen, E. and Bakker, J., eds. *International Perspectives on Countering School Segregation*. Leuven: Garant. 261–273.

Bakker, J., Denessen, E. and Brus-Laeven, M. (2007) Socio-economic background, parental involvement and teacher perceptions of these in relation to pupil achievement. *Educational Studies*, 33(2), 175–190.

Bakker, J., Denessen, E., Dennissen, M. and Oolbekking-Marchand, H. (2013) *Leraren en ouderbetrokkenheid. Een reviewstudie naar de effectiviteit van ouderbetrokkenheid en de rol die leraren daarbij kunnen vervullen.* Nijmegen: BSI/Radboud Docenten Academie, Radboud Universiteit Nijmegen.

Biesta, G.J.J. (2010) Why 'what works' still won't work: From evidence-based education to value-based education. *Studies in Philosophy and Education*, 29(5), 491–503.

Bourdieu, P. (1973) *La Distinction. Critique sociale du jugement.* Paris: Les Éditions de Minuit.

Carter, S. (2002) *The impact of parent/family involvement of student outcomes.* Eugene, OR: CADRE.

Castelli, S. and Pepe, A. (2008) School-parent relationships: A bibliometric study on 40 years of scientific publications. *International Journal of Parents in Education*, 2(1), 1–12.

Coleman, J. (1988) Families and schools. *Educational Researcher*, 16(6), 32–38.

de Bruïne, E.J., Willemse, T.M., D'Haem, J., Griswold, P., Vloeberghs, L. and van Eynde, S. (2014) Preparing teacher candidates for family–school partnerships. *European Journal of Teacher Education*, 37(4), 409–425.

de la Rie, S., van Steensel, R.C.M., van Gelderen, A.J.S. and Severiens, S. (2016) The role of type of activity in parent–child interactions within a family literacy programme:

Comparing prompting boards and shared reading. *Early Child Development and Care*, 188(8), 1076–1092.
de Vries, P. (2010) *Handboek Ouders in de School*. Amersfoort: CPS.
de Wit, C. (2005) *Ouders als educatieve partner. Een handreiking voor scholen*. The Hague: Q*Primair.
Denessen, E., Driessen, G. and Sleegers, P. (2005) Segregation by choice? A study into group specific reasons for school choice. *Journal of Education Policy*, 20(3), 347–368.
Denessen, E. and Raket, L. (2016) Houdingen van leerkrachten ten aanzien van ouders en hun emoties, reacties en gevoelens van competentie bij verschillende uitingen van ouderbetrokkenheid: Een casusspecifieke analyse. *Pedagogiek*, 36(3), 245–265.
Desforges, C. and Abouchaar, A. (2003) *The impact of parental involvement, parental support and family education on pupil achievement and adjustment: A literature review*. Report Number 433, Department of Education and Skills.
Epstein, J.L. (1995) School, family, and community partnerships: Caring for the children we share. *Phi Delta Kappan*, 76(9), 701–712.
Fantuzzo, J.W., Davis, G.Y. and Ginsberg, M.D. (1995) Effects of parent involvement in isolation or in combination with peer tutoring on student self-concept and mathematics achievement. *Journal of Educational Psychology*, 87, 272–281.
Freire, P. (1970) *The Pedagogy of the Oppressed*. London: Penguin Books.
Green, C.L., Walker, J.M.T., Hoover-Dempsey, K.V. and Sandler, H.M. (2007) Parents' motivations for involvement in children's education: An empirical test of a theoretical model of parental involvement. *Journal of Educational Psychology*, 99(3), 532–544.
Green, T.L. (2017) From positivism to critical theory: School-community relations toward community equity literacy. *International Journal of Qualitative Studies in Education*, 30(4), 370–387.
Heath, S.B. (1983) *Ways with Words: Language, Life and Work in Communities and Classrooms*. Cambridge: Cambridge University Press.
Hujala, E., Turja, L., Gaspar, M.F., Veisson, M. and Waniganayake, M. (2009) Perspectives of early childhood teachers on parent–teacher partnerships in five European countries. *European Early Childhood Education Research Journal*, 17(1), 57–76.
Inspectie van het Onderwijs (2016) *De staat van het onderwijs 2014/2015* [*The state of education 2014/2015*]. Utrecht: Inspectie van het Onderwijs.
Kassenberg, A., Petri, D. and Doornenbal, J. (2016) Competenties van leerkrachten in het samenwerken met ouders: een literatuurstudie. *Pedagogiek*, 36(3), 211–226.
Kloosterman, R., Notten, N., Tolsma, J. and Kraaykamp, G. (2011) The effects of parental reading socialization and early school involvement on children's academic performance: A panel study of primary school pupils in the Netherlands. *European Sociological Review*, 27(3), 291–306.
Lareau, A. (2002) Invisible inequality: Social class and childrearing in black families and white families. *American Sociological Review*, 67(5), 747–776.
López, G.R. (2001) The value of hard work: Lessons on parent involvement from an (im)migrant household. *Harvard Educational Review*, 71, 416–437.
Lusse, M. (2013) *Een kwestie van vertrouwen* [*A matter of trust*]. Rotterdam: Rotterdam University Press.
Onderwijsraad. (2008) *Partners in onderwijsopbrengst* [*Partners in educational outcomes*]. The Hague: Onderwijsraad.
Onderwijsraad. (2010) *Ouders als partners* [*Parents as partners*]. The Hague: Onderwijsraad.
Posey-Maddox, L. and Haley-Lock, A. (2016) One size doesn't fit all: Understanding parent engagement in the contexts of work, family, and public schooling. *Urban*

*Education*, 1–28. Available at: https://journals.sagepub.com/doi/abs/10.1177/0042085916660348 (accessed 30 Jan. 2019).

Sieben, I. and van Ginderen, N. (2014) De keuze voor tweetalig onderwijs: De rol van sociale achtergrond. *Mens en Maatschappij*, 89(3), 233–256.

Smit, F. and Driessen, G. (2009) Creating effective family–school partnerships in highly diverse contexts. Building partnership models and constructing parent typologies. In: Deslandes, R., ed. *International Perspectives on Contexts, Communities and Evaluated Innovative Practices: Family–School-Community Partnerships*. London and New York: Routledge. 64–81.

Tienken, C.H. (2013) Neoliberalism, social darwinism, and consumerism masquerading as school reform. *Interchange*, 43, 295–316.

van der Wolf, K. and Everaert, H. (2005) Challenging parents, teacher characteristics and teacher stress. In: Martínez-González, R-M., Pérez-Herrero, M. and Rodríguez-Ruiz, B., eds. *Family School-Community Partnerships Merging into Social Development*. Oviedo: Grupo SM. 233–253.

# 6 Norway

Parental involvement in Norway – ideals and realities

*Unn-Doris K. Bæck*

## 1 Introduction

In Norway, parents' rights to be part of and influence their children's schooling are emphasised in governmental education policy documents and stated by law through the Education Act. In theory, therefore, Norwegian parents have a lot of say in education. This chapter begins by describing the national legislative and regulative context concerning parental involvement in Norway and shows that efforts have been made to ensure parents' position in schools. The chapter also presents current empirical research in this area from a Norwegian context, which highlights that despite formal rights for parents and efforts by the education authorities to include them, parents' actual opportunities to contribute in school can be questionable (Nordahl, 2003; Bæck, 2010b). From a critical point of view, the chapter therefore problematises the tensions between ideals and realities when it comes to parents' opportunities to engage in their children's schooling in Norway. Furthermore, it presents new research that identifies challenges within teacher education as one factor contributing to this tension, leading to suggestions on possible solutions to the problem.

## 2 The Norwegian education system

Compulsory schooling in Norway starts at the age of 6. Prior to that, around 90 percent of 1–6 year olds attend kindergarten. For the age group 6–19, the system is divided into three different levels: primary, lower secondary and upper secondary school. In primary and lower secondary school, years 1 to 10 are compulsory for students aged 6–16, and based on the principle of one comprehensive school for all. There is no segregation or streaming, and all pupils, including those with special needs, are integrated into the same comprehensive school system. Upper secondary school is not compulsory, but more than 90 percent of the students graduating year 10 will continue straight to upper secondary education. In upper secondary education there is a choice between three-year general/academic study programmes *or* three or four years of vocational study (depending on whether one chooses to do all the three years in school *or* two years of schooling and two years of in-company training in order to complete a journeyman's certificate), with 40 percent of the students choosing the latter.[1]

The Norwegian education system is mainly public, with less than 3 percent of the students attending private schools. Compared to many other countries, the Norwegian state allocates considerable funding to the education system, and even private educational institutions receive most of their funding from public sources. Public education is free, from first grade and throughout higher education. In kindergarten, the parents pay a fee with a maximum cost set by the Norwegian authorities.

The Norwegian Parliament (*the Storting*) and the Government define the goals and decide the framework for the education sector, and in this sense the Norwegian education system can be regarded as centralised. The Ministry of Education and Research is responsible for carrying out national educational policy. National standards are ensured through legislation, regulations, curricula and framework plans. The state bears the overall responsibility for the Education Act, including regulations, content and the financing of primary and secondary education and training. However, even though national legislation and regulations, including the National Curriculum, form a binding framework, municipal and county authorities, schools and teachers can influence the implementation of education and training within this framework. This means, for example, that there is considerable local autonomy when it comes to methods of instruction, choice of learning materials, curriculum development and organisation of instruction. Thus, the Norwegian education system also shows decentralised characteristics and can be regarded as both centralised and decentralised at the same time.

## 3 Parental involvement in school in Norway

### 3a Terminology

Parents are involved in their children's education in a myriad of different ways and many different terms are used in education policy documents and in the research literature to describe parents' role in education. In the current Norwegian education context, the relationship between home and school is depicted as a form of cooperation, with 'home–school cooperation' as the dominant terminology used in official education policy documents.

A shift from a focus on 'parent contact' to a focus on 'parent cooperation' in the legal texts, as described below, serves to illustrate a shift in the way education authorities relate to parents in children's schooling. Also, putting the 'home' first in the phrase serves to further emphasise the vital role that parents are seen to play in this relationship.

'Parental involvement' is the other frequently used term in the Norwegian education context, and can be understood as parents' participation and involvement in activities that are initiated by the school. The school invites parents to be involved in their activities, and parents respond to the invitations initiated by the school.

The terminology used by educational authorities and by schools in their outreach to parents is important because it gives some direction to how the defining party understands the home–school relationship. Following this, emphasising cooperation may give certain expectations, both to parents and teachers, when it comes to the nature of parental involvement, as true cooperation can be understood to signify a mutual and balanced relationship between two equal partners.

## 3b National legislative and regulative context

The foundation for cooperation between home and school was set with the introduction of the Primary and Lower Secondary Education Act of 1969 (Holthe, 2000). §1 of the 1969 Act states that the purpose of primary and lower secondary education should be carried out in agreement and cooperation with the home. Also, the Act states that each school will have a parent council consisting of all parents who have children in the school. The parent council will then elect a working committee among the parents and coordinating committees whenever necessary. The 1969 Act also introduced parents' committees for primary and lower secondary education: a national committee appointed by the Ministry of Education, which was implemented in 1976 and known today as 'National Parents' Committee for Primary and Secondary Education' (*Foreldreutvalget for grunnopplæringen*). While acknowledging the role of parents in their children's education, the 1969 Act did not award parents any formal position in the governing of schools, for example in the education committee that was compulsory in each municipality. Neither was it very clear what the mandate of the parent council and the parent working committee would be.

Since the 1969 Act, however, the role of parents and their position and formal rights in school have been clarified and extended. The subsequent legal texts show a movement from addressing these issues in terms of 'contact' between home and school to 'cooperation' between home and school. Following this, official education policy documents in Norway currently employ the term 'cooperation' when the relationship between school and home/parents is discussed. The current Education Act of 2006 (§ 1–1 and § 13-3d) states that there should be 'cooperation' between school and home and that facilitating for 'parent cooperation' is the responsibility of the educational authorities.[2] 'Parent' is the term used for defining those persons who are responsible for the children.

The 2006 Act (§ 20–1) states that the purpose of parental cooperation is to contribute to positive support when it comes to the academic and social development of the student. Both academic and social development are considered crucial for the motivation and well-being of the student, and important elements for the successful completion of children's education. It is emphasised that successful parent cooperation is an important resource for the school in order to strengthen the development of good learning environments and to create successful learning results.

The 2006 Act (§ 20–3) states concrete regulations for parental cooperation in primary, lower and upper secondary education, and these are based on three principles. Firstly, the primary responsibility for children's education and upbringing lies with the parents, emphasised as a right as well as an obligation in the policy documents. From this follows that parents should also have a right to some form of participation and co-determination within the education system. Secondly, schools are responsible for facilitating cooperation between home and school. The realisation of both of these principles is sought through the implementation of a number of formal forums for home–school cooperation, to be described below. The third principle underlines that the best interest of the child should guide all decisions when it comes to educational matters.

### 3c Formal fora for home–school cooperation

As mentioned above, the Education Act of 2006 states that schools are given the responsibility to facilitate contact and cooperation between home and school, and several forums have been established to make contact and cooperation possible. Schools are obliged to arrange for parent meetings for all parents at least once a year. Parent representatives may be asked to take the lead on parts of the meeting. To ensure parents' contact with the teacher about the individual child, individual parent–teacher conferences are held twice a year (these are in fact student–parent–teacher conferences, as students have a right to participate from the age of 12). These conferences are to be planned and structured, and there are detailed requirements about what kind of information parents should receive and what kind of topics should be addressed. Firstly, the conversation should be about how the student works on a daily basis, and secondly the teacher should account for how the student is doing in relation to the relevant competence requirements in each subject. Furthermore, the conversation should address how the student, school and parents can cooperate in order to facilitate for the students' learning and development and how parents can contribute to helping the student with their schoolwork. This aspect was emphasised further in the 2010 changes to the Act of 2006, as the intention is to increasingly involve parents in the schoolwork of the students. Parent meetings and parent–teacher conferences are very well attended in Norwegian schools and make up the corner-stones for the contact between home and school (Bæck, 2010a).

When it comes to parental possibilities for co-determination within the education system, there are also forums in place. Parent representatives are elected among the parent body for each school year, and on behalf of the parent body they keep closer contact with teachers and school administration. Parent representatives are expected to organise the rest of the parents to contribute to different school events, such as open days. They also represent the parent group in the Parents Working Committee (*FAU Foreldrerådets arbeidsutvalg*) and in the Coordinating Committee (*SU Samarbeidsutvalget*). The Parents Working Committee (FAU) is required by law and is put together by all the elected parent representatives to ensure that parents have real influence in school. Among other things, the FAU works to ensure a good school environment, inform and listen to all parents about current issues, and cooperate with the school and other relevant organs such as the student council, principal and teachers. The FAU can also address relevant issues from school or from the municipality, for example in regards to rules of conduct.

The Coordinating Committee (SU) is the school's highest advisory body, in which all the parties in the school are represented: pupils, parents, teaching staff, other employees, and representatives from the local authority (one of which must be the principal of the school). This Coordinating Committee has the right to issue statements on all matters concerning the school, such as budget proposals, activity and development plans for the school, plans for home–school cooperation, school assessment, plans for alterations to and maintenance of the school's facilities, the school's information activities, principles for selecting books for the school library, leisure activities, school transport, traffic conditions, as well as rules concerning conduct and behaviour. The Coordinating Committee does not have the authority to make decisions and can only advise. However, the municipality (the school owner) can delegate such authority to the committee. The municipality can also choose to elect the committee as a board for the school.

Since the implementation of the 2006 Act, changes to the law in 2010 further introduced elements meant to strengthen parents' position in education. Schools are obliged to maintain contact with the home throughout the school year (§ 20–3). This implies that formal parent–teacher conferences and parent meetings are not necessarily regarded as sufficient for ensuring contact between school and parents. The purpose of the change is to further ensure the information exchange between home and school, as this is considered crucial for parents' opportunities to follow-up on the academic and social development of their own child. Schools are responsible for the contact throughout the school year, but the Act does not state anything specific when it comes to the organisation of this contact, which is left to the individual school. Also, the additions to the Act emphasise that there is a limit to how much contact schools can be expected and directed to have with the parents.

The additions and changes to the 2006 Act are also more specific when it comes to the type of information parents are entitled to receive from the school (§ 20–3, part two), including information about the school, contents of the curriculum, possibilities for parental participation, school routines and other issues relevant for parents. It is interesting to note that with this addition to the Act, the concept of 'participation' (*medvirkning*) is starting to replace 'cooperation' as the preferred term in policy documents.

## 4 Existing research on parental involvement

As shown above, parents' formal rights have been strengthened through parents' representation in cooperative and decision-making bodies in school, and studies show that the majority of parents are satisfied with the home–school cooperation they take part in (Nordahl, 2003; Bæck, 2009). Legal texts and policy documents can be said to represent an ideal situation when it comes to home–school cooperation in a national context. Empirical research in Norway has contributed to critically exploring and problematising how the *ideals* hold up when confronted with *reality*, and a number of studies have indicated that there are indeed challenges. Several of these studies have been based in a critical, sociological framework. Also, research has contributed to knowledge about the factors and mechanisms that are relevant in order to understand the distance between ideals and realities in home–school cooperation. At the same time, it is probably fair to say that describing and exploring challenges when it comes to successful home–school cooperation still holds precedence over, for example, research investigating and testing different measures or innovations seeking improvements in the field. In that sense, home–school cooperation as a research and development field can be described as somewhat immature in Norway.

Westergård's study of challenges for developing successful home–school cooperation in Norway represents one example of the critically framed research approach (Westergård & Galloway, 2004, 2010; Westergård, 2010). The author finds that increased expectations of schools regarding cooperation with parents and including them as partners in the educational project also demand more openness from the teachers and increased competence from both parents and teachers. Westergård (2010) identifies five barriers for good communication between home and school: (1) when parents have expectations that the schools are not able to fulfil; (2) when teachers experience stress and work-pressure; (3) when one of the parties in the cooperation (parent or teacher) feel that they are under attack by the other; (4) when neither of the parties are willing to relate to the other's point of view; and (5) when parents or teachers lack motivation or strategies necessary to cooperate with the other. Increasing the authority and rights of parents, as has been done in Norway, demands knowledgeable and competent teachers, and Westergård therefore suggests specific professional development related to parent relations for teachers. This may include learning how to develop strategies when it comes to critique from parents, learning conflict management and how to build fruitful cooperative partnerships with parents.

My own research has been preoccupied with the relationship between parents and teachers, both from the point of view of parents (Bæck, 2009, 2010a) and from the point of view of teachers (Bæck, 2010b, 2013, 2015), and in what way social background factors influence this relationship, which can often be described as distanced. A main finding from this research is that even though social background factors are significant for understanding the relationship between teachers and parents, distance can also be considered a more general characteristic of this relationship irrespective of parents' socio-economic background. The research suggests that aspects related to teachers' working conditions contribute to this situation, as will be elaborated towards the end of this chapter.

Norwegian studies have also investigated the cooperation between home and school when children have academic difficulties and emotional or conduct problems. These studies show, for example, that good home–school cooperation is of particular importance for these families, but that the relationship can sometimes be especially challenging (Nordahl, 2003; Drugli & Onsøien, 2010; Westergård, 2010; Drugli, 2012; Kirkhaug et al., 2013). Parents will often experience the parent–teacher conferences as draining because the conversations are centred around negative aspects (Drugli & Onsøien, 2010). At the same time, the teachers in Kirkhaug et al.'s study (2013) reported higher levels of bonding in terms of more frequent contact initiatives with parents of children with conduct problems than with parents of children who did not display such problems. According to these authors the explanation for this may be that during the past few decades in Norway there has been an increased focus on reducing child conduct problems in schools. Teacher competence in this field has therefore been enhanced in various ways, including highlighting parental involvement as one strategy in the training programmes offered.

## 5 New research perspective: home–school cooperation as a topic in teacher education in Norway

### 5a Background

The remainder of the chapter will focus on some new research that approaches this from a different angle, through looking at how these issues are addressed in teacher education. This is important as the teacher is such an important actor when it comes to ensuring successful home–school cooperation. Following from the emphasis on home–school cooperation and parents' roles in school in national education policies in Norway, we would expect to find a clear focus on these issues in teacher education. International research on this topic, however, indicates that this is not necessarily the case, showing that emphasis on these issues is rather limited in teacher education in many countries (Baum & McMurray-Schwarz, 2004; Daniel, 2011; Saltmarsh et al., 2015). The aim of the current project is therefore to investigate whether topics connected to home–school cooperation have found their way into teacher education programmes in Norway, and, if so, how such topics are addressed.

### 5b Teacher education in Norway

Norwegian teacher education is highly centralised and nationally regulated (Munthe et al., 2011) – more so than teacher education in the rest of the

Scandinavian countries (Hammerness, 2013). Norway has a tradition of teacher preparation both at university colleges and at universities, and there are several paths to becoming a teacher for grades 1–13. Broadly speaking, the main routes are either a five-year integrated masters degree programme (introduced nationally from autumn 2017), qualifying for a teaching career in grades 1–7, 5–10 or 8–13, or to study subjects at a college or university followed by a one-year Post-Graduate Certificate of Education (PGCE), qualifying for a teaching career in grades 5–13. There are currently ten institutions that offer integrated masters degree programmes in teacher education, while the PGCE can be completed at 19 different institutions.

Universities and university colleges that wish to offer primary and lower secondary teacher education programmes for grades 1–7 must be accredited in accordance with the Act Relating to Universities and University Colleges (Sections 1–2 and 3–1). The National Framework Plan for Teacher Education is established by the Ministry of Education and Research, describing the overall direction for teacher education in Norway. This document constitutes the foundation for the National Guidelines for Teacher Education, set up by the National Council for Teacher Education. The National Guidelines provide specific instructions and standards for courses and study points as well as learning outcomes for practice placement. The goal is to ensure a nationally coordinated teacher education that fulfils certain quality demands. The boards of the individual institutions adopt programme plans for the teacher education programmes that they offer, taking the National Framework Plan and the National Guidelines into account.

## 5c *The study*

The data material consists of documents describing national policies for teacher education in Norway as well as local programme plans and course plans for primary and lower secondary teacher education years 1–7 for institutions offering this form of teacher education. At the national level, these are the National Framework Plan and the National Guidelines for Teacher Education. At the local institutional level, we have analysed programme plans as well as course descriptions for individual courses in ten teacher education institutions. Through document analyses, we have investigated the extent to which national policies of teacher education integrate and consider topics related to home–school cooperation, and to what extent these can be found again in local plans and guidelines.

## 5d *Findings*

*Focus on home–school cooperation in national and local plans in teacher education*
In the study, we find that in the National Framework Plan, the National Guidelines as well as in the local plans, home–school cooperation has

a modest focus. In the National Framework Plan, for example, the topic is not mentioned explicitly in the initial introduction nor in the overall statements on the scope and objectives of teacher education. In the National Guidelines, the topic is emphasised when it comes to practice placements. The Guidelines states, that as part of the candidates' skills after practice they should be able to interact with students, parents/guardians, colleagues and other external and internal actors. In addition, they should be able to employ their knowledge and skills in order to involve and build relations towards students and parents/guardians.

As mentioned above, the National Guidelines provide specific instructions, standards and learning outcomes for courses and practice placement. It is compulsory that all teacher education students in Norway have 60 study points in a course called 'Pedagogy and pupil related skills', and it is here that topics related to home–school cooperation is primarily touched upon. A central focus in this course is on how teachers can ensure good learning environments in classrooms characterised by social, religious and cultural diversity. According to the Guidelines, the course should provide teacher education students with the skills to maintain dialogue with parents/guardians about pupils' learning and development in a reflective and professional manner.

Practice teaching is an important part of the training teacher education for students, and they have between 110 and 115 days of practice during the course of their study. Home–school cooperation is included as a topic in practice teaching from year 2, or even as late as from year 3. One of the institutions in the study states the following about the subject content of practice teaching in year 3: 'The main theme for practice teaching in year 3 is the exploration of one's own practice. Another main theme will be the planning of one's own teaching, while using national and local plans as a starting point. In addition, the focus is on school as a learning organisation and on home–school cooperation.' This is followed up in the learning goals, describing the skills and general competences that the students are expected to acquire. The students should acquire the skills to plan, carry out and evaluate parent meetings, and to cooperate with colleagues, school management, parents and other actors in school.

The structure and content found in the national plans and guidelines are echoed in the local programme plans. While some of the institutions include their own elaborations on learning goals related to home–school cooperation, most do not elaborate much at all, and these topics are not very well covered in courses or practice teaching, where other, and mainly pupil-centred issues, stand out as much more central.

*Approaches to home–school cooperation in programmes and course plans*
A central part of teacher education is to teach the candidates what the professional role of being a teacher entails and how to take on this role. In relation to the aforementioned obligatory course, 'Pedagogy and pupil related skills', emphasis is put on the importance of developing a professional teacher identity and the necessary competence enabling the students to handle different

challenges they may face when exercising their profession. Students should develop social and relational competence necessary to encounter pupils, parents/guardians, colleagues and other cooperation partners in a professional manner. This means learning approaches that will help them to relate to parents, communicating and cooperating in a way that is based on teachers' professional knowledge. As shown in previous works (Bæck, 2010b, 2015), for some teachers the balance between keeping parents close, maintaining professional authority and prioritising between different parts of the job can be challenging. Sometimes insisting on professionalism is misconstrued as maintaining distance towards parents, and instead of approaching parents as a resource, they are seen as a potential threat. The groundwork for fruitful home–school cooperation is laid down in teacher education, but preservice teachers' misconceptions about families during their undergraduate training experiences have been studied (Baum & McMurray-Schwarz, 2004), and a limited focus on professionalism may add to such misconceptions. Another approach to home–school cooperation in teacher education could be to view parents as potential supporters and resources in the teaching and learning processes that are taking place in school. Such an approach would demand that the student teachers would be equipped with knowledge about how parents can function as resources in this way, and the students would need skills necessary to engage parents' resources. The studies showed that very few of the programme and course plans included any mention of parents as potential resources in teaching and learning processes. Only one institution had included a separate theme on home–school cooperation and parental involvement. This course included a focus on family-groups, student–parent–teacher-conferences and parent meetings, cooperation at individual, group and system level, as well as conflict management and bullying. In this course, there was a perspective on parents as a partners and resource in teaching and learning, and the course plan stated that the student should gain understanding of how to communicate and analyse professional ethical challenges together with the home and other partners. This was not, however, representative of how the topics were addressed in the other teacher education institutions.

## 6 Conclusions

As shown above, the Norwegian educational system with its policy documents and the Education Act in many ways lay down a solid and promising foundation for the realisation of good and fruitful home–school cooperation, and of parents' continued and increasing roles when it comes to cooperation and decision-making processes. There is also potential for increased formal power if the municipalities choose to grant the coordinating committees decision-making authority. At the same time, research in Norway shows the reality when it comes to home–school cooperation may be quite different from what is depicted in policy documents. Both from the parents' and teachers' point of view, this relationship is challenging and draining for some. A number of researchers therefore question parents' actual opportunities to be involved with and to influence what goes on in school.

With an emphasis on home–school cooperation in national education policies in Norway, we would expect this to be a focus area in teacher education. However, the current study on how such issues are approached in teacher education, as presented above, shows that there is little focus on topics related to home–school cooperation in teacher education programmes in Norway, making this a major policy challenge pertaining to parental involvement in this national context. When such topics are addressed, the focus is often on teaching the students methods to *cope* with parents and ways to *relate* to parents in a professional manner. Teaching students how to *engage* parents as partners in pupils' learning processes and how to *engage* parents as partners in school, seem to be less common. The lack of attention that this topic has attracted in teacher education programmes in Norway, inevitably communicates to teacher students that home–school cooperation is not a particularly important part of the teaching job. Such a message can be established as a master narrative or meta-narrative among novice teachers, who are in the process of establishing a professional identity and a belief in their own professional abilities. We can conclude that teacher education programmes could do more to prepare novice teachers for this part of the teaching job.

The situation described throughout this chapter is likely to have an impact on teachers' insecurities when it comes to home–school cooperation. This can ultimately be part of the explanation behind the high levels of teacher attrition that have been documented, both nationally and internationally (Fantilli & McDougall, 2009; Roksvaag & Texmon, 2012), and especially among novice teachers (Meister & Melnick, 2003; Fantilli & McDougall, 2009). A lack of focus on these issues in teacher education, where the groundwork for high-quality teaching is founded, contributes to making the transition from education and into the teaching profession harder than necessary. This affects the novice teachers themselves, but also families and pupils.

Stronger emphasis on such topics in teacher education would serve to create a common understanding of the importance of home–school cooperation among teachers and future school leaders. Consequently, it would contribute to lifting the responsibility for this task off the shoulders of the individual teacher and direct it to the institutional school level, where it belongs. Thijs and Eilbracht (2012) also argue that there should be more emphasis on preparing teacher candidates for the realities they will encounter as teachers, and that teacher students among other things need to learn how to become more impervious to negative and frustrating interactions with parents instead of focusing on trying to change them. Teacher education students need to have the opportunity to develop interpersonal skills and abilities to cooperate and communicate with parents, and this should be built into teacher education. Engaging in informed discussions about role clarifications and expectations, beliefs about parenting and parenting practices among parents from different social and cultural backgrounds, will help novice teachers in their encounters with parents. In addition, knowledge on how to engage parents is necessary, as opposed to a limited focus on strategies for 'dealing with' parents.

As the analyses in this chapter are based solely on the study of documents, it is clear that the issue at hand is dealt with in more ways in teacher education than the documents reveal. Further studies of home–school cooperation as a topic in teacher education in Norway and elsewhere therefore need to include different kinds of data in order to build a broader picture of the situation in teacher education.

## Notes

1 Currently under revision.
2 In the official English translation of the Education Act, the Norwegian term for cooperation (*samarbeid*) is translated as 'participation', which is a term that has a slightly different meaning. Here I have chosen to relate to the Norwegian version of the law text and employ my own translation of relevant terms.

## References

Bæck, U.-D.K. (2009) From a distance. How Norwegian parents experience their encounters with school. *International Journal of Educational Research*, 48(5), 342–351.

Bæck, U.-D.K. (2010a) Parental involvement practices in formalized home–school cooperation. *Scandinavian Journal of Educational Research*, 54(6), 549–563.

Bæck, U.-D.K. (2010b) 'We are the professionals': A study of teachers' views on parental involvement in school. *British Journal of Sociology of Education*, 31(3), 323–335.

Bæck, U.-D.K. (2013) Lærer-foreldre relasjoner under press [Teacher-parent relations under pressure]. *Barn*, 31(4), 77–87.

Bæck, U.-D.K. (2015) Beyond the fancy cakes. Teachers' relationship to home–school cooperation in a study from Norway. *International Journal about Parents in Education*, 7(1), 37–46.

Baum, A.C. and McMurray-Schwarz, P. (2004) Preservice teachers' beliefs about family involvement: Implications for teacher education. *Early Childhood Education Journal*, 32(1), 57–61.

Daniel, G.R. (2011) Family–school partnerships: Towards sustainable pedagogical practice. *Asia Pacific Journal of Teacher Education*, 39(2), 165–176.

Drugli, M.B. (2012) Skole-hjem-samarbeid når eleven har atferdsvansker [School-home-cooperation when the pupil has behavioral challenges]. *Bedre skole*, 4, 32–37.

Drugli, M.B. and Onsøien, R. (2010) *Vanskelige foreldresamtaler - gode dialoger* [*Difficult Parent Conversations – Good Dialogues*]. Oslo: Cappelen Damm.

Fantilli, R.D. and McDougall, D.E. (2009) A study of novice teachers: Challenges and supports in the first years. *Teaching and Teacher Education*, 25(6), 814–825.

Hammerness, K. (2013) Examining features of teacher education in Norway. *Scandinavian Journal of Educational Research*, 57(4), 400–419.

Holthe, V.G. (2000) *Foreldreinnflytelse i skolen* [*Parental Influence in School. Rights, Negotiation and Compromise*]. Oslo: Universitetsforlaget.

Kirkhaug, B., Drugli, M.B., Klöckner, C.A. and Mørch, W.-T. (2013) Association between parental involvement in school and child conduct, social, and internalizing problems: Teacher report. *Educational Research and Evaluation*, 19(4), 346–361.

Meister, D.G. and Melnick, S. (2003) National new teacher study: Beginning teachers concerns. *Action in Teacher Education*, 24(4), 87–94.

Munthe, E., Malmo, K.-A.S. and Rogne, M. (2011) Teacher education reform and challenges in Norway. *Journal of Education for Teaching*, 37(4), 441–450.

Nordahl, T. (2003) *Makt og avmakt i samarbeidet mellom hjem og skole* [Power and powerlessness in the cooperation between home and school]. NOVA Report 13/03. Oslo.

Roksvaag, K. and Texmon, I. (2012) *Arbeidsmarkedet for lærere og førskolelærere* [*The labour market for teachers and pre-school teachers*]. SSB/Statistics Norway.

Saltmarsh, S., Barr, J. and Chapman, A. (2015) Preparing for parents: How Australian teacher education is addressing the question of parent-school engagement. *Asia Pacific Journal of Education*, 35(1), 69–84.

Thijs, J. and Eilbracht, L. (2012) Teachers' perceptions of parent-teacher alliance and student-teacher relational conflict: Examining the role of ethnic differences and 'disruptive' behavior. *Psychology in the Schools*, 49(8), 794–808.

Westergård, E. (2010) *Parental disillusionment with school: Prevalence, correlates, development and prevention*. PhD-thesis. Norway: University of Stavanger.

Westergård, E. and Galloway, D. (2004) Parental disillusionment with school: Prevalence and relationship with demographic variables, and phase, size and location of school. *Scandinavian Journal of Educational Research*, 48(2), 189–204.

Westergård, E. and Galloway, D. (2010) Partnerships, participation and parental disillusionment in home–school contacts: A study in two schools in Norway. *Pastoral Care in Education*, 28(2), 97–107.

# 7 Portugal

Family involvement and participation in schools in Portugal: the difficulty in sharing responsibilities

*Eva Gonçalves*

## 1 Introduction

Since the 1980s, education policy in Portugal has sought to promote shared responsibility between central government and local communities for the regulation of schools, an approach that follows the general trend in European countries with highly centralised education systems (Batista, 2014). This policy direction has contributed to a redistribution of responsibilities concerning both families and teachers: families can now choose in which schools they want to enrol their children,[1] thereby assuming the role of 'consumers'; they are represented in school management structures where they assume the role of 'stakeholders' who regulate school decisions and practices, and they are also considered 'partners' who must engage in school activities. Teachers are held accountable for everything that happens in a school and have to accept other figures as partners within schools.

This chapter begins with an overview of the Portuguese education system, outlining its organisation and describing some of its distinctive characteristics (Section 2). Sections 3 and 4 consider the evolution of the school–family relationship in Portugal in legislation and research, presenting some of the main findings, theoretical frameworks, and dominant discourses adopted by researchers. This is augmented in Section 5 with details of a specific research project on the school–family relationship in Portugal that examines how teachers and families have adopted their new roles in different schools with different socioeconomic contexts and academic performance records in three municipalities.[2]

## 2 Overview of the Portuguese education system

The Portuguese education system remains highly centralised and regulated by the State, whereby central government retains control of financing, teacher recruitment, resources, planning, management and the national curriculum. However, a decentralisation process that began in 2008 has reassigned some responsibilities to the municipalities, e.g. for infrastructure maintenance, school-related social services and non-teaching staff (Law No. 75/2008) and local authorities can now finance the costs for managing education facilities, public transport for students, extra-curricular activities (mainly for lower primary schools), and some of the non-teaching staff (OECD, 2014a, p. 16).[3] While the PISA results indicated that the level of autonomy over curricula and assessments granted to school principals in Portugal was among the lowest in OECD countries (OECD, 2014b), these schools have since been granted far greater autonomy over curricula, and teachers have a relatively high level of autonomy over teaching and classroom methods. National exams at the lower and upper secondary levels are the only instruments that regulate school performance, with few consequences for schools with lower averages (aside from their image in the media after publication of the rankings).

Although most schools in Portugal are run by the State, the country also has one of the highest percentages of students enrolled in private schools (13.4 percent) in Europe (Eurydice, 2012). These private schools are mainly located in coastal regions and are only accessible to families from higher socioeconomic backgrounds who can afford the tuition fees. State schools are free, and students from low socioeconomic backgrounds receive support to pay for teaching materials, school meals and transport. While legislation in Portugal allows families to apply to up to five schools of their choice, proximity to the family residence remains the main criterion for enrolment (Law No. 137/2013). Furthermore, since Ministry of Education figures for 2018 indicate that around 53 percent of municipalities have only one school cluster (162 municipalities out of 308), freedom of school choice in Portugal is still very limited (CNE, 2016).

Portugal has a formal early childhood care and education (ECCE) system in which there is almost universal participation (OECD, 2017). State schools are inclusive, comprehensive and structured into four sequential levels: 1) lower primary (age 6–9 years); 2) upper primary (age 10–12 years); 3) lower secondary (age 12–14 years); and 4) upper secondary (age 15–18 years). Since 2012, children have been required to complete 12 years of compulsory schooling (i.e. from the age of 6 to 18 years).

As part of a 2005 modernisation project, schools in Portugal were reorganised: lower primary schools with less than ten students were closed, and schools were amalgamated into clusters that offer the full range of education facilities from pre-schools to lower or upper secondary schools (CNE, 2017).

## 3 The school–family relationship in Portugal

### 3a The problem of terminology

All students up to the age of 17 in Portugal must have a so-called 'guardian' (*encarregado de educação*), a specific term used in Portuguese legislation. This guardian is officially responsible for all decisions regarding the student's school life or education choices and is the designated contact person for the school (e.g. for information about grades, disciplinary measures, subjects, school activities, school policies, etc.). The texts of most legislative documents usually refer to 'parents and guardians'. Since the introduction of the new autonomy, administration and management model for state schools in 2008 (Law No. 75/2008), legislation has also increasingly used the term 'partners' to define the roles of teachers and guardians in schools.

In Portuguese education research, 'parents' or 'families' remain the preferred terms used, although some recent studies do use the term 'guardian' in order to cover all possible scenarios (mother, father, grandparent, neighbour, friend, or others). In Portuguese, the term 'home' (*casa*) refers to the physical place where the family resides. Furthermore, the many different designations (involvement, relationship, participation, interaction, engagement, partnership, etc.) and definitions used by researchers in Portugal to describe school–family dynamics make it difficult to understand and compare studies.

In this chapter, the school–family relationship is defined as all possible dynamics between teachers and families. This relationship can be classified as one of 'involvement' if the joint activities of teachers and families centre on students and one of 'participation' when their joint activities centre on the class and/or school (Davies, Marques, & Silva, 1997). Involvement is divided into two types: 'familiar', portraying how families get involved/guide/monitor their child's education path within the family space, and 'scholarly', focusing on how families communicate with schools and teachers concerning their own child only (Silva, 2007). Participation, in turn, can be 'informal' when families engage in activities that help all students (such as organising and participating in school events, fundraising or helping with school maintenance) or 'formal' when families participate in the General Council or Parent Association at a meso level and the Class Council at a micro level.

### *3b Legislative change in the school–family relationship in Portugal*

The school–family relationship was first mentioned in Portuguese legislation in 1835,[4] when education became a legal duty of the central government. The corresponding legal document assigned families the responsibility of sending their children to school every day. For many years, Portugal's economic and social structure, which was based on subsistence farming and characterised by high illiteracy rates, made families less likely to invest in education as a way to improve their lives (Candeias, 2005).[5] The reforms introduced by Veiga Simão (the Minister of Education in the XI Portuguese Government) in the late 1960s with the aim of granting access to education to the whole population regardless of socioeconomic status were accompanied by changes to the legislation. Since 1968,[6] all schools have had to designate a class teacher (*diretor de turma*) to establish regular communication between schools and families (Silva, 2003). However, the role of families in education remained incipient in Portuguese legislation until 1977. Parents only had two duties: to send their children to school every day and to meet the class teacher when requested; they could not participate in schools – either on an informal or a formal basis. Since then, Portuguese school legislation has gone through four stages of transformation.

The '*first stage of transformation*' began in 1977 with the legitimation of parents' associations (PA) and the introduction of freedom of school choice. The role of parents was emphasised in line with national and European calls for the decentralisation of highly centralised education systems (Batista, 2014) and following the end of the Salazar regime (the dictatorship that ruled Portugal from 1933 to 1974). After 1977, parents could legally form PAs (prohibited during the Salazar regime), which gave them a means to issue statements about the education system and school management. However, they remained without representation in school management structures. According to data from the Ministry of Education, until 1990 less than 20 percent of schools had a PA,[7] and most of those schools that did were located in urban and middle-class areas where families had a level of cultural capital similar to teachers (Martins, 2003). By 2013 almost 70 percent of state schools had a PA (Figure 7.1).

In the 1980s, Portuguese legislation introduced the possibility for families to choose a school. This was intended as a regulatory instrument to guarantee school quality (Silva, 2003). However, it remains essentially a limited right, particularly for families with low socioeconomic backgrounds (who are less able to send their children to private schools or schools in other locations and are more likely to be excluded by school strategies to select students) and because many municipalities only have one school (Sebastião, 2008; CNE, 2017).

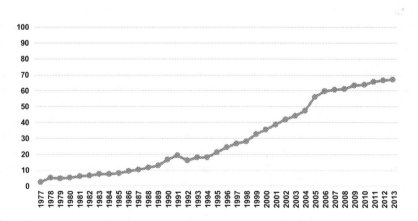

*Figure 7.1* Schools with a legally formed parents' association registered with the National Confederation of Parents Associations (percentages)★

Source: Gonçalves (2015, p. 110).

★ These percentages refer to individual schools (no data is available for school clusters) and include all registered parents' associations (including those that are inactive).

A '*second stage of transformation*' began in 1990 with the reinforcement of the power of PAs, facilitated by the fact that Portugal began to receive extra funding from the European Union.[8] New legislation gave families the right to formally participate in schools for the first time: they could now form a PA free of charge (see an increase in the percentage of PAs post 1992 in Figure 7.1) and assume a role in school management. However, families still remained 'outsiders' because this legislation was optional, and only 50 percent of schools decided to apply it (Silva, 2003).

In 1998, a '*third stage of transformation*' began with the introduction of legislation that focused on the responsibilities of families. As already mentioned, education policy in Portugal has been shaped since the 1980s by a decentralisation movement that promotes the sharing of responsibilities between central government and the local actors (Batista, 2014). Accordingly, the new legislation gave guardians the right to receive all information about school policies and school and classroom activities, thus bringing them closer to the role of partners. A law on 'student status' (Law No. 270/98) introduced a set of rights and duties for students, teachers and families to ensure that all actors acted correspondingly. It included not only existing duties that were a matter of common sense, such as family responsibility for student punctuality and behaviour, but also new responsibilities that accentuated family duties related to the school's pedagogical mission (for example, to engage in the Educational Project[9] and to elect their own representatives). During this stage, the participation rights of families were enlarged, giving them the right to contribute to school strategic policy documents and to vote on all matters pertaining to the school.

The '*final stage of transformation*' started in 2008 by reinforcing parental involvement in students' education paths and consolidating formal parental participation in schools. As part of the decentralisation policy, a new school autonomy, administration and management model[10] was introduced that changed the way schools are managed. This reform established three councils in schools: the General Council for operational and strategic planning and monitoring, the Pedagogical Council to supervise and coordinate pedagogical activities, and the Administrative Council, responsible for administrative and financial matters. This model assigned families a regulatory role in schools by requiring them to elect and appoint their own representatives on the General Council, the Pedagogical Council (although this right was revoked in 2013) and the Class Councils (a management structure at the micro level where teachers and family representatives work together to define the strategies for each class). Through their representatives on the General Council, families have the right to approve all monitoring and assessment documents, and all projects and activities (including those organised by the Pedagogical and Administrative Councils), and they also have the right to vote for the election of the school principal. They are therefore viewed as stakeholders who regulate teaching activities (Sliwka & Istance, 2006). In Class Councils, families have the right to participate in the development of pedagogical projects but the actual carrying out of these projects does not require their approval.

The afore-mentioned law governing 'student status' was developed during this stage (Law No. 51/2012). This focuses on the notion of (co)responsibilities between teachers and families on a multitude of items, including the right/duty of teachers and families (primarily class teachers and guardians) to work together to define a student's academic career path.

Another development during this stage concerned parental freedom of school choice within the state education system: parents can now apply to five state schools of their choice. The schools, in turn, select their students based on a list of criteria defined by legislation (Law No. 5048-B/2013), which requires them to prioritise students who live nearby, then students with accessibility issues, then students with older siblings at the school, before moving on to other applicants. However, since the return to a left-wing government in 2018, it has become harder to enrol children in a state school that is not located near their guardians' home or work address (enrolment now depends on the guardian's fiscal address).

## 4 Research on the school–family relationship in Portugal

The first studies into the school–family relationship in Portugal were conducted in the 1980s and shared a common heterogeneity in discourse because they focused on the cultural diversity of Portuguese families and on how each cultural class interacted with schools in different ways (Benavente et al., 1987; Marques, 1988), showing different strategies correlating to specific performance levels in school (Davies & Johnson, 1996). This earlier research set out the positive reasons for promoting school–family relationships. First, regular communication between teachers and families facilitates the interpretation of the roles that each must play, increases teachers' knowledge of their students' situations and helps families to appreciate how teachers work, thus diminishing conflicts (Marques, 1996; Silva & Vieira, 1996). Second, knowing about family backgrounds helps teachers to define adequate strategies to improve student performance and advise families on their expectations for their children (Marques, 1996; Villas-Boas, 1996).

In the early 2000s, research moved away from highlighting the effects of cultural and socioeconomic background on the school–family relationship and began to centre on the impact that schools as organisations might have on teacher–family dynamics using mainly micro perspectives and qualitative methodologies (Diogo, 1998; Silva, 2003). The findings of this research show how schools as organisations can influence those dynamics, primarily following the opinions and practices of their principals (Silva, 2004). Some studies showed how teachers and families engage in conflicts from opposing positions: teachers want all students to succeed, while families demand that attention is focused on their own children to raise their academic performance (Silva, 2003). These studies view families as individual entities trying to secure the best futures for their children to succeed by making the best academic choices but neglect the fact that families from different socioeconomic backgrounds have different capacities to access and interpret information about schools and the available choices (Sebastião, 2008).

In recent years, a growing number of studies have looked at the shared regulation processes between central government and the local communities in line with the trend in 21st-century discourse towards democratisation and active citizenship. These studies show that schools and teachers have difficulty in accepting 'outsiders' as stakeholders who must approve and can influence their decisions and practices (Lima & Sá, 2002; Barroso, 2005; Batista, 2014; Gonçalves, 2015). On the family side, research findings indicate a low level of family participation in school assemblies[11] (Barroso, Almeida & Homem, 2001) and PAs (Delicado, 2002), confirming international studies that show very low levels of civic and democratic behaviour in Portuguese society (European Social Survey, 2012).

In general, research shows that the involvement and participation of families differs according to their socioeconomic backgrounds (Diogo, 1998), that guardians and families are neither motivated nor prepared to be stakeholders (Gonçalves, 2015), and that teachers lack the training and motivation to assume many of their new responsibilities – especially being accountable – and to accept families as partners and stakeholders (Lopes, 2006; Oliveira, 2010; Gonçalves, 2015).

## 5 New research perspective: Is the school-family relationship an effective partnership or a mere approximation?

### 5a Context and research questions

Portuguese legislation implemented several changes towards decentralisation and school autonomy that redistributed responsibilities between central government and the local communities and identified new roles. As a result, families and teachers are now defined as partners (Sá, 2000), and families must assume the role of stakeholders (Sliwka & Istance, 2006) in the school's General Council and Class Councils. They also serve as consumers, who hold schools to account when choosing where to enrol their child(ren) (Estevão, 1998).

The research project described in this section adopts a sociological approach, comparing schools and families from different municipalities with diverse socioeconomic and education backgrounds. It is embedded in the discourse on democracy and active citizenship, focusing thereby on how teachers and families adopt the role of partners and how families adopt the role of stakeholders. The study is divided into three parts: (1) a macro analysis of the national guidelines relating to the school-family relationship provided in the legislation outlined above; (2) a meso analysis to explain how schools and PAs define their strategies as organisations by following or not following national guidelines; and (3) a micro analysis of cooperation between class teachers and guardians to elucidate how they interpret their defined roles in national and school guidelines.

The analysis model used in this study (as illustrated by Figure 7.2) was influenced by two main theoretical concepts: Margaret Archer's morphogenetic cycle (1979) and Anthony Giddens' theory of structuration (1984). According to Archer (1979), education systems are part of the structure of a society (macro context), simultaneously defined by the history and sociocultural context of a country and determining all social dynamics at lower levels (meso and micro). To analyse the dynamics between schools and families in Portugal, the researchers also had to study the history of the Portuguese education system, especially the changes in legislation that could have had an impact on the school–family relationship.

Giddens' theory of structuration refers to the influence that institutions like schools and PAs can have on the daily dynamics between teachers and families, particularly through how they re-interpret the national education policy guidelines and (re)contextualise them in their local school context (Zanten & Ball, 2000). Both school guidelines, which are the product of the principal's and PA's interpretation of national guidelines (Zanten & Ball, 2000), and the dynamics between school and family representatives (Perrenoud & Montandon, 1988) at an institutional (meso) level, are influenced by national guidelines and can influence the school–family relationship at a micro level.

The model shown in Figure 7.2 also includes student characteristics, i.e. their education paths (success or unsuccessful) and their socioeconomic backgrounds (Silva, 2003; Diogo, 2008). In other words, class teachers and guardians may or may not choose to follow national and school guidelines or may even change or create new guidelines in their daily cooperation in line with student education paths and socioeconomic backgrounds.

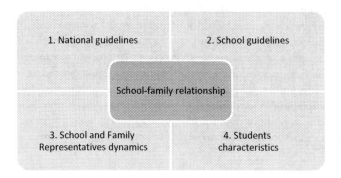

*Figure 7.2* Influences on the school–family relationship
Source: Gonçalves (2015, p. 41).

98  Eva Gonçalves

At the meso and the micro levels, both Archer (1979) and Giddens (1984) maintain that individuals can act as 'agents' when they change/create new guidelines or decide not to follow the given rules but that they usually choose to be 'actors' who follow such guidelines since they have a practical consciousness that helps them to act according to their internalised rules (Giddens, 1984). This research aimed to determine whether or not schools, PAs, class teachers and guardians had internalised their new roles as partners and stakeholders and explain why this was the case.

### 5b Methodology and data collection

The research was split across two stages. First, an analysis of 67 legal documents (dating from 1835 to 2014) and a number of international reports (Eurydice and OECD) was carried out to study the history of the Portuguese education system. This was then followed by a multiple-case study involving six schools from three different municipalities: three located near the coast, one that was the only school in a small municipality in the centre of the country, and two from the east and closer to Spain (one from a rural and the other from an urban area). In each school, most students have distinct socioeconomic backgrounds and the academic success rates vary across schools.

Fieldwork for the meso analysis included analysing the schools' strategic documents (education projects and internal regulations), conducting semi-structured interviews with the principals and chairs of the PAs and attending General Councils as a non-participating observer to gather information on how principals interpret national guidelines and create school guidelines and identify the dynamics between schools and their PAs.

For the micro analysis, fieldwork consisted of semi-structured interviews conducted with three students, their guardians and their class teachers in each school (54 interviews in total) and non-participatory observations of Class Councils to gather data on how guardians and class teachers interpret the roles assigned to them in national and school guidelines.

The data was then analysed using the thematic content analysis approach (Cohler & Hostetler, 2002) using the MAXQDA program (a software program for qualitative and mixed methods research). The categories used to analyse documents and discourses was transformed into categorical variables to allow the application of multiple correspondence analyses (exploratory multi-variable statistical analysis) using SPSS software (Statistical Package for Social Sciences). The main goal was to identify the characteristics of parent representatives in General and Class Councils and the types of relationships between class teachers and guardians.

### 5c Main results

This section presents the main results of the case study, beginning with the meso analysis and then moving on to micro analysis, organised according to the four school–family relationship types already presented: familiar involvement, scholarly involvement, informal participation and formal participation.

The results at the *meso level* confirm that most schools and PAs tend to perform their roles as defined in the national guidelines – as predicted in the theories proposed by Archer (1979) and Giddens (1984). However, there were also some exceptions. Family socioeconomic background seems to have an influence on how principals adopt national guidelines for 'familiar involvement'. In schools where more families come from privileged socioeconomic backgrounds, principals tend to define guidelines for teachers that focus exclusively on improving students' academic performance and maintain a distance to their family lives. In contrast, guidelines in schools with students from non-privileged socioeconomic backgrounds also include activities that hold teachers accountable for the development of students as citizens and promoting the involvement of their guardians in their school and personal lives.

The way principals interpret legal documents on the 'formal participation' of families through representation in General Councils also seems to have an influence on school guidelines. In some cases, principals design specific procedures to guarantee that teachers act as accountable partners and families as effective stakeholders. In such cases, principals add guidelines to cover what was determined at the macro level. When they consider it to be the responsibility of families to define how they engage in formal participation, schools tend to follow national guidelines, which ultimately translates into families not acting as partners and stakeholders.

With regard to the dynamics in formal participation, the study results reveal three different profiles of family representatives in General Councils: 1) 'stakeholders' in schools with students from privileged socioeconomic backgrounds and highly educated families (with the emergence of conflicts when teachers attempt to limit their participation); 2) 'partners' in schools with students from average socioeconomic backgrounds (with their discourse showing an alienation from the families they should represent); 3) 'non-participants' in schools with students from adverse socioeconomic backgrounds, where family representatives tend to accept teachers' proposals and rarely put forward their own opinions. One important finding is that families continue to resist 'formal participation' instruments: in general the membership of PAs is low, which leads to a lack of validation when negotiating with principals.

As far as 'scholarly involvement' is concerned, school guidelines follow national guidelines by using the instruments prescribed in national legislation (teacher webpages, e-mails, phone calls) to communicate and share information with families. School and parents' association guidelines for 'informal participation' refer to sporadic activities and events, which is consistent with the fact that this type of participation is not as developed in legislation as the others.

At the *micro level* of analysis, the findings for 'scholarly involvement' and 'informal participation' are similar: teachers and guardians use the same channels of communication prescribed in national and school guidelines; teachers rarely or never promote informal activities, and most guardians tend not to participate in these rare events.

In the case of 'familiar involvement', teachers and guardians seem to follow their own set of rules regardless of the existence of any specific school guidelines. When a student's academic performance is poor, interactions between the teacher and guardian tend to be more collaborative and regular in nature, and they discuss a variety of topics (success, behaviour, friendships, daily habits, etc.) even if the school guidelines indicate that teachers should focus solely on academic topics. When a student's academic performance is good, teachers and guardians tend to meet less frequently and only discuss academic performance, even if the school guidelines indicate that teachers should help families with other topics. At the micro level, student characteristics (academic performance) therefore have more influence on the dynamics of interaction between teachers and guardians than national and/or school guidelines.

When it comes to 'formal participation', a difference can be seen between schools that have corresponding guidelines in place and those that do not. In the former, guardians appear to be able to assume their role as stakeholders in Class Councils, since the schools provide an appropriate forum for communication. In the latter, the representatives of the guardians rarely intervene in Class Councils and usually do not have any communication channels open to them to talk to the families they represent.

The results from the *meso* and *micro levels* confirm that most families have difficulties in taking up their new roles as partners and as stakeholders. There are several reasons for this: 1) a lack of time due to work commitments; 2) non-availability of private or public transport; 3) difficulties with new technologies; 4) a lack of awareness of the existence of family representatives on school councils; 5) a lack of trust in family representatives to discuss matters about students; 6) a lack of communication channels between guardians and their representatives; and 7) a low level of civic participation leading to the non-existence of or low number of members in PAs.

## 6 Conclusions

In the early years of the Portuguese education system, families did not get involved with schools, and all decisions were entrusted to teachers. Since 1977, the legislative discourse has changed completely: from a total separation of school and family to a shared responsibility for education (at home and at school), school management and education policies. The national guidelines for the rights and duties of schools and families with regard to parental involvement date from 30 years ago (with a recent revision in 2012), and the current instruments for formal participation in all state schools have only been in place for ten years. While the legislative changes might be recent, it is nonetheless important to study their influences on the dynamics of interaction between schools and families.

The combination of the recent changes in the legislative discourse and a highly centralised and bureaucratic education system (Justino & Batista, 2013) might well explain why most actors follow a bureaucratic-administrative rationality that is far removed from developing a real partnership between schools and families and becoming agents of school regulation. Most school principals and family representatives (meso level) and class teachers and guardians (micro level) show little motivation and capacity to adopt their new roles as partners and stakeholders. Principals appear to be at a loss about what schools must do to facilitate having family representatives in their classrooms and school decision-making processes, showing a lack of training in how to accept and work with new actors within the school. Families, on the other hand, seem to have little knowledge of national and school guidelines and thus show little capacity to embrace their new roles as partners and stakeholders.

Nevertheless, the research project described in this article has highlighted some exceptions. Some actors do seem capable to shape and adapt their roles to their own specific context (socioeconomic background, academic achievement in the school) by augmenting or adapting the national guidelines for school–family relationships, especially in the case of familiar involvement and formal participation.

Further research into the school–family relationship will be important because the decentralisation process remains ongoing, bringing further challenges for teachers and families. Researchers can help schools and families through action research projects directed at creating guidelines for collaborative practices, training teachers and families to promote effective partnerships and mobilising regulation instruments, thus benefitting all students. Further studies into the individual types of school–family relationships – using qualitative methods to collect more insights into daily practices and quantitative methods to gather the data necessary to draw an overall picture for the whole country – would also be very beneficial.

## Notes

1 To a limited extent, as will be explained later in the chapter.
2 This research was carried out as part of a PhD programme (Gonçalves, 2015).
3 Infrastructure maintenance at some upper primary, lower secondary and upper secondary schools remains under central government control because of other ongoing projects (Parque Escolar).
4 Law dated from 7 September 1835.
5 Portugal did not achieve a 100 percent school enrolment rate until the 1960s.
6 Law No. 48 572.
7 A fee had to be paid to form a legal association.
8 Portugal joined the European Community (European Union) in 1986.
9 A strategic document mandatory for state schools.
10 Law No. 75/2008.
11 School assemblies are not mandatory and usually take place in schools which do not have a Parents' Association.

# References

Archer, M. (1979) *Social Origin of Educational Systems*. London: Sage Publications.
Barroso, J. (2005) O Estado, a Educação e a Regulação das Políticas Públicas. *Educ. Soc.* [online], 26(92), 725–751.
Barroso, J., Almeida, A. and Homem, L. (2001) As Assembleias de Escola em discurso directo. In: Barroso, J., ed. *Relatório Global da Primeira Fase do Programa de Avaliação Externa*. Lisboa: Centro de Estudos da Escola, FCPE/ U, 100–119.
Batista, S. (2014) The redistribution of responsibilities in five european educational systems: From global trends to national arrangements. *European Educational Research Journal*, 13(2), 181–198.
Benavente, A., et al. (1987) *Do outro lado da Escola*. Lisboa: Edições Rolim/Instituto de Estudos para o Desenvolvimento.
Candeias, A. (2005) Modernidade, Educação e Estatísticas na Ibero-América nos Séculos XIX e XX: Estudos sobre Portugal. *Análise Social*, 176, 477–498.
CNE (2016) *Liberdade da Escolha da Escola: instrumentos da liberdade*. Lisboa: CNE – Conselho Nacional de Educação.
CNE (2017) *Organização escolar: os agrupamentos*. Lisboa: CNE – Conselho Nacional de Educação.
Cohler, B.J. and Hostetler. A. (2002) Linking life course and life story. Social change and the narrative study of lives over time. In: Mortimer, J.T. and Shanahan, M.J., eds. *Handbook of the Life Course*. New York: Kluwer Academic Publications.
Davies, D. and Johnson, V., eds. (1996) *Crossing Boundaries: Multi-National Action Research on Family–school Collaboration*. Report 33. Baltimore, MD: Center on Families, Communities, Schools and Children's Learning.
Davies, D., Marques, R. and Silva, P. (1997) *Os professores e as famílias: A colaboração possível*. Lisboa: Livros Horizontes.
Delicado, A. (2002) Caracterização do Voluntariado Social em Portugal. *Seminário Olhares sobre o voluntariado: análises e perspectivas para uma cidadania activa*. Lisboa: 10 e 11 May 2002, ISSCOOP, 127–140.
Diogo, A.M. (1998) *Famílias e escolaridade: representações parentais da escolarização, classe social e dinâmica familiar*. Lisboa: Ed. Colibri.
Diogo, A.M. (2008) *Investimento das famílias na escola – dinâmicas familiares e contexto escolar local*. Porto: Celta Editora.
Estevão, C. (1998) *Gestão Estratégica nas Escolas, Cadernos de Organização e gestão Curricular*. Lisboa: Instituto de Inovação Educacional.
European Social Survey (2012) Round 6: European Social Survey. Data file edition 1.0. Norwegian Social Science Data Services, Norway – Data Archive and distributor of ESS data.
Eurydice (2012) *Key Data on Education*. Brussels: Education, Audiovisual and Culture Executive Agency.
Giddens, A. (1984) *The Constitution of Society*. Cambridge: Polity Press.
Gonçalves, E. (2015) *A Escola e a Família, uma parceria ou uma simples aproximação? Uma análise comparada de políticas, estratégias, práticas e resultados*. PhD thesis completed in Lisboa: ISCTE.
Justino, D. and Batista, S. (2013) Redes de escolas e modos de regulação do sistema educativo. *Educação, Temas e Problemas*, 6 (12-13), 41–60.

Lima, L. and Sá, V. (2002) A Participação dos Pais na Governação Democráticas das Escolas. In: Lima, J.A., ed. *Pais e Professores, um Desafio à Cooperação*. Porto: Edições ASA. 25–95.

Lopes, F. (2006) *Participação Organizacional e Educativa dos Pais na Escola do 1º Ciclo do Ensino Básico: Potencialidades e limites*. Masters' dissertation completed in Braga: Instituto de Educação e Psicologia da Universidade do Minho.

Marques, R. (1988) *A Escola e os Pais: Como Colaborar?* Lisboa: Texto Editora.

Marques, R. (1996) Rumo ao Futuro elementary school: A Portuguese school of choice. In: Davies, D. and Johnson, V., eds. *Crossing Boundaries with Action Research: A Multinational Research on Family–School Collaboration*. Baltimore: Centre of Families, Communities, Schools, and Children's Learning, Johns Hopkins University. 36–46.

Martins, M.F. (2003) *Associações de pais e encarregados de educação na escola pública. Contributos para uma análise sociológica-organizacional*. Lisboa: Departamento de Educação Básica.

OECD (2014a) *Educational Policy Outlook in Portugal*. Portugal: Educational Policy Outlook.

OECD (2014b) *PISA 2012 Results in Focus: What 15-Year-Olds Know and What They Can Do With What They Know*. Paris: OECD Publishing.

OECD (2017) *Education at a Glance 2017: OECD Indicators*. Paris: OECD Publishing.

Oliveira, M.C. (2010) *Relação Família-Escola e Participação dos Pais*. Master thesis completed in Lisboa: Instituto Superior de Educação e Trabalho.

Perrenoud, P. and Montandon, C., eds. (1988) *Qui maîtrise l'école? Politiques d'institutions et pratiques des acteurs*. Lausanne: Realités Sociales.

Sá, V. (2000) Políticas educativas e participação dos pais na escola: novos direitos ou velhos deveres? *IV Congresso Português de Sociologia Passados Recentes, Futuros Próximos*. Coimbra.

Sebastião, J. (2008) *Democratização do Ensino, Desigualdades Sociais e Trajectórias Escolares*. Lisboa: Fundação Calouste Gulbenkian.

Silva, P. (2003) *Escola-Família, uma Relação Armadilhada. Interculturalidade e Relações de Poder*. Porto: Edições Afrontamento.

Silva, P. (2004) A condição híbrida dos pais- professores. In: Vieira, R., ed. *E agora professor? – A transformação na voz dos professores*. Porto: Profedições.

Silva, P. (2007) Associações de pais, interculturalidade e clivagem sociológica: algumas questões. *Revista Electrônica de educação*, 1(1), UFSCar, 3–30.

Silva, P. and Vieira, R. (1996) A dialogue between cultures: A report of school–family relationships in Pinhal do Rei Elementary School. In: Davies, D. and Johnson, V., eds. *Crossing boundaries – Multi-National Action Research on Family–school Collaboration*. Baltimore: Center of Families, Communities, Schools, and Children's Learning, Johns Hopkins University. 47–68.

Sliwka, A. and Istance, D. (2006) Parental and Stakeholder 'voice' in schools and systems. *European Journal of Education*, 41(1), 29–43.

Villas-Boas, M.A. (1996) The role of Indian parents in their children's literacy acquisition. In: Davies, D. and Johnson, V., eds. *Crossing boundaries – Multi-National Action Research on Family–school Collaboration*. Baltimore: Center of Families, Communities, Schools, and Children's Learning, Johns Hopkins University. 69–97.

Zanten, A. and Ball, S. (2000) Comparer pour comprendre: globalisation, réinterprétations nationales et recontextualisations locales des politiques éducatives néolibérales. *Revue de l'Institut de Sociologie*, ULB, 1(4), 112–131.

# 8 Slovenia

Overprotective parenthood: parental involvement in the educational trajectories of their children in Slovenia

*Andreja Živoder and Mirjana Ule*

## 1 Introduction

This chapter explores parental involvement in the educational transitions of children in Slovenia, with a focus on the social, institutional and specific historical-political context. In the last three decades, both familial life and educational trajectories have undergone many changes, some of which are global societal trends (e.g. individualisation, familialisation), while others are more country-specific (such as the legacy of egalitarianism, the specific mix of individualism and collectivism, familial and neighbourly links, and institutional changes to the education system).

These changes enlarged the responsibility of parents who face societal pressure and unanswered questions raised by the new risks of the uncertainty and unpredictability of future social trends and precarious employment markets on one hand, and the individualisation of these risks on the other. Moreover, Slovenia is a country characterised by very strong family ties – placing it in the southern European (Mediterranean) cultural model (Ule, 2004) – and it can be expected that family life, including the manner and forms of parental involvement, will be strongly affected by these new risks. In fact, research shows that children and parents in Slovenia are increasingly turning to the private sphere (Ule, 2013), away from the forms of help foreseen by society. In the education setting for example, research reveals that parents and children in Slovenia rarely resort to the very generous and diverse counselling help available in schools but instead prefer to take educational decisions within the immediate family circle (Ule et al., 2015). Hence, they are attempting to solve crucial educational and life questions individually that are actually socially and systematically structured. All of the above results in what we may describe as overprotecting parenthood in terms of parental involvement in educational trajectories.

Based on policy analysis (the national legislative and regulative framework) and qualitative and quantitative empirical data gathered in the European project GOETE (Governance of Educational Trajectories in Europe), this chapter aims to analyse and contextualise these contemporary processes and interpret the practices of parents in terms of their involvement in their children's education from a social and institutional perspective.

## 2 Overview of the education system in Slovenia

A major reform of Slovenia's education system began after Slovenia declared its independence in 1991. These developments are based on two White Papers on Education in the Republic of Slovenia. In addition to introducing new comprehensive legislation regulating the entire education system from preschool to university, the first White Paper (1995) provided the fundamental principles of the Slovenian education system: the right to education, equal opportunities and non-discrimination, freedom of choice, fostering of excellence, education quality, increases in teacher and school autonomy and professional responsibility, cultural plurality, values and knowledge, and lifelong learning (Krek, 1995; Peček Čuk, 2017). Although the system framework along with its basic premise is now established, the country's education system is continually changing in an attempt to address the new demands (Peček Čuk, 2017). This also explains why in 2011 the second White Paper on Education in the Republic of Slovenia was published, which offers a systematic consideration and analysis of the education system in order to find solutions for the future (Krek & Metljak, 2011).

Slovenia provides comprehensive compulsory basic education that lasts nine years; students begin school at the age of 6 years. The education system is almost fully financed by the state, which funds all forms of schools: state schools, accredited private schools and, to the extent determined by law, also other private schools. Nevertheless, almost the whole student population (99.1 percent) attend public basic and upper secondary schools (Peček Čuk, 2017).

The Slovenian education system is inclusive, comprehensive and comprises the following levels: preschool education, compulsory basic education, upper secondary education, tertiary education, and adult education. A distinctive feature of the education system is its late tracking (there is no actual transition that would entail any choice between primary and lower secondary education), which begins in upper secondary education (typically at the age of 15). According to Allmendinger's typology of transition regimes (1989), which links the education system to labour market outcomes based on the two measures (standardisation and stratification of the education system), the Slovenian system is marked by high standardisation and low stratification. These characteristics, coupled with the fact that the majority of students attend public basic and upper secondary schools, indicate that there are only minor regional differences among schools (basic schools are usually chosen according to the principle of proximity) and there is no typical distinction of affluent, average or disadvantaged schools or school contexts.[1] In this respect, schools differ mostly by ethnic heterogeneity and the region's socio-economic background in systemic terms and with respect to the subjective, individual differences in teachers, principals and their teaching methods.

## 3 Parental involvement in Slovenia: policy and terminology

### 3a Terminology

In the field of education, there is no general consensus on the terms used to identify those persons who are responsible for children or to describe their involvement in children's educational trajectories. Nevertheless, and despite the new and various forms of families and parenthood (Švab, 2001; Rener et al., 2006), the most common term remains 'parents' *(starši)*. Legal language, for example, identifies the following categories: 'parents', 'guardians' *(skrbniki)* and other persons with whom a child is in care and then proceeds to use the term 'parents' for all of the listed categories (Elementary School Act, 1996). In the scientific literature and sociological discussions, two terms are employed: 'parents' *(starši)* and 'family' *(družina)*, although the former prevails. The term parents is used to describe parental involvement in children's education (e.g. Žakelj et al., 2013; Ule, 2015; Ule et al., 2015) and for parental participation with school (e.g. Kalin, 2008; Kalin et al., 2009). The term family is more often used when referring to the structural position of the family in education and society (e.g. Žakelj & Švab, 2011) and in discussions of the reproduction of social inequalities in education and access to education (Razpotnik, 2011; Turnšek et al., 2016).

Likewise, there is no single term to describe the relationship between parents/ guardians and the school. However, both the scientific discourse (sociological and educational literature) and the practical use in schools typically use the term *sodelovanje,* which in Slovenian language stands both for 'cooperation' and 'participation' and accentuates the equal position of both partners (school and parents). Here, more variants of this term are in use, i.e. cooperation between parents and the school (Kalin et al., 2009), cooperation of parents with the school or cooperation of the school with parents (Martinšek, 2012) or, in the school setting, simply cooperation with parents. In some cases, the term 'partnership' *(partnerstvo)* is employed to highlight the benefits of building a high-quality partnership between parents and teachers/the school (i.e. Kalin, 2008). Use of family in this respect occurs much less often or is uncommon, for example when describing the work of a social pedagogue at school.

### 3b National legislative & regulative context

Educational and school legislation in Slovenia is based on two White Papers on Education (1995, 2011). The relationship and basic framework for the cooperation between school and parents is regulated in several acts[2] and provisions and regulations at all levels of education, which set out the possibilities of parental influence on life and work at schools.

In terms of parents' cooperation at the systemic decision-making school level, Slovenian legislation enables two forms of participation: parents' councils and school councils. Parents' councils are formed to realise the interests of parents in every public school and kindergarten. They consist of a representative of all parents for each school department. The main tasks are to propose higher standard programmes, give an opinion on proposed school development programmes and annual work plans, discuss the principal's reports on educational work, and elect representatives to the school council, etc. (Organisation and Financing of Education Act, 1996). *School councils* consist of three representatives of the founding entity,[3] five school representatives and three parent representatives. These councils have many tasks, including the appointment and dismissal of school principals, implementing the school development programme, working on the annual work plan and reporting on its realisation, decision-making on the introduction of academic programmes, dealing with reports on upbringing or educational issues, and deciding on various complaints concerning educational work at the school etc. (Organisation and Financing of Education Act, 1996).

In terms of the individual participation of parents, there are several formal and informal types of parental cooperation with the school. Formal types of parental cooperation (together with participation in the school and parents' councils described above) include parental meetings and consultation hours for parents, as well as written, phone and e-mail communication between parents and teachers. There is a multitude of diverse informal forms of participation that vary from school to school. They include activities such as attending open days, pedagogical workshops, projects and workshops, excursions, parents' participation in the educational process, social gatherings, exhibitions, and parents' clubs, amongst others.

## 4 Research on parental involvement in Slovenia: theoretical framework, empirical research and dominant discourses

Recent research on family patterns and the relationship between parents and children in Slovenia demonstrates important changes are taking place in family upbringing patterns, which can be described as a shift from the model of an upbringing family to the model of an emotional and supportive family – a process some authors describe as familialisation (Ule et al., 2015). This process began in the mid-1990s because of a specific transition from an egalitarian welfare society to a competitive individualistic society (Ule, 2013). This means the role of the family has shifted – it is no longer predominately a place of reproduction, a place of strict upbringing patterns or authoritarian control, but increasingly serves as a place to escape from the tensions and demands of the outside competitive world. At the end of the 1990s, youth research in Slovenia found that parents, especially mothers, were the most trusted persons in the eyes of children and that the relationship between parents and children was becoming exceptionally protective and symbiotic (Ule, 2013). Such a relationship is well matched by the tendency to prolong children's dependence on their parents that is found all around the developed world (Nelson, 2010).

In terms of the relationship between parents and the school, two ideologies traditionally characterise Slovenia: strong family ties coupled with prolonged care for the upbringing of children, and the high evaluation of the relevance of education. These two belief systems originate from the predominantly middle-class population in Slovenia, which holds the assumption that social promotion in social mobility is achieved through education. This ideology was further strengthened during the period of individualisation in the neoliberal social frameworks when parents in Slovenia assumed not only the responsibility for raising children but also for their transition to adulthood (educational and career planning, solving the housing problems of adult children etc.). In this way, we can talk about actual over-parenting.

What is more, in this ideological setting also marked by an economic environment with insufficient youth employment opportunities and strong competition for good jobs, parental involvement in the education of their children is a self-evident, even rational process, which is why theoretical frameworks or studies of parental involvement are lacking. We first thoroughly analysed this phenomenon in Slovenia in the European project GOETE (Walther et al., 2016), where we confirmed parents' strong involvement in education and, further, its uniqueness in the European context. For example, only in Slovenia did teachers complain that parents are too involved in schoolwork. There is also a growing discourse on the premature biographisation of children, about hurried childhood, overly ambitious parents who start planning their child's educational path, and how children are excessively burdened by school and extracurricular activities at an early age. Parents, in addition, adapt their lives, leisure and social activities to the (perceived) needs of their children.

Thus, parents in Slovenia believe they can best serve their children in a modern competitive society if they facilitate their acquisition of as much education (titles, diplomas, certificates) as possible and if they involve them early in various forms of training and education. According to research data, the educational wishes and aspirations of both children and parents in Slovenia are among the highest in Europe (Ule et al., 2015). In this regard, the social-liberal policy in Slovenia during the 1990s satisfied their needs and ambitions. That is, it expanded the possibilities of general education at the secondary and tertiary levels to the wider population and also established an 'informal agreement' with parents on extended child-care in the family of origin, i.e., that parents will take care of the children's (housing, financial etc.) needs for a longer period of time. By enabling the extended schooling of children (for all social strata), politics temporarily solved the labour market problem (i.e. it reduced the pressure of unemployed young people on the labour market). Consequently, children are also remaining in prolonged dependency on their original family (Ule, 2004). Unfortunately, the socialisation patterns in society today encourage and accept as very 'desirable' socially immature and only seemingly autonomous young people. The model of socially immature and non-autonomous youth carries through into adulthood, influenced by a modern consumer culture that cultivates the cult of un-reflected private individualism, which entails a mixture of narcissism and conformism with current society.

It seems that in Slovenia there is precisely the mode of education that was critically illuminated by Côté (2007) in his studies on the development of identity capital: both school and parents mainly act as young people's 'guardians of access' to different types of educational achievements and stages of adulthood, rather than as sources of positive motivation for children and young people to achieve emotional stability and sensitivity, openness to others, empathy, critical thinking and mature moral judgement. Moreover, since the involvement of parents in schoolwork and educational trajectories is considerable and crucial, it functions as a new factor in the social differentiation of children. The accessibility or absence of a family support network reproduces social inequality and creates a gap between those who are well-equipped and those who are not (Ule, 2013). The existence and quality of family support structures is without question one of the most vital factors in young people's social differentiation today. Emotional and supportive parents are more emphatic regarding the changed needs of growing-up children and are more willing to conform to them (Tzanakis, 2011; Ule et al., 2015).

We can say in this sense that social inequality is being extended from inter-class to intra-class differentiation (Ule, 2004). This certainly does not mean that class differences are becoming less important, but other factors are strengthening the differentiation between the young generations. Intra-class differentiation is often more painful for a young person to endure than inter-class differentiation. Some studies also suggest that the lack of parental support for children is closely linked to the early abandonment of further education or with children choosing less demanding education (Kintrea et al., 2011). In particular, parents from the social margins exclude certain possible choices, schools, courses of study or careers as opportunities for their children, even though their children would choose them or be able to successfully complete them.

## 5 New research perspective: overprotecting parenthood?

### 5a Introduction, data and methodology

The empirical analysis draws on qualitative data gathered within the European project GOETE[4] that explored interactions between structural, institutional and individual contexts of educational trajectories with quantitative and qualitative methodology. The project was carried out in eight European countries (Finland, France, Germany, Italy, the Netherlands, Poland, Slovenia, and the UK).[5] It focused on the educational period between the end of the lower secondary education and transitions to the upper secondary level of education. The project's theoretical tool was a life course perspective through which the main themes were analysed: access to education, coping with educational demands, relevance and governance of education (Walther et al., 2016).

We concentrate on comparative quantitative data and Slovenian qualitative data. Standardised individual surveys were carried out with students (N = 6390) aged between 13 and 16 years. In Slovenia, 9th grade students were surveyed, aged 14–15, in 20 basic schools[6] in three Slovenian regions.[7] The Slovenian survey included 725 students and 419 parents. In terms of qualitative material, we focus only on the Slovenian data: essays (written by students), interviews and focus groups with students (aged 14–15 years), their parents, teachers and other school staff that took place between April and November 2011. In total, 101 interviews and 12 focus groups were conducted, with students writing 105 essays.[8]

Based on the theoretical framework and comparative aspect of this chapter, we aim to answer the following research questions: How and why are parents in Slovenia involved in their children's education? What are the country-specific aspects of parental involvement in Slovenia? How do the (overprotective) parenthood practices influence parental involvement in education? In analysis of the empirical data, we follow the distinction of Pomerantz et al. (2007) between *school-based* and *home-based involvement*.

### 5b Home-based involvement: parents are to be fully trusted

There is a wide range of parental practices and activities that belong to home-based involvement in child schooling; in fact, as some of these practices are subtle and/or very general (such as e.g. parental style), it is unwarranted to accept that theoretical or empirical reasoning can encompass them all. They differ in location (they happen outside the school, usually but not always at home, they can occur in social events, family gatherings, holidays etc.) and in content (they can be more or less directly related to school, e.g. assistance with homework, school projects, course/school selection, discussing school issues, or general well-being of the child).

What parents and children talk about and what they do together is a key component of the family's cultural and social capital (Bourdieu, 1986); this importantly shapes both the educational performance and outcome as a reproduction of educational inequality, which was also confirmed by our data (McDowell et al., 2016; Walther et al., 2016). Further, it directly influences both the skills and motivational development of the child.

As shown in Table 8.1, the data indicate that, comparatively speaking, parents in Slovenia are more involved in their children's daily school life in terms of the frequency of conversations about experiences at school, schoolwork and future education. However, it is unclear whether this is an unconditional positive involvement that benefits the child's education and life in general. It could also be a response to the general fears and worries about uncertainties and unpredictability of their children's future life and integration into society, rather than merely a positive interest in the child's schooling, aimed at developing their skills, abilities, interest social and cultural capital. For instance, given that parents in Slovenia less frequently than in other countries discuss social and political questions with their children or take them to the theatre, museum or

Table 8.1 How often in the past 12 months, have you talked about or done the following things with your child?

|  | Slovenia | | Total* | |
| --- | --- | --- | --- | --- |
|  | Daily | Weekly | Daily | Weekly |
| Talked about their experiences at school[a] | 74% | 21% | 64% | 26% |
| Discussed their school work with them[b] | 68% | 26% | 44% | 33% |
| Talked about their future education or career options[c] | 13% | 49% | 21% | 41% |
| Discussed current political or social issues with them[d] | 7% | 22% | 16% | 33% |
| Talked about their life in general[e] | 31% | 40% | 39% | 35% |
| Visited relatives or family friends[f] | 6% | 49% | 2% | 34% |
| Done an activity like playing a sport or going to a movie[g] | 3% | 25% | 3% | 22% |

\* All countries, including Slovenia.
a Sig.=<0.000, Cramer's V 0.250;
b Sig.=<0.000, Cramer's V 0.246;
c Sig.=<0.000, Cramer's V 0.152;
d Sig.=<0.000, Cramer's V 0.171;
e Sig.=<0.000, Cramer's V 0.099;
f Sig.=<0.000, Cramer's V 0.175;
g Sig.=<0.000, Cramer's V 0.132.

opera (60 percent had not done so in the year of the survey, 2011, while the average for EU countries was 50 percent), both of which are considered as activities directly linked to improving a child's cultural capital, this might confirm the latter.

Nevertheless, another comparison is also indicative: parents in Slovenia much more often take their children to visit family or friends, showing the importance of strong familial and neighbourly links and ties – a confirmation of the Slovenian family described as the southern European (Mediterranean) cultural model (Ule, 2004). In terms of education and parental involvement, this means that as part of confronting the new risks, children and parents are turning to the private, familial sphere where they prefer to attempt to solve any educational questions (e.g. also in terms of educational decision-making) within the sphere of the family and friends first, and only later turn to outside experts or help.

The above questioning of the (positive) involvement of parents in Slovenia is further substantiated by the findings about parental worries (worries related to falling into bad company, employment opportunities, being poor, doing badly at school, illness, addictions, or loneliness). They show that parents in Slovenia are, on average, more worried than seen in other researched countries in all studied categories of worries, pointing to an increased level of anxiety concerning overall risks and uncertainties and also to the low level of general trust, for instance in the country's employment system.

To a certain extent, this is explicable within the framework of the economic, political and social transition in the early 1990s – the onset of radically changed value sets and rules of life, coupled with the processes of the individualisation, de-standardisation and deregulation of growing up as common western contemporary processes, have made individual life planning an impossible task. This might be exacerbated in Slovenia, where people have been used to fully trusting the political and social system to take care of them (e.g. full employment, free health care, education etc.).

These findings also related to the increased sense of individualism and competitiveness that was detected in the empirical results. For example, when parents were asked how much they agree that children at their child's school are competitive amongst each other, parents in Slovenia scored the highest (mean value 2.65, EU average 2.31). The interviews showed a similar picture:

> But this peer help. Here [a break] it's hard to overcome the barriers. Individualism is so strong that there are all those barriers for written tests so that nobody can copy from another. [...] Very egoistic, right. So, we also encourage them to help each other if the children are absent, bringing in notebooks [to copy over the lesson notes].
> (Pedagogue Counsellor, Interview 86)

However, this increased competitiveness has to be put in context, especially from a comparative perspective. Namely, one must keep in mind that competitiveness in Slovenia has in fact to some extent increased as a 'side effect' of the transition from a socialist to a capitalist regime (and its implications) occurring in the early 1990s. In this regard, it is important to highlight that there might be a psychological moment of increased awareness of competitiveness, again, due to the transition. This means that parents from other countries with a long tradition of capitalism, for example the Netherlands, may perceive the same (objective) level of competitiveness as being substantially lower than parents in Slovenia. Nevertheless, the fact remains that the conditions of daily school life and educational pathways in Slovenia have changed – greater individualism has also led to greater competitiveness, and lower readiness to help each other.

Another distinctive feature of parents in Slovenia, also related to the increased competitiveness and change in the regime, are their high educational aspirations for their children. Namely 80 percent of parents in Slovenia would like their child to achieve at least a tertiary level of education[9,10] whereas the average for other respondent countries is 62 percent.

> I see it this way: for my children, I want them to attain a high education, right. And if there is even more, then even better.
> (Mother, Interview 33)

> Now every parent wants that their child would have completed, I don't know, a university, a faculty, not so much because of the title but because of the easier life afterwards.
> (Mother, Interview 42)

In order for their children to have the best learning conditions possible, many parents are willing to make many sacrifices, e.g. in terms of their resources (paying for additional lessons, post-curriculum activities, buying good equipment), investing their time (helping with school work, attending school activities etc.), or simply by relieving their child of any other commitments or duties. As one father stated in the interview: '*She has no other obligations when she comes home. She only has to study. That's all*' (Father, Interview 29).

Still, these lofty ambitions do not always go hand-in-hand with their child's abilities, interests, and sometimes even without regard to their wishes. As a psychologist highlighted: '*Because now it looks like everyone can go to a faculty, but that isn't so! Maybe everyone can enrol, but then they quickly come back home*' (Psychologist, Interview 88).

Thus, parental good intentions and high hopes might in some cases amount to psychological pressure to perform well and meet the high standards set by their parents (and themselves), leading to adverse, including long-term, consequences in terms of the child's emotional stability, feelings of self-efficacy, self-esteem, future planning etc. For example, as one student wrote:

> The family, teachers and above all myself have always thought and expected that I would enrol in a gymnasium, but I've been slacking at school in recent years and my school performance has declined. Many people have been disappointed about this because they held much greater expectations for me and I also had much higher goals. I'm determined to make much more effort in secondary school, put in more effort and goodwill and show that I can do it.
> 
> (Student, Essay 75)

What adds another variable to the equation of parental influence (and pressure), as the empirical evidence suggests, is that parents are students' number one confidants and advisors. Namely, with respect to whom parents think their child would turn to should they have problems with life in general and schoolwork, the data show that Slovenian parents expect children to rely more on their close family members than in other countries (i.e. more than 98 percent expect that children would turn to their mothers in the event of problems in life in general and school work, with the total average for included EU countries being 96 percent and 94 percent, respectively). Similar results are found for fathers: 80 percent of parents expect the child would turn to their father in the case of life problems (all countries average 77 percent) and 77 percent for problems with school work (all countries average 73 percent).

The same question was also posed to the students themselves. The results show an even greater deviation from the EU countries' average: 89 percent of students in Slovenia claimed they would turn to their mothers in the case of problems in life in general (all countries 80 percent), 71 percent to fathers (all countries 60 percent); while 85 percent would seek advice from their mothers on school work problems (all countries 79 percent) and 71 percent from their fathers (all countries 64 percent).

Analogous results emerged from a qualitative study on trust among young people carried out in Slovenia in 2010 (Ule, 2013). For the majority of respondents, the most trustworthy figures are parents, especially mothers, where young people emphasise and value the unconditionality of help and support.

Similarly, the students in our sample also stressed the fact that only parents help them unconditionally and that they can always rely on them, because no one else cares as much for them as their parents; hence, their support is not only valuable, but also all that can be fully trusted. For example: '*In life, in my decisions, I know that they* [the parents] *will support me in my decisions. Friends come and go, but my family will always stay by my side*' (Student, Essay 83).

### 5c School-based involvement: overly involved parents?

The school-based involvement of parents encompasses those activities that require them to make actual contact with the school (Pomerantz et al., 2007), such as attending parental meetings and consultation hours for parents, or initiating other communication with teachers or other school staff, attending the parents' council and the school council, participating at school events (e.g. open days, science fairs), and volunteering at school.

The survey included only a little information about the participation of parents at school. In variables such as communication between parents and the school and parents' perception of the impact they have on the governance of schools, parents in Slovenia do not differ significantly from the total average of all researched countries.

Table 8.2 below, however, shows what the children said about their parents attending school activities.

Here, parents in Slovenia differ significantly from the total countries' average: according to students, both mothers and fathers attend activities at school much

*Table 8.2* Over past 12 months, how often has your mother/father supported you by attending activities at school? (Scale 1=Not Applicable; 2=Never; 3=Rarely; 4=Sometimes; 5=Frequently; 6=Always)

|  | Slovenia | | | Total* | | |
| --- | --- | --- | --- | --- | --- | --- |
|  | Never | Frequently | Always | Never | Frequently | Always |
| Mother[a] | 18% | 24% | 20% | 23% | 18% | 14% |
| Father[b] | 29% | 14% | 16% | 39% | 11% | 11% |

\* All countries, including Slovenia.
a Sig.=<0.000, Cramer's V 0.100;
b Sig.=<0.000, Cramer's V 0.109.

more often and, conversely, also considerably less frequently never attend such events.

Further, the qualitative data support this finding. Unlike findings in other countries where teachers often complained about the lack of parental involvement, teachers in Slovenia particularly highlighted the problem of overly involved parents, i.e. parents who meddle with teachers' work and autonomy:

> Because parents want one thing, but the abilities are another thing. And then they are looking for errors, what we [teachers, school] do poorly. They do respect our autonomy, but only to a certain extent. I think that it is very difficult for us because they meddle in the teaching process where we really should have autonomy.
> (Teacher of mathematics, Interview 64)

## 6 Conclusions

The changing and often too complex demands of parental responsibility are, in the Slovenian context, coupled with the transformed dominant societal discourse: from an egalitarian discourse to an individualistic, competitive discourse. As the empirical evidence demonstrated, this transformation is clearly seen in the altering practices of educational pathways of children and accompanying parental involvement, for example, in terms of high educational aspirations, growing competitiveness among students, and the bigger and more intense parental involvement in all spheres of the child's educational pathways. However, a specific paradox appears: while on the one hand Slovenia has a comprehensive, standardised, non-competitively-oriented and inclusive education system, on the other hand, competition emerges from within the system – through intensive parental involvement and support in children's education. This means that parents, through their various forms of involvement (e.g. helping with schoolwork, hiring paid tutors), enforce the differentiation of students within the inclusive system. And it is precisely on this that the specific complaints by teachers in Slovenia are focused: compared to other countries, where teachers more often complain about the lack of parental involvement, teachers in Slovenia complain about parents who are excessively involved (Ule et al., 2015; Walther et al., 2016).

Too involved, too ambitious or too protective parents are not individual decisions or acts – we cannot simply dismiss this behaviour as acts of vanity and egotism. On the contrary, this reflects the demands of a social and political situation in which parents are trying to do their best to protect their children's interests. Unfortunately, such involvement does not culminate (always or at all) in the desired outcome (a happy, successful, educated child), but has many other adverse effects (overburdened children, unsatisfied teachers, blame and guilt). As Gill (2007) highlighted, overprotective parenthood is a result of a lack of confidence in oneself and the outside world. Constantly trying to maximise the 'good and beneficial' while minimising the 'bad and dangerous' can lead to enormous amounts of energy being spent in order to gain and be in control of the many variables that simply cannot be controlled, also at the cost of children's freedom to explore, learn, be independent, self-confident and to enjoy their childhood.

As the empirical evidence suggests, parents in Slovenia are strongly involved in their children's education and have a great influence on their child's educational decisions and plans (Ule et al., 2015). We can best describe the great majority of Slovenian parents' rationale as 'Only the best for my child!'. However, the 'parents' best wishes' and their full support is not always beneficial for the child as parents' expectations, and aspirations are often very high and thus not always attuned to their child's abilities or wishes.

Yet this raises other issues. For example, one of the side effects of familialisation is strong control over children's everyday life as well as their life course, which makes children dependent, limits their autonomy and prolongs their dependency. Accordingly, today when parents try to support the young to cope with the demands of late modernity, they unfortunately also prevent them from learning how to cope independently with such demands in their future life course. Such a parental attitude is certainly also inhibiting the educational and career choices of children. Parents make decisions for children or are projecting their own desires on to their children, often in the belief they are only doing everything 'in children's best interest' (Segrin et al., 2012). In a climate of over-anxious protection, children feel immature and overly dependent on their parents; they thereby do not develop their autonomy, own assessments and decisions on viable life problems during childhood and youth. Another, and not inconsiderable big societal shift is emerging that should not be overlooked, supported by the processes of familialisation and individualisation: families are actually taking over the roles and responsibilities of the welfare state (Ule et al., 2015).

Moreover, the increased role of parents is not accompanied by any moral guidance or traditional patterns on which parents can lean on while leading their and their children's life courses. In the absence of such guidance, parents seek some measure of control over their predicament by way of overparenting (Furedi, 2008). Due to social pressures on the adults, which force them towards atomisation, mutual isolation and competition, they are losing mutual trust and thus increasingly turning to their children in the belief that relationships with them are less vulnerable and more stable. The potential professional counselling additionally undermines parental self-confidence (Furedi, 2008). The professionalisation and politicisation of parenthood has similar effects. Parents are generally quite helpless in the face of these cultural influences that undermine their self-confidence and authority, all of which adversely affects the upbringing of their children. Such attitudes well corroborate the tendency to prolong children's dependency on parents that is seen all around the developed world.

Slovenia 117

## Notes

1 When such a division is required, for example, for the purposes of international comparison such as in the GOETE research project (Walther et al., 2016), the distinction is made according to other external school criteria such as the affluence of statistical regions in which schools are based, as in this project.
2 Preschool Institutions Act, Elementary School Act, Vocational Education Act, Gymnasium Act, Higher Education Act, Placement of Children with Special Needs Act, Organisation and Financing of Education Act, School Inspection Act.
3 Public kindergartens and schools are founded by local communities or the state, while private kindergartens and schools can be founded by physical persons or legal entities.
4 Governance of Educational Trajectories in Europe, 2010–2012 (www.goete.eu). The project was established by the EU under the 7th FP. For more information about the project and its results in an international perspective, see Walther et al. (2016).
5 UK (parental sample) quantitative data were excluded following considerations of the small and biased sample.
6 Basic education in Slovenia lasts nine years and comprises three cycles – two cycles of primary education (6 years) and one cycle of lower secondary education (3 years).
7 Osrednjeslovenska, Obalno-kraška, and the Pomurska region.
8 The topic of the essays was wishes, worries and barriers regarding their future and the role and support of their family, friends and school.
9 ISCED 5 and 6.
10 The actual educational attainment of the general population in 2015 in Slovenia was as follows: 25 percent tertiary education, 56 percent upper secondary education, 19 percent primary and lower secondary education (EU-28 average was 25 percent, 45 percent, and 29 percent, respectively) (SURS, 2017: 19).

## References

Allmendinger, J. (1989) Educational systems and labour market outcomes. *European Sociological Review*, 5(3), 231–250.
Bourdieu, P. (1986) The forms of capital. In: Richardson, J., ed. *Handbook of Theory and Research for Sociology of Education*. New York: Greenwood. 241–258.
Côté, J. (2007) Youth and the provision of resources. In: Helve, H. and Bynner, J., eds. *Youth and Social Capital*. London: The Tufnell Press. 59–70.
Elementary School Act (1996) *The Official Gazette of the Republic of Slovenia, Nr. 81/06*. Available at: https://www.uradni-list.si/glasilo-uradni-list-rs/vsebina/2006-01-3535/ (accessed 16 Oct. 2017).
Furedi, F. (2008) *Paranoid Parenting: Why Ignoring the Experts May Be Best for Your Child*. London and New York: Continuum.
Gill, T. (2007) *No Fear: Growing Up in a Risk Averse Society*. London: Calouste Gulbenkian Foundation.
Kalin, J. (2008) Teacher-parent partnership in the light of ensuring better pupils' learning achievements. *Contemporary Pedagogy*, 5, 10–30.
Kalin, J., Resman, M., Šteh, B., Mrvar, P., Govekar-Okoliš, M. and Mažgon, J. (2009) *Izzivi in smernice kakovostnega sodelovanja med starši in šolo*. Ljubljana: Filozofska fakulteta.

Kintrea, K., St Clair, R. and Houston, M. (2011) *The Influence of Parents, Places and Poverty on Educational Attitudes and Aspirations*. Glasgow: Joseph Rowntree Foundation. Available at: www.jrf.org.uk/sites/files/jrf/young-people-education-attitudes-full.pdf (accessed 5 Dec. 2016).

Krek, J., ed. (1995) *Bela knjiga o vzgoji in izobraževanju v Republiki Sloveniji* [White Paper on Education in the Republic of Slovenia]. Ljubljana: Ministry of Education and Sport.

Krek, J. and Metljak, M., eds. (2011) *Bela knjiga o vzgoji in izobraževanju v Republiki Sloveniji* [White Paper on Education in the Republic of Slovenia]. Ljubljana: Zavod RS za šolstvo.

Martinšek, J. (2012) Vstopanje šole v sodelovalen odnos s starši. *Socialna pedagogika*, 16(4), 355–371.

McDowell, J., Živoder, A. and Tolomelli, A. (2016) Comparing the views of students, parents, and teachers on the emerging notions of relevance of education. In: Walther, A., et al., eds. *Governance of Educational Trajectories in Europe: Pathways, Policy and Practice*. London, New Delhi, New York, Sidney: Bloomsbury. 183–201.

Nelson, M. (2010) *Parenting Out of Control: Anxious Parents in Uncertain Times*. New York: NYU Press.

Organisation and Financing of Education Act (1996) The Official Gazette of the Republic of Slovenia, Nr. 16/07. Available at: https://www.uradni-list.si/glasilo-uradni-list-rs/vsebina/2007-01-0718?sop=2007-01 (accessed 16 Oct. 2017).

Peček Čuk, M. (2017) Slovenia: An overview. In: Corner, T., ed. *Education in the European Union: Post-2003 Member States*. London, New Delhi, New York, Sidney: Bloomsbury Academic. 249–268.

Pomerantz, E.M., Moorman, E.A. and Litwack, S.D. (2007) The how, whom, and why of parents' involvement in children's academic lives: More is not always better. *Review of Educational Research*, 77(3), 373–410.

Razpotnik, Š. (2011) It is all up to me: Access to education and the discourse of individual responsibility. *Teorija in praksa*, 48(5), 1446–1465.

Rener, T., Sedmak, M., Švab, A. and Urek, M. (2006) *Družine in družinsko življenje v Sloveniji*. Koper: UP, Založba Annales.

Segrin, C., Woszidlo, A., Givertz, M., Bauer, A. and Murphy, M.T. (2012) The association between overparenting, parent-child communication, and entitlement and adaptive traits in adult children. *Family Relations*, 61, 237–252.

SURS (Statistical office of the Republic of Slovenia) (2017) *Boljši, slabši, povprečni. Statistični portret Slovenije v mednarodni skupnosti 2017*. Ljubljana: ABO grafika. Available at: www.stat.si/StatWeb/Catalogue/Index (accessed 2 Nov. 2017).

Švab, A. (2001) *Družina: od modernosti k postmodernosti*. Ljubljana: Znanstveno in publicistično središče.

Turnšek, N., Poljšak Škraban, O., Razpotnik, Š. and Rapuš Pavel, J. (2016) Challenges and responses to the vulnerability of families in a preschool context. *CEPS Journal*, 6(4), 29–49.

Tzanakis, M. (2011) Bourdieu's social reproduction thesis and the role of cultural capital in educational attainment: A critical review of key empirical studies. *Educate*, 11(1), 76–90.

Ule, M. (2004) Changes in family life courses in Slovenia. In: Robila, M., ed. *Families in Eastern Europe*. Amsterdam: Elsevier. 87–101.

Ule, M. (2013) 'I trust my mom the most': Trust patterns of contemporary youth. In: Warming, H., ed. *Participation, Citizenship and Trust in Children's Lives*. Basingstoke: Palgrave Macmillan. 174–193.

Ule, M. (2015) The role of parents in children's educational trajectories in Slovenia. *Journal of Contemporary Educational Studies*, 1, 10–27.

Ule, M., Živoder, A. and Du Bois-Reymond, M. (2015) 'Simply the best for my children': Patterns of parental involvement in education. *International Journal of Qualitative Studies in Education*, 28(3), 329–348.

Walther, A., Parreira do Amaral, M., Cuconato, M. and Dale, R., eds. (2016) *Governance of educational trajectories in Europe: Pathways, policy and practice*. London, New Delhi, New York, Sydney: Bloomsbury.

Žakelj, T., Mencin Čeplak, M. and Švab, A. (2013) The role of parents in young people's educational trajectories in Slovenia. Annales. *Series historia et sociologia*, 23(2), 317–328.

Žakelj, T. and Švab, A. (2011) Rely on yourself and your family: How 9th grade students in Slovenia cope with educational demands. *Teorija in praksa*, 48(5), 1466–1485.

# 9 Sweden

## Parental involvement in Sweden exemplified through national policy on homework support

*Marie Karlsson, Stina Hallsén and Johanna Svahn*

## 1 Introduction

With this chapter, we wish to contribute to the field of research on parental involvement in education. The chapter first provides an overview of the Swedish education system and the role of parental involvement. It then presents the dominant fields in Swedish research on parental involvement and discusses the preliminary findings from a current study on changing policies on homework support in Sweden as well as its implications for ideas on parental involvement outside of school.

## 2 Overview of education system in Sweden

Sweden has, together with other Nordic countries, a long and strong tradition of public childcare and education (Karlsson & Perälä-Littunen, 2017). Beginning in the 1990s, Sweden has undertaken several national reforms to decentralise the education system and shift the responsibility for education, and funding of the school sector to local government (municipalities). Today the National Agency for Education prepares the knowledge requirements, regulations, general recommendations and national tests for education; and the municipalities use their allocated state funds to organise and execute the central guidelines and regulations.

As a result, the subsequent development of the school system has been characterised by deregulation and freedom of choice. This gave parents greater freedom to choose schools for their children, making school choice an important aspect of parental involvement. The reforms also allowed independent schools to be established. Today many primary (*grundskolor*) and upper secondary schools (*gymnasieskolor*) in Sweden are privately run independent schools (*friskolor*), which receive public funding for each student at a level similar to that of public schools. During the school year 2016/2017, approximately 20 percent of the primary schools and 33 percent of the upper secondary schools were independent (Swedish National Agency for Education). While the Swedish schools are mainly inclusive, there are also nine special needs schools with a total enrolment of 640 students.

In Sweden, most children attend preschool (*förskola*) for four to five years before entering the compulsory school system in the autumn of the year they turn 6. They must attend compulsory school for ten years. However, in reality, most Swedish students attend school for at least 13 years as they spend additional three years in upper secondary school. After-school care is offered to all children aged 6 to 12, before and after scheduled school activities and often in school facilities. In 2016, 84 percent of all children ages 6–9 and 58 percent of children ages 6–12 were enrolled in formal after-school care (The National Agency for Education, 2018). Education is free throughout the public school system; this includes teaching materials, school meals, health services and transport (for more information, see skolverket.se, the Swedish National Agency for Education).

## 3 Parental involvement in Sweden

### 3a Terminology

In the Education Act, the legal term used to define who is responsible for a child is 'legal guardians' (SFS, 2010:800), who often are the child's biological parents. The terms 'parent' (*förälder*) and 'guardian' (*vårdnadshavare*) are often used interchangeably. Terms used to describe relationships between parents and schools are often 'home–school cooperation/collaboration' (*samverkan/ samarbete mellan hem och skola*) as well as 'parents' influence' (*föräldrainflytande*). The term 'family' is used less frequently.

### 3b National legislative and regulative context

While there are no statutory obligations for parents to educate their children in the Swedish context, in the 1960s, the first compulsory school curricula strongly emphasised home–school collaboration in education in terms of shared responsibility for the upbringing of children. The home–school collaboration was described in general terms, for example, requesting that differences between home and school be bridged. The curriculum clearly states that the school has the main responsibility for making this collaboration possible by, for example, arranging parent meetings and by initiating and maintaining a student journal to be shared with parents. In the following two decades, political attention was directed towards parental involvement in education, and national regulations emphasised its importance more strongly. However, it was not until the 1970s that one-to-one discussions between the home and school were realised. From the 1970s onwards, teachers were expected to hold individual parent–teacher conferences every semester (*kvartsamtal*). During this period, home–school collaboration was regulated in state policy. Since the 1990s, regulation for parental involvement has been mainly locally anchored, and regulations may occur at both the municipal and school levels. Therefore, the forms this involvement takes may differ between different local contexts. In addition, the decentralisation of the education system has contributed to regulation of home–school collaboration being limited at the national level. A pilot project was initiated in 1995 by the Swedish government, aimed at enforcing the possibility of local schoolboards with parent majority (Proposition, 1995/96:157). However, this did not come to have any real practical impact, and today the Swedish Education Act states that municipalities may establish local school boards with parent participation, but parents must not be in the majority (SFS, 2010:800). The Act also states that all school units must organise forums for joint consultation where parents are invited to participate. Overall, the degree of parental involvement in school in Sweden is still high, due, for example, to teachers in compulsory school being obliged to hold parent–teacher–student conferences (*utvecklingssamtal*) with every student and their legal guardians twice a year.

Although the education system has undergone several major reforms over the last 50 years, the main principles for home–school collaboration from the 1960s still stand as a foundation for policies on parental involvement. The principles are shared responsibility and the importance of bridging differences. The Education Act (SFS, 2010:800) regulates the rights and duties of children, students and their legal guardians. According to the main curriculum for compulsory school (Lgr 11), legal guardians and schools share the responsibility for creating the best conditions possible for students' development and learning. The curriculum also addresses the right as well as the obligation of parents to be involved in the education of their children. Moreover, in Sweden divorced parents often share the custody of their children and therefore have equal rights to be informed about and make decisions on behalf of their children.

Schools may provide at least five opportunities for parental involvement in Sweden today. The parent–teacher–student conference is one such opportunity, and the Swedish National Agency for Education provides advice and guidelines for how they may be carried out and addressed. These conferences are to be based on a written individual development plan (*individuell utvecklingsplan*), focusing on both student achievements and forward-looking planning (SFS, 2010:800). Second, schools organise voluntary parent meetings (*föräldramöten*) often twice a year and, third, more entertainment-related activities in which the children participate. A fourth example, emphasised in the curriculum (Lgr 11, 8), is the school's responsibility to keep parents informed. Further, municipalities, or even local schools may have policies that regulate the possibilities and obligations of parental involvement. For example, municipalities may establish local school boards with parent participation, as previously stated.

## 4 Existing research on parental involvement in Sweden

Research on parent–school relationships in general and on parental involvement in particular is conducted in many disciplines and within many different theoretical frameworks. In this chapter, we discuss research on parental involvement in compulsory primary schools, leaving out research on preschools and upper secondary schools. In contrast to trends in international research on parental involvement (cf. Jeynes, 2011), little research in Sweden has focused on parental involvement in schools in relation to student academic achievement (one exception is Niia et al., 2015). Rather, there are four other dominant fields of inquiry about parental involvement with schools: (1) parental choice of schools, (2) what facilitates and hinders parental involvement in schools, (3) parent–teacher communication, and (4) relationships between parents and schools in the national education policy. Researchers within these fields take their points of departure from different theoretical frameworks, ranging from sociological theories on social reproduction to social psychological theories on communication.

*Parents' choice of schools* can be seen as a form of parental involvement within the political context of privatisation and marketisation of the Swedish education system. Parental choice and its consequences for student achievement and social integration and segregation has been a major research field since parental choice and independent schools were introduced in the early 1990s. This research often targets parental choice as related to residential, social and ethnic segregation (cf. Bunar, 2010; Trumberg, 2011) or to public education as part of the welfare state (Blomqvist, 2004). Other research has focused on the introduction of independent schools and its impact on student academic achievement in municipal schools (Lindbom, 2010).

The second research focus on parents and schools asks *what facilitates and hinders parental involvement in schools*. Within this discourse, the focus can be on groups of parents, such as minority parents (Bouakaz, 2007), middle-class parents (Forsberg, 2007) or parents of children with special needs (Roll-Pettersson, 2001; Andersson, 2003). Other topics within this discourse are teachers' perspectives on parental involvement (Tallberg Broman, 2009) and on tools for facilitating parental involvement, such as school web sites (Gu, 2017) or homework (Forsberg, 2009).

The third research field targets the social practices of *parent-teacher communication* by looking closely at how parent-teacher-student conferences are conducted locally as conversations in institutional settings (Hofvendahl, 2006). The fourth field focuses on changes in the *national education policy* in the discourse on relations between parents and schools (Erikson, 2004). Some studies in this field examine how policy discourses on parental involvement are used in other contexts, such as the marketing of private education services (Hallsén & Karlsson, 2018).

In summary, the Swedish research findings make evident that parental involvement in schools, although a taken-for-granted good, is a complex phenomenon that has to be approached thoughtfully, because what may facilitate a type of parental involvement in one context may have the opposite effect in another. Parents have different resources to draw on when they are expected to choose a good school. Teachers may struggle with how to invite uninvolved parents to participate in school-based and home-based activities. At the same time, they may feel that the very involved parents demand the impossible and even question their professionalism (Tallberg Broman, 2009). Parents may find their relationship with teachers and schools supportive and constructive or oppressive and degrading (Andersson, 2003). Research on minority parents shows that language and cultural and religious beliefs can be barriers to parental involvement (Bouakaz, 2007), while research on middle-class parents' involvement shows that mothers tend to be more directly involved with their children's education than fathers (Forsberg, 2007). Results from the research on the effects of parents' school choice on student achievement and social integration and segregation point to the marketisation of education. Other research suggests that the introduction of independent schools tends to increase social inequality and segregation, affecting already marginalised groups in ways that may have a negative impact on student achievement (cf. Trumberg, 2011).

In the following section, we will present an example of research from the fourth field of study, an ongoing study of parental involvement in schools through the lens of national policy on homework support. It will make visible how changing policies on what homework is, where it should be done and by whom it should be supported produce normative ideas about parental involvement in home-based school activities.

## 5 New research perspective: homework support as parental involvement outside of school

In Sweden, as in many other countries (Borgonovi & Montt, 2012), homework is a recurrent form of home-based and academically related parental involvement in children's education. Helping with homework is a child-centred form of parental involvement that in Sweden can be seen as a taken-for-granted parental duty.

Homework (*läxor*) was established as a term as early as in the 16th century in Sweden, and the first governmental regulation (*Skolordning*) overseeing the occurrence of homework in schools was issued in 1611 (Lundahl, 2004). The meaning of the term is much the same today: homework is schoolwork performed outside of school, often in children's homes. Throughout history, parents were responsible for making sure their children did their homework, while the priest (and later the schoolteacher) was responsible for testing whether it was properly done (Strandberg, 2013).

Homework was regulated in Swedish national curricula for compulsory education in the 1960s, the 1970s and the early 1980s. The next two curricula, 1994 (Lpo 94) and 2011 (Lgr 11), did not mention homework, and neither did the Swedish Education Act (SFS, 2010:800). Yet, it remains a well-established practice. Homework resurfaced in a new policy arena in 2007 with the introduction of a tax reform (RUT tax deduction). Within this legal framework, it was possible, until August 2015, for parents to make tax deductions for homework support as a household service. This newly awakened political focus on homework actualised ideas on parental involvement in education.

### 5a Homework and parental involvement in Sweden

Internationally, much research on parental involvement in homework argues that it can have a positive effect on student learning and achievement (Epstein, 1986; see research reviews by Hoover-Dempsey et al., 2001; Patall, Cooper, & Robinson, 2008). Other research argues the opposite effect or advocates taking a more critical approach, showing that parental involvement can be understood as being conditioned by gender and class structures (David, 1980; Lareau, 2000) in ways that have a direct impact on parents' involvement in their children's homework (Hutchison, 2012).

Both these lines of argumentation can be found in Swedish research on homework and parental involvement. However, the emphasis in the Swedish context has largely been on students' and parents' experiences of and views on the phenomenon. The research also illuminates the tensions existing between the pedagogical and social dimensions embedded within homework as a form of parental involvement (e.g. Gu & Kristoffersson, 2010; Wingard & Forsberg, 2009). These studies and others (e.g. Strandberg, 2013) can be connected to a more profound discussion that lies at the core of the Swedish research on homework and parental involvement – a discussion on the very benefit of homework. Another aspect of this discussion is that the circumstances in which parents assist their children with homework and the challenges that brings vary greatly between different groups of parents, affecting the impact of the parents' involvement (e.g. Österlind, 2001; Bouakaz & Persson, 2007; Strandberg, 2013; Svensson, Meaney, & Norén, 2014).

Homework deserves to be studied as an aspect of parental involvement in education that has a bearing on both student achievement and social equality. Homework support is a Swedish term for supplementary tutoring and means help with homework and other schoolwork outside of regular school hours. Today homework support is provided by for-profit companies, non-profit organisations and since 2015 by some, but not all, primary and secondary schools. We still know little about the how many students, or the characteristics of families and students, who avail of either form of homework support in Sweden. In the next section, we present preliminary results from an ongoing study of how changes in national policy on homework support produces normative ideas about parental involvement in education.

### 5b From responsible consumers to unreliable providers of homework support – parental involvement in national policy

Changes in government policies on homework support provide an opportunity to gain insight into changing normative ideas on parental involvement in education. An ongoing study on changing national programmatic policy ideas on homework support in Sweden has revealed changes in political views on parental involvement between 2007–2012 and 2013–2017. Through a few empirical examples, we illuminate how two sets of reforms that changed policies on homework support also have implications for normative ideas on parental involvement in education outside of school.

The data selection was made through a search of policy documents dealing with homework support. The policy formulations regarding homework support were read in three steps. First, after locating the text explicitly dealing with homework support in each policy document, we focused on the content of the formulations. Then we related the content to the policy areas and thus contextualised them as programmatic policy ideas (Schmidt, 2008) aimed at solving specific problems. Finally, we traced how the programmatic ideas had changed over time within and between different policy arenas. Within the theoretical framework of discursive institutionalism (Schmidt, 2010), we thus looked at changing national policies on homework support as programmatic ideas (Schmidt, 2008) as they sought to solve different kinds of problems in society. In turn, these problems are related to different normative policy ideas on parental involvement in education.

a) *First reform period: parents as providers and consumers of homework support in the home*

During the first reform period (2006–2012), homework support was initially mentioned in the right-wing government Proposition (2006/07:94) within the context of a suggested system for tax relief. A tax deduction would be allowed for the costs of hiring people to perform household services that were normally performed by family members and that did not require specialist skills, such asccleaning, gardening and baby-sitting.

The suggested tax relief system was proposed for a number of reasons. One was to weaken black market sales of domestic services. Another was to relieve families of economic burdens and, as a consequence, free mothers from household duties that prevented them from taking part in the labour market under the same conditions as men. Another was to create job opportunities for young unskilled workers.

The law on tax reliefs for household services, which was instated in 2007 (SFS, 2007:346), included baby-sitting services. In this context, homework support was described as a task that baby-sitters might do. The proposition thus claimed that homework support is a form of home-based childcare.

> The same is true in the case of a baby-sitter helping the child with homework or other forms of schoolwork. However, it should not include the hiring of a private tutor or similar for the child's benefit. In such a case, it is a matter of work that demands expert knowledge that is normally not conducted within the household. It is therefore not a question of care or supervision but teaching.
>
> (Proposition, 2006/07:94, 43, translation by authors)

In its budget proposition for 2013, the government modified the arguments underlying the claim that homework was a form of home-based childcare (2012/13:1). It stated that the description of homework support as a household service should be separated from that of baby-sitting. It also stated that the legislation on tax relief for household services should make this clearer in order to facilitate its application so that people other than baby-sitters could perform the task.

We argue that during this first reform period, policies on homework support as a form of home-based childcare produced normative policy ideas on parents as providers and consumers of homework support. Parents were depicted as being responsible for making sure that their children *did* their homework at home, but not necessarily providing homework support. Parents could have other adults actually supporting their children. While previously, the normative construction of the role of the 'good' parent was to support their child with their schooling and homework, thus, the role of parents now changed to the ability to purchase homework support under the guise of home-based childcare (Svensson, Meaney, & Norén, 2014). However, this reform that offered tax relief for parents to buy homework support from external agents (including private providers) continued to reproduce a view of homework as a parental responsibility.

b) *Second reform period: parents as unreliable providers of homework support in the home*

In the second reform period (2012–2017), this depiction of homework support as a form of home-based childcare was challenged by policies arguing that many children lacked sufficient support from their parents in purchasing homework support as a form of home-based childcare. These policies highlighted social inequities, and argued that homework support should be seen as a form of supplementary education, facilitating student learning and social equality, which could be performed by different agents in contexts *outside the homes*. This change in claims about the nature of homework support where it should be performed and by whom also produced changes in normative ideas on parental involvement.

During the second reform period (2012–2017), the programmatic ideas on homework support, and thus normative ideas on parental involvement, were gradually redefined. The changes began with a report from the Parliamentary Tax Committee (SkU, 2012/13:10), on which the government based its proposition to separate the services of homework support and baby-sitting (Proposition, 2012/13:1). The legislation was approved by the Parliament. In addition, the report challenged the original claim that homework is a form of home-based childcare by listing schools, after-school centres, non-profit organisations and cooperation between these operators as possible contexts outside of the family homes in which children could receive homework support.

> Homework support of this sort may be organized within schools or leisure centres with teachers or educators or after school hours by help of non-profit organisations such as the Centre for Mathematics (*Mattecentrum*), the

Foundation for Homework Support (*Stiftelsen läxhjälpen*) or the Red Cross (*Röda korset*), etc. The homework support may also occur in collaboration between the school and non-profit organisations. In this context, the committee wishes to particularly emphasise the most valuable work of non-profit organisations in relation to homework support and other forms of help with schoolwork for children and youth. Yet another way for students to gain support with homework or other forms of schoolwork outside of school is through private providers. The committee looks very positively at any efforts that may increase the students' knowledge and increase the goal achievement in the primary school and the secondary school.

(SkU, 2012/13:10, 14, translation by authors)

As can be seen, the question about homework support had turned from a fiscal to an educational issue with homework support described as one of many ways to facilitate student learning. Everything supporting the education of children was viewed positively, including tax relief for homework support as a household service.

The claim that homework was a form of home-based childcare was further challenged in the Budget Bill for 2014 (2013/14:1), which contained a suggestion to set aside state funds that schools and non-profit organisations providing homework support could apply for. Here, homework support policy had shifted from supporting home-based child-care to supporting out-of-home supplementary education for students who lacked the necessary home-based support.

Additional support and assistance from home contributes to high performance and the committee is aware that all students do not have access to it. The committee believes that if the school provided homework support it could compensate the students who do not have access to homework support in their homes, and simultaneously contribute to an increase in goal completion and equivalence.

(Prop. Proposition, 2013/14:1, 59, translation by authors)

The Budget Bill for 2015 (2014/2015:1) suggested that even more state funds be set aside for school-based homework support and that the regulation governing tax relief for homework support as a household service should be cancelled. The programmatic idea that homework support was a form of out-of-home supplementary education was to prevail as the left-wing government came into power in 2015. In the Budget Bill for 2016 (2015/16:1), it was suggested that a portion of the funds financing school-based homework support would be earmarked for non-profit organisations providing homework support.

During this second reform period, the policies on homework support as a form of out-of-home supplementary education produced normative ideas on parents as potentially uninvolved in their children's education and thereby as unreliable providers of homework support. In this policy discourse, parental responsibility was not taken for granted in the way it had been in the first reform period. Here, society was to compensate for parents who failed to provide homework support. Some parents no longer have to pay for homework support in the home – instead they can send their children free of charge to a homework support provided by schools, funded by the state.

These preliminary findings show that normative ideas on the forms and content of parental involvement in education may be produced by policies from arenas other than education. This example also shows that research on parental involvement in education may benefit from looking more closely into national and international policies regulating and allocating resources among and between families, welfare institutions and civil society (non-profit organisations). Parental involvement in and out of school, such as assisting with homework, may be facilitated or hindered by seemingly unrelated programmatic policies aimed at solving problems in society. This seems to be the case with the Swedish law on tax deductions for household services.

## 6 Conclusions

In Sweden, assisting with homework has for a long time been an undisputable parental duty, which has not really offered any other possible subject positions other than that of a responsible parent (cf. Forsberg, 2007). Most parents go to parent–teacher–student conferences, attend parent meetings and assist with homework on a regular basis. Because of this, Swedish research rarely investigates parental involvement *per se*, but instead focuses on practices of parental involvement such as parents' choices of schools (Bunar, 2010), parent–teacher–student conferences (Hofvendahl, 2006) or parents' assistance with homework (Forsberg, 2007). As parental involvement is, to some extent, taken for granted in Sweden, researchers want to understand and remedy unequal opportunities for parental involvement among different groups of parents (Bouakaz, 2007; Forsberg, 2007).

As shown in research, homework is one of the most complex areas for parental involvement in education because not all parents can meet the assumption behind the assigning and assessing of homework: that all children have parents or guardians that are able to support them in their tasks (Corno, 1996; Forsberg, 2007).

Our ongoing study focuses on how government policy, even outside of education policy, may make an impact on how parental involvement in education is perceived. In the case of the second reforms, the change came out of a regulation on taxes. The preliminary findings from our study show that the reform giving tax relief for parents buying homework support from private providers reproduced a view on homework as a parental responsibility, while later reforms somewhat questioned this view. The regulations in the second reform period seem, to some extent, to have relieved parents of what had been a taken-for-granted responsibility. Instead, schools and non-profit organisations were expected to take on the responsibility to make sure that children were given the support they needed to succeed in school.

How are we to understand that the Swedish government made schools and non-profit organisations responsible for what researchers have described as the most obvious dimension of parental involvement in their children's education? Our study points to changes through which parents have gone from being pictured as responsible providers and consumers of homework support to potentially uninvolved parents, endangering the provision of equal opportunities for schoolchildren's learning and development. In fact, the whole idea of state funding of homework support rests on an assumption that some children lack support from parents. The responsibility for remedying problems with uninvolved parents is left to the local municipalities and schools, while the state targets the problem of providing equal opportunities in education through the provision of funding for homework support.

The now well-established homework support market in Sweden, in which private and non-profit organisations offer various forms of services (Hallsén & Karlsson, 2018), has turned homework into a boundary object (Strandberg, 2013) for more actors than just students, parents and schools. As our preliminary results show, parents are also deemed an unreliable source for support in ways that may even take the 'home' out of homework. The implications this will have for how we understand homework as a taken-for-granted aspect of parental involvement in education in Sweden are yet to be seen.

## References

Andersson, I. (2003) *Föräldrars möte med Skolan*. Individ, omvärld och lärande/Forskning nr 15. Institutionen för individ, omvärld och lärande, Lärarhögskolan i Stockholm. Stockholm.

Blomqvist, P. (2004) The choice revolution: Privatization of Swedish welfare services in the 1990s. *Social Policy and Administration*, 38(2), 139–155.

Borgonovi, F. and Montt, G. (2012) *Parental Involvement in Selected PISA Countries and Economies*. OECD Education Working Papers, No. 73. OECD Publishing. Available at: http://dx.doi.org/10.1787/5k990rk0jsjj-en.

Bouakaz, L. (2007) *Parental Involvement in School: What Promotes and What Hinders Parental Involvement in an Urban School*. Doctoral Thesis, Malmö Studies in Educational Sciences 30.

Bouakaz, L. and Persson, S. (2007) What hinders and what promotes parents' engagement in school? *International Journal about Parents in Education*, 1, 97–107.

Bunar, N. (2010) Choosing for quality or inequality: Current perspectives on the implementation of school choice policy in Sweden. *Journal of Education Policy*, 25(1), 1–18. DOI:10.1080/02680930903377415.

Corno, L. (1996) Homework is a complicating thing. *Educational Researcher*, 25(8), 27–30.

David, M. (1980) *The State, the Family and Education*. London: Routledge.

Epstein, J. (1986) Parents' reactions to teacher practices of parent involvement. *The Elementary School Journal*, 86(3), 277–294.

Erikson, L. (2004) *Föräldrar och skola*. V Frölunda: DocuSys. PhD Dissertation. Örebro Studies in Education 10.

Forsberg, L. (2007) Homework as serious family business: Power and subjectivity in negotiations about school assignments in Swedish families. *British Journal of Sociology of Education*, 28(2), 209–222.

Forsberg, L. (2009) *Involved Parenthood. Everyday Lives of Swedish Middle-Class Families*. PhD Dissertation. Linköping Studies in Arts and Science No. 473.

Gu, L. (2017) Using school websites for home–school communication and parental involvement? *Nordic Journal of Education Policy*, 3(2), 133–143.

Gu, L. and Kristoffersson, M. (2010) *Hemma blir som skola – elevperspektiv på hemläxor*. Stockholm: Institutionen för barn- och ungdomsvetenskap vid Stockholms universitet.

Hallsén S. and Karlsson, M. (2018) Teacher or friend? Consumer narratives on private supplementary tutoring in Sweden as policy enactment. *Journal of Education Policy*. DOI:10.1080/02680939.2018.1458995.

Hofvendahl, J. (2006) *Riskabla samtal – en analys av potentpp.iella faror i skolans kvarts- och utvecklingssamtal*. PhD Dissertation. Linköping Studies in Arts and Science. 338.

Hoover-Dempsey, K., Battiato, A., Walker, J., Reed, R., DeJOng, J. and Jones, K. (2001) Parental involvement in homework. *Educational Psychologist*, 36(3),195–209.

Hutchison, K. (2012) A labour of love: Mothers, emotional capital and homework. *Gender and Education*, 24(2), 195–212.

Jeynes, W.H. (2011) *Parental Involvement and Academic Success*. New York and London: Routledge.

Karlsson, M. and Perälä-Littunen, S. (2017) Managing the gap – Policy and practice of parents in child care and education. *Nordic Journal of Education Policy*, 3(2), 119–122.

Lareau, A. (2000) *Home Advantage. Social Class and Parental Intervention in Elementary Education*. Lanham, Maryland: Rowman and Littlefield Publishers.

*Lgr 11. Läroplan för grundskolan, förskoleklassen och fritidshemmet 2011*. Stockholm: Skolverket.

Lindbom, A. (2010) School choice in Sweden: Effects on student performance, school costs, and segregation. *Scandinavian Journal of Educational Research*, 54(6), 615–630.

*Lpo 94. Läroplan för det obligatoriska skolväsendet*. Stockholm: Utbildningsdepartementet.

Lundahl, C. (2004) En läroplansteoretisk och läroplanshistorisk analys av kunskapsbedömning i Sveriges första läroverksstadgar 1561–1724. *Studies in Educational Policy and Educational Philosophy*, 2, 1–31.

Niia, A., Almqvist, L., Brunnberg, E. and Granlund, M. (2015) Student participation and parental involvement in relation to academic achievement. *Scandinavian Journal of Educational Research*, 59(3), 297–315.

Österlind, E. (2001) *Elevers förhållningssätt till läxor: en uppföljningsstudie*. Falun: Högskolan Dalarna.

Patall, E., Cooper, H. and Robinson, J.C. (2008) Parent involvement in homework: A research synthesis. *Review of Educational Research*, 78(4), 1039–1101.

Proposition 1995/96:157 Regeringens proposition 1995/96:157. *Lokala styrelser med föräldramajoritet inom skolan* [Government proposition on Local school boards with parent majority]. Sweden: Ministry of Education.

Proposition 2006/07:94. Regeringens proposition 2006/07: 94 *Skattelättnader för hushållstjänster m.m.* [Government proposition on tax deductions for household services]. Sweden: Ministry of Finance.

Proposition 2012/13:1 Regeringens proposition 2012/13:1. *Budgetpropositionen för 2013*. [*Budget Bill for 2013*]. Sweden: Ministry of Finance.
Proposition 2013/14:1 Regeringens proposition 2013/14:1. *Budgetpropositionen för 2014*. [*Budget Bill for 2014*]. Sweden: Ministry of Finance.
Proposition 2014/2015:1 Regeringens proposition 2014/15:1. *Budgetpropositionen för 2015*. [*Budget Bill for 2015*]. Sweden: Ministry of Finance.
Proposition 2015/16:1 Regeringens proposition 2015/16:1. *Budgetpropositionen för 2016*. [*Budget Bill for 2016*]. Sweden: Ministry of Finance.
Roll-Pettersson, L. (2001) *Between open systems and closed doors. The needs and perceptions of parents of children with cognitive disabilities in educational settings*. Doctoral thesis. Stockholm Institute of Education. HLS Förlag.
Schmidt, V. (2008) Discursive institutionalism: The explanatory power of ideas and discourse. *Annual Review of Political Science*, 11, 303–326.
Schmidt, V. (2010) Taking ideas and discourse seriously: Explaining change through discursive institutionalism as the fourth 'new institutionalism'. *Political Science Review*, 2(1), 1–25.
SFS 2007:346 Lag om skattereduktion för hushållsarbete [Swedish Code of Statutes no. 2007:346. Tax Reduction for Household Services]. Stockholm.
SFS 2010:800 Skollagen [Swedish Code of Statutes no. 2010:800. The Education Act]. Stockholm.
SkU 2012/13:10 Skatteutskottets betänkande – Skattereduktion för läxhjälp [The Committee of Taxation Report – Tax Reduction for Homework Support]. Stockholm.
Strandberg, M. (2013) *Läxor om och för kulturell mångfald med föräldrars livserfarenheter som resurs – några kritiska aspekter*. Doctoral Thesis in Didactics 23. Stockholm Institute or Education and Didactics.
Svensson, P., Meaney, T. and Norén, E. (2014) Immigrant students´ perceptions of their possibilities to learn mathematics: The case of homework. *For the Learning of Mathematics*, 34(3), 32–37.
The Swedish National Agency for Education (2018) National Agency for Education Official Website. Available at: www.skolverket.se (accessed 15 Apr. 2018).
Tallberg Broman, I. (2009) 'No parent left behind': Föräldradeltagande för inkludering och effektivitet. *Educare*, 2–3, 221–240.
Trumberg, A. (2011) *Den delade skolan: segregationsprocesser i det svenska skolsystemet*. Doctoral thesis. Örebro Studies in Human Geography no. 6.
Wingard, L. and Forsberg, L. (2009) Parent involvement in children's homework in American and Swedish dual-earner families. *Journal of Pragmatics*, 41, 1576–1595.

# 10 Switzerland

Parental involvement and career decision-making: the case of Switzerland

*Markus P. Neuenschwander*

## 1 Introduction

There is an ongoing debate in Switzerland on how parents should be involved in their children's schools. In general, parents in Switzerland have a positive attitude towards school. Nevertheless, teachers and principals have become more engaged with parents in recent years to further enhance this relationship. After all, if parents have a positive attitude towards school, it boosts student satisfaction and performance levels and reduces teacher stress (Neuenschwander et al., 2005). Accordingly, cooperation between teachers and parents has been the subject of attention at governmental, school, class and individual levels in research, state policy, teacher training and the daily work of principals and teachers.

This chapter begins with a description of the legal rights of schools and families in Switzerland regarding cooperation between parents and teachers. It discusses how Swiss law regulates family–school relationships and which research activities dominate in this legal framework, then presents a review of Swiss research on parental involvement. Finally, an example of an ongoing study is used to estimate the effects of parental expectations regarding their child's achievement and their cooperation with teachers on student achievement and track selection.

## 2 The Swiss education system

Switzerland has a federal school system, and, as a result, the school structure varies widely between the cantons (states). However, in the majority of cantons, children enter kindergarten at age 4 and move on to full-day primary school two years later. Around half of the 26 cantons have inclusive school systems in which students with special needs are included in regular classrooms. In the others, students with special needs are taught in separate classes or separate schools.

After grade six (at about age 12), students in most cantons move on to tracked lower secondary education. The track they are assigned to is determined in a performance-based selection process through a combination of test results, teacher evaluations and recommendations from parents/guardians. The number (one to five) and organisation of these tracks vary between cantons. Most parents in Switzerland send their children to state schools; only about 5 percent of Swiss children attend a private school,[1] and home schooling is very rare. Children in the state school system have to attend the school they are assigned to by the state or communal authorities. In other words, there is no free choice of school. After two years of kindergarten and nine years of compulsory primary and lower secondary schooling, approximately 96 percent of students move to upper secondary education at around the age of 16 (Schweizerische Koordinationsstelle für Bildungsforschung, 2018).

There are several options at upper secondary level. First, the result of a performance-based selection process determines whether a student can attend a *gymnasium* and achieve the so-called *maturität* leaving certificate (about 20 percent of the age group; Babel & Lagana, 2016). Secondly, based on a performance-based selection process, students can attend a specialised upper secondary school (about 7 percent of the age group) and receive a specialised school certificate or additionally a specialised baccalaureate (*Fachmaturität*). Thirdly, after a successful application procedure, students can participate in a dual VET/apprenticeship (training company, VET school and intercompany courses) or a full-time course at a vocational secondary school and complete their schooling with a certificate or diploma (about 68 percent of the age group). Some students in this group also gain the federal vocational baccalaureate (about 17 percent of the group). In all, about 5 percent of students do not obtain an upper secondary qualification.

At the tertiary level, students with a *maturität* qualification can study at a cantonal or federal university. Students with a *baccalaureate* can attend a cantonal university of applied sciences or a cantonal university of teacher education. Students with a VET certificate or diploma can start a *baccalaureate* course, a professional education and training course (PET), a preparation course for a federal PET diploma, or an advanced federal PET diploma.

## 3 Parental involvement in schools in Switzerland

### 3a Terminology

At the federal level, the term 'legal guardian' (*Erziehungsberechtigte*) is used in legislation to indicate the person(s) responsible for a child. In most cases, this will be the child's biological parents.[2] Following a divorce, legal guardianship may in some cases be assigned to only one parent. Legal guardians can also be adoptive parents or the person(s) who officially care for a child (*Vormund*).

While the term 'family' in legislation includes parents and all the children they are responsible for, its definition varies in educational, psychological and sociological research (Ecarius et al., 2011). Some researchers define a family as the intimate relationship between family members (Schneewind, 1994) or a lasting intense interaction between persons of two or more generations who typically live together (Herzog et al., 1997). Parents are members of the older generation in this family system.

Various terms in legislation and public institutions are used to describe the relationship between family and school, depending on the interests of the institutions and parties who shape it. Parent organisations often use terms like 'parental involvement' (*Elternmitwirkung*) or 'parental participation' (*Elternpartizipation*). School-related legislation, in turn, often uses the terms 'cooperation with parents/legal guardians' or 'cooperation between the school and the family' (*Elternhaus*). These terms indicate that – in the legal context – parents and teachers collaborate on the same hierarchical level and share information. Some research studies in Switzerland have also adopted these legal terms, while others use a subjective definition of parent by asking participating children to indicate the adults who are their parents.

## *3b National legislative and regulative context*

According to the Swiss Civil Code (Schweizerisches Zivilgesetzbuch) of 1907, parents, as primary caregivers, are responsible for raising their children until the age of 18 and serve as their legal representatives. However, they have to allow their children to attend school and complete an appropriate education that fits their abilities and interests. They also have to cooperate with their children's teachers – an amendment to the law that only came into force in 1978.

Additional legal provisions regarding cooperation between parents and teachers can be found in cantonal laws. Cantons are allowed to enact laws that are consistent with federal law and the respective cantonal constitution. Thus, legal provisions on parent–teacher cooperation differ between cantons and have changed frequently in the last 40 years. In most cantons, teachers and parents are obliged to cooperate. However, Swiss schools are autonomous and have the right to define how this cooperation is organised. Accordingly, it is the teachers and parents – and not the legislation – who define the intensity, form and content of their cooperation.

In recent decades. particular attention has been paid by parents, teachers and politicians to the role teachers and parents (should) play in school decisions. In the 1970s, teachers and school principals made the decisions regarding school. However, in the 1980s parents were given more power to influence their children's school career decisions in line with their interests and aptitudes. In some cantons this power shift has been reversed in the last few years, with teachers and school principals once again making these decisions and then simply informing parents.

As outlined below, there are some recurring provisions in Swiss legislation regarding cooperation between parents and teachers.

Schools are obliged to inform parents annually about their curriculum, organisation and special events (*information,* typically at a parents' evening at the beginning of the school year). They also have to provide parents with direct information about their child's academic and social learning in the classroom on an annual basis (typically in the mid of the school year). In some cantons, these information sessions have legally replaced the annual mid-term report in the first years of primary school. In addition to their regular contact sessions, teachers and parents can arrange separate meetings to discuss specific situations or characteristics pertaining to the child (e.g. health problems, misbehaviour, social problems, learning problems, grades, etc.). To a limited extent, the issues discussed with the teachers can also refer to home-based parental activities. However, teachers do not have the right or the duty to counsel parents or change family activities: their duties are restricted to child-centred information.

Most cantons have detailed rules on how to involve parents in *school career decision-making* (child-centred activities). Parents are involved in deciding the type of lower and upper secondary tracks to which their children are assigned. They are also involved in deciding whether their children will repeat or skip grades and whether they are assigned to special needs classes. The manner of this involvement varies from canton to canton.

In most cantons, parents are not involved in *the organisation of teaching and classroom activities* and do not have the right to influence them; it is up to the teachers to decide how they involve parents in this matter.

Another set of rules based on federal and cantonal law outlines school intervention procedures in the event of a suspicion that a child is being neglected or abused by their parents or that their welfare is at risk (*control*). In such cases, teachers confront the respective parents with their observations. They then begin an investigation in conjunction with the school principal and the communal authorities. If it is determined that parents are not fulfilling their duty to raise their children in the latter's best interests, cantonal authorities have the right to assign those children a legal assistant or guardian.

In most Swiss cantons, the municipal school authority defines local school strategies and hires principals and teachers. Typically, the municipal school authority is made up of a small group of citizens (representatives, often parents), who are elected in a democratic process. In addition to the municipal school authority, some cantons allow – or even require – schools to install official parent councils (*parental organisation at school level*). These councils are not child-centred but rather responsible for coordinating parental interests in school and improving communication between parents and teachers at the school level. They do not, however, have the right to make school-related decisions.

## 4 Existing research on parental involvement in Switzerland: theoretical frameworks, empirical research and dominant discourses

In Switzerland, parental involvement in schools is not a core research topic, although activities in this field have grown continuously since the 1970s, with researchers conducting quantitative and qualitative research from the educational, psychological, sociological and economic perspectives. As parents of kindergarten and primary school children are more involved in school, there has been more research activity on kindergarten and primary school children than on secondary school students.

Based on reviews of Swiss studies (Cusin & Grossenbacher, 2001; Zweidler & Haller, 2012) and an internet search on research in Switzerland since 1980, we identified six key research areas in the field of parental involvement. While these areas do not derive deductively from a theoretical framework, they do illustrate prototypical research questions that are examined using specific theoretical backgrounds and research methodologies.

### 4a Structural and functional aspects of school and family

A number of studies have used qualitative methods to explore the relationship between schools and families from the sociological, historical and educational perspectives (Chartier et al., 2014). In this regard, researchers have analysed and compared the varying roles, functions and perspectives of parents and teachers. Chartier and Payet (2014), for instance, conceptualised teachers as professionals in teaching and learning, and parents as representatives of their children as individuals, i.e. as partners with separate expertise in a non-hierarchical relationship. Other researchers have used qualitative and quantitative studies to compare the perspectives of teachers and parents (Egger et al., 2015; Neuenschwander et al., 2005) and found that parents tend to attribute more positive characteristics to their children than teachers.

### 4b Cooperation between parents and teachers

The most prevalent area of research activity focuses on the nature of the cooperation between parents and teachers (Hofstetter, 2017; Steinert & Maag Merki, 2009). Research in this area examines the strategies, attitudes and behaviours encountered in interactions between parents and teachers, including when making decisions regarding lower secondary track.

Although teachers and parents have different perspectives and interests, research has found that Swiss parents generally have a positive attitude towards schools (Neuenschwander et al., 2005). While severe conflicts rarely arise between parents and teachers in Switzerland, nonetheless, conflicts with parents still remain the most frequent reason for teachers to leave their jobs (Ludwig-Tauber et al., 2000). School rules and demands communicated by teachers can also be a source of stress for parents, especially those of low achievers or children who do not adhere to the rules (Kern et al., 2012). Studies likewise show that a high level of cooperation influences the attitudes of parents and teachers towards school. Thus, the primary functions of cooperation between parents and teachers are to improve the acceptance of school among parents and reduce teacher stress (Neuenschwander et al., 2005).

### 4c Effects of family on student motivation and achievement

Another key area of research uses quantitative methods to examine the effects of family dynamics and parental beliefs and behaviour on student motivation, achievement and behaviour. Studies in this field examine school effectiveness and effective family functions and find that parents can differ quite substantially in how they support their children's academic learning and behaviour in school.

First, parents directly influence their children through their attitudes and behaviours at home, which affect the latter's self-images, motivation, achievements and behaviours in school; this is a form of *home-based, child-centred parental involvement* (Buff et al., 2011; Neuenschwander, 2017). Research has found that parental expectations have a similar influence on student achievement in mathematics and German in both Switzerland and the USA (Neuenschwander et al., 2007).

Second, parents' attitudes affect their children's attitudes towards school and teachers. This represents another form of *home-based, school-centred parental involvement*. Parents who appreciate a school encourage their children to have a positive attitude towards it. Those children, in turn, exhibit a greater motivation to learn and contribute to a more positive classroom atmosphere.

Third, through cooperation parents can directly affect teachers' attitudes towards their children, which influence the latter's learning, achievement and behaviour in class – a form of *school-based, school-centred parental involvement* (Niederbacher & Neuenschwander, 2017).

Finally, parents directly influence classroom processes by visiting the class or establishing strategies in cooperation with the teacher that influence the child's learning and behaviour in school (*school-based, child-centred parental involvement*). However, intense cooperation between parents and teachers does not necessarily have a direct effect on student motivation and achievement. The frequency of parent–teacher contacts typically correlates negatively with student achievement (Neuenschwander et al., 2005). Parents of low-achieving students do, however, need to cooperate with teachers more intensively than other parents.

### 4d Effects of family on school career – social inequality

Another area of intense research activity is social inequality. Research in this field looks at how family background influences students' school career decisions and vocational choice processes and often refers to human capital theory, rational choice theory or Bourdieu's habitus theory (1993). Many quantitative studies have shown that, in Switzerland, assignment to a specific track in lower secondary education and the decision to opt for an academic or a vocational track in upper secondary education depend on the student's socioeconomic status, migration background and gender – even after controlling for academic achievement (Bäriswyl et al., 2006; Becker & Hecken,

2009). The extent of the effect of socioeconomic background on school track assignment in lower secondary and upper secondary education varies between cantons and is stronger in areas where parents are more involved in career decisions (Bäriswyl et al., 2006; Neuenschwander, 2014). In other words, research in the Swiss context finds that parents with a high socio-economic status (SES) are more likely to be engaged in their children's learning (home-based, child-centred parental involvement). Thus, these children achieve more and attain higher grades, reflecting the primary effect of social disparity as highlighted by Boudon (1974). In addition, parents with a high SES ensure that their children are assigned to school tracks with high scholastic demands, thus reflecting the secondary effects of social disparity (ibid.).

### 4e Education, counselling and support for parents regarding educational topics

Most parents consider their children's success at school to be very important, hence their interest in acquiring information on how to assist their children in learning. However, low SES and immigrant parents have less knowledge about the education system and how to go about supporting their children effectively. Given the large number of immigrant parents in Switzerland, key research areas include how to involve low SES and immigrant parents in such programmes (Bader & Fibbi, 2012; Giuliani, 2013) and the conceptualisation of effective programmes for this target group (Neuenschwander et al., 2016). Typically, teachers are not key players in such programmes because their primary tasks lie in the classroom.

Several quantitative and qualitative studies have investigated new training programmes for parents and how they can effectively support their children's learning (Niggli et al., 2009) and career choice processes (Neuenschwander et al., 2016). Such programmes seek to empower parents to support their children at home. Research has also examined the effects of private tutoring (*Nachhilfe*) and of boarding school (*Tagesschule*) on academic achievement and track selection. The findings show a corresponding small effect of attending either private tutoring (Grunder et al., 2013) or boarding school (Schüpbach & Herzog, 2009).

### 4f Training to prepare teachers for collaboration with parents

Some recent research focuses on how teachers are prepared for effective and successful cooperation with parents, and investigates the struggles and perceived stress teachers face when they attempt to cooperate with parents. Programmes that seek to prepare student teachers to cooperate successfully with a diverse range of parents are still rare in Switzerland. One of the few such programmes uses role-playing exercises to equip student teachers with the social competences they need to cooperate with parents (Schütz, 2016). An evaluation of this programme using training and control groups shows that it increased teachers' belief in their self-efficacy when cooperating with parents. However, there is a need for more research and programme evaluations in order to improve the quality of parent–teacher cooperation and ensure it is beneficial and effective for both groups.

## 5 New research perspective: parental effects on achievement and school track decisions in lower secondary education

The review above refers to research on the effects of parental expectations on student achievement and track assignment in lower secondary education (Eccles & Harold, 1996; Neuenschwander, 2014), an area where research findings are still limited in the Swiss context. As indicated above, parents can influence academic achievement and track selection through child-related home- and school-based activities. Similarly, Krumm (1996) reports that parental beliefs and activities have stronger effects on student achievement than intelligence. Accordingly, we will now contrast the strengths of the effects of socioeconomic background and parental beliefs and activities with those of intelligence on student achievement in mathematics and German and on track assignment at lower secondary level.

Boudon (1974) postulates that parental SES, expectations and self-efficacy in supporting their children's learning affect student achievement in mathematics and German (primary effect). He also maintains that parental SES affects education choices and track assignment – even after controlling for achievement (secondary effect). Parents with a high SES try to assign their children to tracks with high scholastic demands, while those with a low SES tend to opt for tracks with low demands, even if the students' achievement levels are the same. Moreover, parental involvement research indicates that both parental child-centred attitudes and parental activities to support their children at home and in school contribute to academic performance, education choices and track assignment. Highly intelligent children learn new information quickly and thoroughly (Sternberg, 1997). The achievement gain is higher if children achieve high scores in intelligence tests.

### 5a Data and method

The study draws on data from the Swiss longitudinal study on the 'Effects of Tracking' (WiSel). After grade 6, students in Switzerland transition from primary school into one of three lower secondary tracks. The concepts used in these analyses were operationalised by items in questionnaires and tests that were analysed using multivariate statistical procedures.

A sample of 51 primary schools in the cantons of Bern and Lucerne were chosen at random in 2011 to participate in the study. We asked grade 5 students to fill out a questionnaire and complete achievement tests in mathematics and German in a classroom setting (wave 1). In total, 985 grade 5 students agreed to participate in the study (mean age=11 years, 48 percent female, 76 percent Swiss nationals). We also asked their parents to fill out a questionnaire at home. In wave 1, the parent sample consisted of 84 percent mothers, 13 percent fathers and 3 percent other parental representatives (response rate: 95 percent of students).

One year later, we asked the same students to participate in the study again (wave 2) and complete new achievement tests in mathematics and German.

For the purposes of our study, achievement tests in mathematics and German were completed by students in grades 5 and 6 and represented a key dependent variable (items taken from Moser et al., 2011). Anchor items from the grade 5 tests were used again in their grade 6 counterparts. The other items in both tests varied, although the concept remained the same. The tests were analysed using item response theory (Yen & Fitzpatrick, 2006). The grade 6 achievement test scores were used as the dependent variable, while the grade 5 scores served as an independent variable. The key dependent variable used to test the effects of parental expectations on track assignment in lower secondary education, was obtained by asking grade 6 teachers to report the students' tracks in grade 7 (track with basic demands = 'low track', track with expanded demands = 'medium track', track with high demands = 'high track').

A range of independent variables were included. Students in grade 5 were asked to complete part 1 of the CFT-20-R intelligence test (56 items), a non-verbal matrix speed test (Weiss, 2008). Other key independent variables included parental socio-economic status (SES), which was measured using the professions of the parents based on responses given in the parent questionnaire. The professions were coded using the International Standard Occupation Classification (ISCO-08) (Ganzeboom & Trieman, 2010). Each ISCO code was translated to a value on the Standard International Socio-Economic Index of Occupational Status (ISEI-08).

Other independent variables related to parental beliefs and activities in grade 5. (1) The achievement expectation of parents was measured for both mathematics and German[3] using three items adapted from Wigfield and Eccles (2000). The six-point rating scale ranged from 1 'not well at all' to 6 'very well'. (2) To measure parents' assessment of their self-efficacy in supporting their children (Niederbacher & Neuenschwander, 2017), a single item was used for both mathematics and German.[4] The six-point rating scale ranged from 1 'not well at all' to 6 'very well'. (3) Parental behaviour to cognitively stimulate learning was measured using seven items that we developed ourselves.[5] The six-point rating scale ranged from 1 'not true at all' to 6 'completely true'. (4) Number of class visits: parents were also asked about the number of times they visited their child in the classroom (rating scale from 0 to 5 times). This was a new item developed specifically for our study.

## 5b Findings

We analysed the questions using stepwise regression analyses after imputing for missing data (Table 10.1). While achievement in mathematics in grade 5 was a strong predictor of achievement in this subject in grade 6 (Model 1a), after adding a measure of intelligence to the equation (Model 2a), the gain in explained variance compared to the prior model was 1.4 percent. In Model 3a of Table 10.1, we removed intelligence from the equation and added parental SES,

Table 10.1 Gain in achievement in maths and German (multiple regression analyses)

| N=985 | Maths achievement in 6th grade | | | | German achievement in 6th grade | | | |
|---|---|---|---|---|---|---|---|---|
| | M1a | M2a | M3a | M4a | M1b | M2b | M3b | M4b |
| Maths achievement | .70*** | .64*** | .58*** | .70*** | | | | |
| German achievement | | | | | .67*** | .62*** | .56*** | .66*** |
| Intelligence | | .13*** | | | | .16*** | | |
| Socio-economic background | | | .08*** | | | | .12*** | |
| Parental maths expectation | | | .18*** | | | | | |
| Parental German expectation | | | | | | | .12*** | |
| Parental self-efficacy expectation maths | | | .00 | | | | | |
| Parental self-efficacy expectation German | | | | | | | .10*** | |
| Parental behaviour | | | | -.02 | | | | .09*** |
| Number of class visits | | | | -.03 | | | | -.02 |
| F, df$_1$ df$_2$, p | 940.4***, 1,983 | 496.7***, 2,982 | 265.0***, 4,980 | 314.9***, 3,981 | 813.5***, 1,983 | 441.7***, 2,982 | 241.2***, 4,980 | 279.8***, 3,981 |
| R$^2$ adjusted | 48.8% | 50.2% | 52.0% | 48.9% | 45.2% | 47.3% | 49.2% | 45.9% |

Legend: ***p<.001; **p<.01; *p<.05. df$_1$/df$_2$, degrees of freedom; R$^2$ adj, explained variances adjusted for the number of predictors.

parental expectations of achievement in mathematics and parental self-efficacy expectations in mathematics. The first two of these variables proved to be significant predictors of achievement in mathematics, while the third did not. Compared to Model 1b, the gain in explained variance compared to the prior model was 1.8 percent, indicating that the model explains more variation (52 percent) in the mathematics score than the previous model. These variables were removed from the equation, and Model 3a added cognitive stimulation by parents and number of classroom visits, neither of which proved to be predictors of achievement in mathematics.

A similar procedure was applied for German (see Models M1b to M1d in Table 10.1). Intelligence is a strong predictor of achievement (Model M2b), as are SES, parental expectations and parental self-efficacy (Model M2c). In this model, these parental variables explained 1.9 percent more of the variation in achievement gain in German than the previous model. In contrast to the pattern for achievement in mathematics, parental cognitive stimulation proved to be a predictor of achievement in German.

In summary, our findings show that parental SES, expectations of achievement and expectations of self-efficacy explained more of the variance in achievement in mathematics and German than either intelligence or parental activities. While it should be noted that the explained variances did not differ greatly, parental effects were stronger for achievement in German than for mathematics.

To test the effects on tracking, we conducted stepwise multinomial analyses to predict assignment to the low and high tracks compared to the medium track (Table 10.2). In Model 1, achievement in German and mathematics significantly predicted assignment to the low and high tracks rather than the medium track (Nagelkerke model fit: 38.6 percent). In Model 2, we added the intelligence measure to the equation and found that it was positive and significant. The Nagelkerke model fit was 39.2 percent, indicating a good fit between the model and the data. In Model 3, the variables capturing SES as well as parental achievement and self-efficacy expectations in mathematics and German were added. While SES did not prove to be a significant predictor of track assignment, each of the other two variables did – even when controlling for achievement in mathematics and German in grade 5: the Nagelkerke model fit increased from 39.2 percent in Model 2 to 48.2 percent in Model 3. Finally, in Model 4, the variables capturing parental cognitive stimulation and number of classroom visits were added. While the number of parental visits was significant, the Nagelkerke model fit decreased in comparison to the previous model.

The results show that achievement in mathematics and German in grade 6 (after controlling for achievement in these subjects in grade 5) and track assignment in lower secondary school are better predicted by parental SES, parental achievement expectations and parental self-efficacy expectations to support their children, than by intelligence. In contrast, parents' reported activities at home and in school are at times significant but explain less of the

Table 10.2 Multinomial Regression of school track assignment in 7th grade (Odds Ratios)

| N=985 | Model 1 | | Model 2 | | Model 3 | | Model 4 | |
|---|---|---|---|---|---|---|---|---|
| | Low track | High track | Low track | High track | Low track | High track | Low track | High track |
| German achievement | .39*** | 1.57*** | .40*** | 1.53*** | .44*** | 1.61*** | .38*** | 1.68*** |
| Maths achievement | .42*** | 1.2* | .44*** | 1.17 | .48*** | .96 | .42*** | 1.29* |
| Intelligence | | | | 1.01* | | | | |
| Parental socio-economic status | | | | | .99 | 1.00 | | |
| Parent maths expectation | | | | | .92 | 1.74*** | | |
| Parent German expectation | | | | | .51*** | .95 | | |
| Parental self-efficacy expectation maths | | | | | .79* | 1.32** | | |
| Parental self-efficacy expectation German | | | | | .75** | 1.07 | | |
| Parental cognitive behaviour | | | | | | | 1.0 | .74* |
| Number of parental class visits | | | | | | | .86* | 1.32*** |
| Chi², df | 411.9***, 4 | | 420.2***, 6 | | 549.1***, 14 | | 445.0***, 8 | |
| R² Nagelk | 38.6% | | 39.2% | | 48.2% | | 41.0% | |

Legend: Reference category: medium track. ***p<.001; **p<.01; *p<.05.

variation in the outcome variables. In line with Boudon (1974), our results confirm the primary and secondary effects of SES and parents' beliefs on academic achievement and school track decisions. In general, child-centred parent attitudes are better predictors of changes in academic achievement and track assignment than child-centred behaviour and intelligence, especially in the case of German.

## 6 Conclusions

This chapter summarises the main legislation regarding parental involvement in schools in Switzerland, where the shared responsibility of teachers and parents for the education of children is regulated by law. While the regulations pertaining to schools are very detailed, families are considered private and are thus weakly regulated by law.

Challenges in the cooperation between parents and teachers have motivated researchers to analyse the relationship between school and family using qualitative methods, especially for the French-speaking part of Switzerland. However, there has been little research as of yet into parental organisations at the community level. There is no systematic knowledge of how these organisations work and cooperate with school principals and teachers or whether they affect classroom processes and student learning. Longitudinal studies using quantitative designs and experimental studies are likewise rare. Similarly, few studies as of yet examine how family influences student behaviour in the classroom, student achievement, educational careers, vocational choices and the transition from school to work.

Although parents have a fairly strongly effect on student motivation and achievement, there are very few programmes available in Switzerland to teach parents how to support their children. Accordingly, more such programmes are needed, especially those that enable parents with a low income, a migration background, ill health or disabilities to support and assist their children. These would improve opportunities for all children in their education careers and support children who grow up in disadvantaged families. This should also be backed up with more research that shows how legislation and the provision of such programmes help children from disadvantaged families to grow up, find good jobs and become responsible members of society.

## Notes

1 www.expatica.com/ch/education/Education-in-Switzerland_100021.html
2 The term parent is used to refer to the person with the legal rights to raise a child.
3 Item 1: How well will your child perform in mathematics in this school year? Item 2: How well can your child learn something new in mathematics? Item 3: How well would your child fit in a profession that requires good mathematics skills?
4 How well can you help your child learn in the following subjects: Mathematics? German?
5 For example, I keep drawing my child's attention to new things. Or, I discuss with my child topics that they are interested in.

## References

Babel, J. and Lagana, F. (2016) *Der Übergang am Ende der obligatorischen Schule*. Neuchâtel: Bundesamt für Statistik.

Bader, D. and Fibbi, R. (2012) *Kinder mit Migrationshintergrund: ein grosses Potenzial*. Neuchâtel: Université de Neuchâtel.

Bäriswyl, F., Wandeler, C., Trautwein, U. and Oswald, K. (2006) Leistungstest, Offenheit von Bildungsgängen und obligatorische Beratung der Eltern. *Zeitschrift für Erziehungswissenschaft*, 9(3), 373–392.

Becker, R. and Hecken, A.E. (2009) Higher education or vocational training? Empirical test of the relational action model of educational choices suggested by Breen and Goldthorpe and Esser. *Acta Sociologica*, 52(1), 25–45.

Boudon, R. (1974) *Education, Opportunity, and Social Inequality: Changing Prospects in Western Society*. New York: Wiley.

Bourdieu, P. (1993) *Sozialer Sinn*. Frankfurt am Main: Suhrkamp.

Buff, A., Reusser, K., Dinkelmann, I. and Steiner, E. (2011) Unser kind ist gut in Mathematik! Zur Bedeutung elterlicher kindbezogener Kompetenzüberzeugungen hinsichtlich Selbstkonzept und Schulerfolg von Schülerinnen und Schülern. In: Hellmich, F., ed. *Selbstkonzepte im Grundschulalter. Modelle, empirische Ergebnisse, pädagogische Konsequenzen*. Stuttgart: Kohlhammer. 209–227.

Chartier, M. and Payet, J.-P. (2014) 'Comment ça se passe à la maison?' Troubles du rôle professionnel dans l'entretien enseignant-parents. *Revue Française de Pédagogie*, 187, 23–33.

Chartier, M., Rufin, D. and Pelhate, J. (2014) L'entretien enseignant-parents: un révélateur de l'hybridation des enjeux de la relation école-familles. *Éducation et société*, 34, 39–54.

Cusin, C. and Grossenbacher, S. (2001) *Im Schnittpunkt der Veränderungen: Die Beziehungen Schule-Familie in der Schweiz* (Vol. Trendbericht 4). Aarau: SKBF.

Ecarius, J., Köbel, N. and Wahl, K. (2011) *Familie, Erziehung und Sozialisation*. Wiesbaden: VS-Verlag.

Eccles, J.S. and Harold, R.D. (1996) Family involvement in children's and adolescents' schooling. In: Booth, A. and Dunn, J. F., eds. *Family–School Links. How Do They Affect Educational Outcomes?* Mahwa, NJ: Lawrence Erlbaum. 3–34.

Egger, J., Lehmann, J. and Straumann, M. (2015) Collaboration with parents isn't a burden. It's just a natural part of my work. Parental involvement in Switzerland. An analysis of attitudes and practices of Swiss primary school teachers. *International Journal about Parents in Education*, 9(1), 119–130.

Ganzeboom, H.B.G. and Treiman, D.J. (2010) *International stratification and mobility file: Conversion tools*. Amsterdam: Department of Social Research Methodology. Available at: www.harryganzeboom.nl/ismf/index.htm (accessed 15 Jul. 2010).

Giuliani, F. (2013) *Accompagner. Le travail social face à la précarité durable*. Rennes: Presses universitaires de Rennes.

Grunder, H.-U., Gross, N., Jäggi, A. and Kunz, M. (2013) *Nachhilfeunterricht in der deutschsprachigen Schweiz*. Bad Heilbrunn: Klinkhardt.

Herzog, W., Böni, E. and Guldimann, J. (1997) *Partnerschaft und Elternschaft. Die Modernisierung der Familie*. Bern: Haupt.

Hofstetter, D. (2017) *Die schulische Selektion als soziale Praxis*. Weinheim: Beltz.

Kern, M., Sodogé, A. and Eckert, A. (2012) Die Sicht der Eltern von Kindern mit besonderem Förderbedarf auf die Zusammenarbeit mit den heilpädagogischen Fachpersonen. *Schweizerische Zeitschrift für Heilpädagogik*, 10, 36–42.

Krumm, V. (1996) Schulleistung – auch eine Leistung der Eltern. Die heimliche und die offene Zusammenarbeit von Eltern und Lehrern und wie sie verbessert werden kann. In: Specht, W. and Thonhauser, J., eds. *Schulqualität*. Innsbruck: Studien-Verlag. 256–290.

Ludwig-Tauber, M., Wild-Naef, M. and Vouets, V. (2000) *Merkmale des Berufsfeldes von Lehrerinnen und Lehrern der 7. bis 9. Klasse*. Bern: Forschungsstelle für Schulpädagogik und Fachdidaktik, Universität Bern.

Moser, U., Buff, A., Angelone, D. and Hollenweger, J. (2011) *Nach sechs Jahren Primarschule. Deutsch, Mathematik und motivational-emotionales Befinden am Ende der 6. Klasse*. Zürich: Universität Zürich.

Neuenschwander, M.P. (2014) Selektionsentscheidungen beim Übergang in die Sekundarstufe I und in den Arbeitsmarkt im Vergleich. In: Neuenschwander, M.P., ed. *Selektion in Schule und Arbeitsmarkt*. Zürich: Rüegger. 63–98.

Neuenschwander, M.P. (2017) Lern- und Leistungszielorientierung beim Übergang in die Sekundarstufe I: Längsschnittliche Befunde zur Bedeutung von Belastungen und Erziehungsverhalten von Eltern. *Schweizerische Zeitschrift für Bildungswissenschaften*, 39(2), 321–336.

Neuenschwander, M.P., Balmer, T., Gasser, A., Goltz, S., Hirt, U., Ryser, H. and Wartenweiler, H. (2005) *Schule und Familie – was sie zum Schulerfolg beitragen*. Bern: Haupt.

Neuenschwander, M.P., Rösselet, S., Cecchini, A. and Benini, S. (2016) *Unterstützung von sozial benachteiligten, bildungsfernen Eltern bei der Berufswahl Jugendlicher*. Bern: Bundesamt für Sozialversicherung (BSV).

Neuenschwander, M.P., Vida, M., Garrett, J. and Eccles, J.S. (2007) Parents' expectations and students' achievement in two western nations. *International Journal of Behavioral Development*, 31(5), 474–482.

Niederbacher, E. and Neuenschwander, M.P. (2017) Wie elterliche Selbstwirksamkeitsüberzeugungen und Lehrpersonenerwartungen die Leistungsentwicklung von Grundschulkindern mit unterschiedlicher Familiensprache erklären. *Zeitschrift für Grundschulforschung*, 10(2), 88–101.

Niggli, A., Wandeler, C. and Villiger, C. (2009) Globale und bereichsspezifische Komponenten eines Elterntrainings zur Betreuung bei Lesehausaufgaben – Zusammenhänge im familiären Kontext. *Unterrichtswissenschaft*, 37(3), 230–245.

Schneewind, K.A. (1994) Erziehung und Sozialisation in der Familie. In: Schneewind, K.A., ed. *Psychologie der Erziehung und Sozialisation*. Göttingen u.a.: Hogrefe, Verlag für Psychologie. 435–464.

Schüpbach, M. and Herzog, W. (2009) *Pädagogische Ansprüche an Tagesschulen*. Bern: Haupt.

Schütz, G. (2016) *Stärkung der Auftretenssicherheit junger Lehrpersonen gegenüber den Eltern*. PhD. Universität Basel.

Schweizerische Koordinationsstelle für Bildungsforschung (SKBF) (2018) *Bildungsbericht 2018*. Zürich/Aarau: GdZ.

Steinert, B. and Maag Merki, K. (2009) Kooperation zwischen Lehrpersonen und Schulen. Empirische Analysen und offene Forschungsfragen. *Beiträge zur Lehrerbildung*, 27(3), 395–403.

Sternberg, R. J. (1997) The concept of intelligence and its role in lifelong learning and success. *American Psychologist*, 52(2), 1030–1038.

Weiss, R.H. (2008) *CFT 20-R. Grundintelligenztest Skala 2 – Revision – (CFT 20-R) mit Wortschatztest und Zahlenfolgentest – Revision (WS/ZF-R)*. Göttingen: Hogrefe.

Wigfield, A. and Eccles, J.S. (2000) Expectancy-value theory of achievement motivation. *Contemporary Educational Psychology*, 25(1), 68–81.

Yen, W.M. and Fitzpatrick, A.R. (2006) Item response theory. In: Brennan, R.L., ed. *Educational Measurement*. Westport: Praeger Publisher. 111–154.

Zweidler, K. and Haller, E. (2012) *Literatur-Recherche zur Empirie, Theorie, Philosophie und Praxis der schulischen Elternarbeit*. Zürich: Hochschule für Heilpädagogik.

# 11 United Kingdom

Divided and United Kingdom: parents in education and the common issue of inequality across the diversity of four nations

*Sarah Christie and Joanna Apps*

## 1 Introduction

This chapter commences its journey in the United Kingdom (UK) over half a decade ago and takes a critical promenade through the societally and politically derived expectations, responsibilities and roles of parents in their children's education amidst an ever inconstant political and social backdrop. Once inside the 21st century and up to the present time, an analysis of research trends and notable studies, including those by the authors, depicts a contemporary portrayal of this important area of research and concludes that there are worrying divisions between what research indicates is valuable, what government narratives suggest and the lived experiences of parents.

## 2 Overview of the education systems in the UK

In order to contextualise our discussion, we offer a brief overview of the education systems that exist in the UK, which comprises England and the devolved nations of Northern Ireland, Wales and Scotland. However, the minutiae of the diversity that exists between the education policies and systems of the four nations and which predates the political autonomy is beyond the scope of this chapter. We recommend a dedicated issue of *Oxford Review of Education* (edited by Furlong & Lunt, 2016) as an excellent overview of the contemporary issues. In this chapter, we take the liberty of drawing on research from across the UK, but we regret that for pragmatic reasons only the policy overview in terms of both the education systems and the role of parents in education is focused largely on that of England with briefer allusions to variations which exist elsewhere.

The UK education system can be understood as federalised and characterised by varying degrees of centralisation within each nation. In England, children must attend school from the term after their 5th birthday (though in practice almost all start at 4) and are required to be in education or training until age 18. In general, primary school is attended to age 10 and secondary from age 11 to 16, followed by two years in a school 'sixth form', further education college or in training. In other parts of the UK, the compulsory age varies only slightly but young people can leave school at 16 or just before without the English requirement to continue in education or training (Government of the United Kingdom, 2017). Across the UK, schools under central or local government control tend to open for around 190 days per year and 25–27 hours per week, with the potential for children to attend for 'a full day' if schools choose to offer breakfast or after-school clubs.

In England, the Conservative government of the 1970s initiated reforms under which the number and type of schools operating independently of the government (but not 'fee-paying') mushroomed. This trend continued under the Labour government of the 1990s and has resulted in a complex contemporary situation in which more than half of secondary schools and around 20 percent of primary schools operate without direct government control, the greatest number in the form of academies. Academies and other such 'free' and grant-maintained institutions are not required to follow the national curriculum (other than core subjects) and operate their own staffing and entry policies; yet they remain 'steered from afar', particularly by a requirement to align themselves with government assessment protocols. Elsewhere, Scotland operates a non-statutory curriculum, a 'modular' qualification system (Scottish Standard Grade and Highers), which is distinct from the UK system of General Certificates of Secondary Education (GCSEs, taken at around age 16) and Advanced Level qualifications (taken at around age 18) (Machin et al., 2013a). In addition, and unlike in England, Scottish local authorities (local government) adopt a prominent role in school management, effectively decentralising the system. Similarly, local authorities in Wales are integral to the governance and administration of schools (Power, 2016). The interpretation of the UK National Curriculum (introduced in 1988 under the Education Reform Act) was always considered to be distinctly progressive in Wales in comparison to the a more traditional approach in England. This distinction has become more pronounced since Welsh devolution, resulting in the development of a curriculum that is considered by many to be distinctly European in flavour and reminiscent of the child-centred approaches of Scandinavia. There are also some differences in the assessment schedules between Wales and England: children in Wales do not take standardised assessment tests (SATs) at 7, 11 and 14 and there is a greater emphasis on course and project work in the GCSE, A level and equivalent qualifications (Power, 2016).

Selectivity by academic aptitude is the most significant distinction between the education system in Northern Ireland and other UK states. Only Northern Ireland (and a small minority of English local authority areas) retains the selection and segregation at age 11 that was first instigated throughout the UK in 1945 but has since been abolished elsewhere (Machin et al., 2013a, 2013b). Additionally, Northern Irish schools still tend to be somewhat segregated by religion (Catholic/Protestant) and also boast the largest proportion of single-sex schools in the UK (Machin et al., 2013b).

Providing an appropriate education for children with special needs is a matter of great contention and current debate in the UK. As in other aspects of education, there are variations in terminology and approach between the nations. In England, just less than half of the children with the highest need (around 3 percent of all children) attend specialist schools and more than half attend mainstream (non-specialist) schools (Department for Education, 2017). In theory, mainstream schools have a duty to accommodate children with all but the most complex needs in their education provision. However, in practice the current situation is one of great disquiet: accusations abound of lack of funding, inadequate and inappropriate educational provision and claims that significant numbers of children have been left without school placements (e.g. Richardson, 2018). Many children with special educational needs fall within the burgeoning numbers of children who do not attend school and are home-schooled.

Across the UK, the greatest appetite for independent ('fee-paying') education is in England, where these schools are attended by around 7 percent of children, rising to 16 percent in the over-17s (Independent Schools Council, 2016). The overall figure reduces to around 4 percent in Scotland (Scottish Council of Independent Schools, 2016) and around 2 percent in Wales (Welsh Government, 2015), whilst the proportion of children attending independent schools in Northern Ireland is negligible. Outside the independent sector, education and teaching materials are free, and meals are free for children in the first three years of school in England and Scotland and for children from families with lower incomes across the UK. In most cases, families arrange and pay for their own transport to school, although some 'disadvantaged' groups of children are eligible for free transport.

## 3 Parental involvement in the UK

### 3a Terminology

Key politically driven changes in parents' involvement in their children's education began only half a decade ago, re-visioned within the strategic aims of each successive government and further splintered by the systematic differences between the four nations' approaches to education. This may, in part, account for the lack of consensus in appropriate terminology in use in legislation, practice and research. In this chapter, we have mainly adopted the term 'parents' involvement in education' as a catch all for the multi-faceted aspects of the interplay between parents, carers and even extended families and schools (and/or children's formal learning).

### 3b National legislative and regulative context

Until the 1960s, the parents' role in their children's education was relatively unacknowledged in legislation or policy in the UK. Parent-teacher contact was limited to annual or biannual 'parents' evenings' (parent–teacher meetings) and school reports on children's progress that were sent home. Parents' evenings themselves had only become established in the 1950s. These served primarily to inform rather than engage with parents and there was little or no acknowledgement of the role played by families in the educational progress of children.

In England, one of the first documents to acknowledge the critical role played by parents in children's education, a government-commissioned review of primary education known informally as the Plowden report, was published in 1967. A chapter of the report focused solely on parental participation, advocating increased agency in education for parents, increased teacher-led communication between parents and schools, and increased roles for schools in the community. The following decades consolidated this political change of direction: The Bullock Report (HMSO, 1975) reiterated the role of parental participation in supporting language and literacy development and progress, and the need for programmes, home visits, contact with schools and even the physical design of schools in supporting this. Under the Conservative government of Margaret Thatcher (1979–1990), two influential White Papers were published: *Better schools: A White Paper* (HMSO, 1985) and *The Education Reform Act* (HMSO, 1988). *Better Schools* proposed continued and increased home–school links and placed a duty on schools to explain their policies and work to parents, whilst *The Education Reform Act* promised parents more information about schools in the form of league tables and positioned parents firmly as consumers through the introduction of 'parental choice'. Schools were considered to be *accountable* to parents for the first time.

This move to accountability intensified in the 1990s, when the *Parents' Charter* (part of the wider *Citizens' Charter*, 1991) stipulated, as mandatory, not just parental rights to information about how their children was progressing but to school performance nationally. Around this time, Ofsted (the Office for Standards in Education, Children's Services and Skills) was established in England as a non-ministerial government department through which education services are inspected and regulated (Government of the United Kingdom, 2017). Similar bodies operate in other parts of the UK: Education Scotland in Scotland (Education Scotland, 2017), the Education Training Inspectorate in Northern Ireland (Education Training Inspectorate, 2017), and Estyn in Wales (Estyn, 2017). Parental involvement had, by 1994, been incorporated into UK schools' development plans (Ofsted, 1994) and by the following year it had been included in the inspection of nurseries and primary schools (Ofsted, 1995). Interestingly and, importantly, *intervention* in parental involvement in the UK grew most rapidly in the late 1990s to mid-2000s under the Labour government of Tony Blair. Reay (2008, 1) considered that this time was 'heralded as a period of increased parental power and growing choice within education' but which, despite this discourse, served instead to widen inequalities. It promoted the concept of 'parenting' and by adopting middle-class notions of 'good' parenting, pathologised and positioned working-class parents within a deficit model where their children are academically disadvantaged and not effectively supported in the home.

Reay (2008) also argued that the discourse of 'parent power' served as an effective mask for increasing shifts in responsibilities away from schools and towards parents. 'Parental involvement' had evolved to mean a wide range of activities (Desforges & Abouchaar, 2003) and many of these placed the onus on parents to proactively engage with their children's schools and learning. A less than subtle sign of this shift took the form of home–school agreements, set out in the White Paper *Excellence in Schools* (HMSO, 1997). These agreements were to take the form of a home–school contract, outlining responsibilities of schools and parents, respectively. Central to these was the parents' responsibility to be active in 'home–school work' such as supporting homework, providing materials, resources and support not just to their individual child but to the school (Crozier & Reay, 2005). The early 2000s saw further regulations around parenting contracts and parenting orders legislating for the prosecution, fining and ultimately imprisonment of parents whose children repeatedly truanted from school.

Today whilst policy continues to place an onus for parental involvement work on schools, there are indications that some schools see parents as failing to conform to their perceived responsibilities in this area and the agenda of the school. One extreme but not exceptional example are schools that grade parents in terms of how engaged they are with their children (Ough, 2016). The regulatory systems have also been accused of encouraging schools to demonstrate their parental involvement through visible events, which fail to take account of the evidence advocating parental support for their child's education in the home (Desforges & Abouchaar, 2003) nor the subtleties of cultural diversities in parenting and home learning practices.

Without the scope to detail the variations in historical aspects of parents' involvement in education across the four nations of the UK, we offer instead an overview of current directions. In Scotland there have been several legislative moves and a large-scale review of these during the first years of this century. The Scottish Schools (Parental Involvement) Act (2006) required local authorities to develop cohesive parental involvement strategies and considered that parental involvement is about supporting pupils and their learning. It focused on parents and teachers working together in partnership to help children become more confident learners. In 2012, Scotland also launched the *National Parenting Strategy*, which supports the Act and focuses on helping parents support all areas of their children's development. In 2017, the *National Parent Forum of Scotland* (NPFS, 2017) reviewed the impact of this legislation and considered the state of parental involvement across Scotland. They found a great deal has been achieved since the Act was passed. In particular, the Act outlines the central role played by parents' councils and these are now firmly embedded in many maintained schools in Scotland. In Northern Ireland, a political focus remains on overcoming historic sectarian divisions in communities (PTA UK, 2017) and parents are viewed as important consultation partners in this journey (Northern Ireland Assembly, 2017). However, there appears to be a lack of progress in developing parent–school partnerships beyond this focus. Finally, the Welsh government launched *Rewriting the Future* in 2014, which was the Education Minister's vision for reducing inequalities in education. The initiative foregrounded parents and families as pivotal to supporting children in their learning and recommends that practitioners at every stage of education work in partnership with the families to ease transitions and improve outcomes.

## 4 Existing research on parental involvement in the UK

As legislation and policy-driven practice in parents' involvement in education has evolved over the past half-century, social inequalities in educational outcomes have persisted (e.g. Clegg et al., 2016) and are comparable in many indicators across the four nations (Machin et al., 2013b). It appears that whilst education systems and approaches to parental involvement become increasingly distinct between the four nations, the UK remains united by social inequalities in education. Policy and practice are not resulting in benefits across the social spectrum: for example, research evidence has consistently indicated that parental socio-economic background is a strong predictor of educational outcomes, particularly progression to higher education (post-18). Parental education, social class and income are all associated with increased chances of a young person entering higher education; the likelihood of going to university for a state-educated young person whose parents have a high level of education (undergraduate and postgraduate degrees) is five times higher than for those whose parents have few or no qualifications (Jerrim & Vignoles, 2012).

Despite these stark statistics, the structural forces that hinder or facilitate the educational trajectories of children from different social groups are typically underplayed in favour of discourses of parental choice and individual agency, along with crude stereotypes of parental involvement. Such stereotypes are unfortunately reinforced in the media where caricatures of 'pushy' middle-class parents (Turner, 2017), relentlessly seeking special support and attention for their children and colonising resources to gain advantage, are positioned against examples of low income 'pyjama parents' (Hinsliff, 2016) who are portrayed as generally disengaged from their children's education and failing to 'respect' school rules and boundaries such as parking considerately in school grounds. These stereotypes belie a reality that is a much more diverse and diffuse.

In the domain of research in the UK on parents in education, funding during this century has supported some large-scale, longitudinal, largely quantitative work. These studies re-confirmed earlier international work that had established parental involvement as a valuable asset in children's educational outcomes and also began the work of unpicking what works best for whom and when. In respect of the youngest children, The Effective Provision of

Pre-school Education (EPPE) studies (Melhuish et al., 2008) considered the quality of the 'home learning environment' as one aspect contributing to a child's academic outcomes at entry to school. Their findings were and remain highly influential in driving the momentum for a focus on parental involvement in education, and sent a clear message that it is not who the parents are in terms of class or education level but what they actually do to support their children's learning that matters to children's outcomes. Likewise, a review paper, again funded by the government (Desforges & Abouchaar, 2003), elicited confident findings about the range of types of parental involvement, what activities were most effective in raising attainment and, significantly, how engagement with these activities was in part dictated by a range of factors relating to socio-economic status, maternal factors and ethnicity.

In the subsequent years, a number of studies and practice-based interventions attempted to do as Desforges and Abouchaar (2003) had recommended, and in 2011 Goodall et al., commissioned by the UK government, reviewed and recommended best practice for practitioners going forward. However, the intention to deploy successful practice as evidence of a successful practice strategy was not unanimously supported. Critics questioned whether 'synthesised' parental involvement could be created through interventions and whether this kind of involvement would be as effective as that which was 'naturally occurring' amongst the families who featured in the studies. Reviews of interventions to improve educational attainment through attempts to increase parental involvement have in fact found little hard evidence that this can be achieved (e.g. Gorard & See, 2013) with the authors advocating for more discerning investment in robust research that would deliver valuable evidence-based findings. The Education Endowment Foundation (EEF) (2015) recently concurred, stating that there is 'mixed and inconclusive' evidence of successful parental engagement interventions and particularly weak evidence on what works with disadvantaged families.

At the end of the last century, a critical voice emerged in the field, which challenged the accepted wisdom of some of the key policies. Carol Vincent, one of the inaugural voices in this arena, opened her influential 1996 book *Parents and Teachers: Power and Participation* by reflecting that policy narratives of 'parent power' and 'parental choice' may not reflect the lived experience of parents. Soon after, Crozier (2000, 2001) challenged the 'one-size fits all' approach to parental engagement work in many schools and later rejected the notion of the 'hard-to-reach' parent in favour of schools that are places for exclusion for many ethnic-minority families (Crozier & Davies, 2007). The latter conclusion was drawn as a result of a large qualitative project with 591 Bangladeshi and Pakistani parents living in the North East of England. They found that Bangladeshi parents, in particular, often had little knowledge of how their children were progressing in the British education system. However, all parents, whatever their socio-economic background, held education in high esteem and this related to their 'Islamic values' and wanting children to do better than they had.

In the years since Vincent, Crozier and colleagues first asserted their critical voices, classrooms in the UK have become even more culturally varied: recent statistics show that classrooms are recording ethnic-minority proportions of between 23 percent and 79 percent (Government of the United Kingdom, 2015). Our own work (Christie & Szorenyi, 2015) sought to capture the nature of the relationships with schools experienced by migrant parents from Eastern and Central Europe, 'in the shadow of one of the most hotly debated and contentious political issues of recent times: the Brexit referendum and the subsequent prospect of a Post-EU era'. We found that parents constructed their relationships with their children's schools around an extremely narrow range of interactions and activities and uni-directional channels of communication (parent approaching school). Issues of poor communication, struggles to understand and work with classroom practices, and concerns about marginalisation and exclusion also dominated the parents' experiences. Our study supported the findings of Sales et al. (2008) in their study of Polish students in London, particularly by highlighting an apparent lack of systematic approaches to working with migrant parents. In both cases, positive and negative experiences of interactions with the schools were mediated by the personal efforts or behaviour of individuals within the school rather than systems of good practice. It seems that in the ten years since Crozier and Davies (2007) wrote about the schools in their study as 'places of exclusion' for ethnic minorities, the same circumstances apply to the newest wave of migrants to the UK.

The majority of UK work on parental influence on the educational outcomes of children in disadvantaged families is focused on early years settings and primary schools. Less work has been carried out on the role and support needs of parents with children in secondary school and less still as their children make post-compulsory education decisions. There are important indications that parents remain influential at these educational stages and parental educational expectations and aspirations are considered to be prime targets for intervention to widen participation in higher education. However, there is a dearth of robust research to support policy and practice (EEF, 2015).

A scattering of UK studies exist that support the important role of parents in educational success at secondary and post-compulsory levels. Goodman and Greg (2010) found that after controlling for family background factors and prior attainment, young people in secondary school (age 11–16) were more likely to do well at GCSE (national examinations usually taken at age 16) if their parents thought they would go on to higher education (post-18). Strand (2007) found that, even after controlling for family background, young people aged 14 whose parents aspired for them to stay in school post-16 achieved higher scores on their Key Stage 3 tests (at age 14), placing them ahead of their peers by the equivalent of four terms of learning. Data from the Avon Longitudinal Study of Parents and Children (ALSPAC) indicated that mothers' aspirations for their children to go to university were one of four key factors that predicted children would stay on in full-time post-compulsory education (Department of Children, School and Families, 2008).

The aspirations of parents from poorer backgrounds with regard to post-18 education are frequently under-estimated, yet Goodman and Greg (2010) found that, at birth, 97 percent of parents aspired for their children to attend university and that the general parental level of aspirations at primary school and secondary school remained high for children of all backgrounds. In their study of families from disadvantaged areas in three cities around England, Kintrea et al. (2011) also found high aspirations amongst the parents for their children's progression to higher education, more than three-quarters wanted their children to go to university when surveyed when their children were 13 years old, and around the same proportion considered it important that their children obtained better qualifications than they possessed. Overall, these findings highlight not only the fluid and changeable nature of parental expectations and aspirations but also that both expectations and aspirations (of parents of all backgrounds) can be high without this always translating into reality.

A study of young people whose parents had never been to university (Passey et al., 2009) found that the probability of the students' progression to higher education was strongly linked to the level of support from parents to stay in education. With this in mind, the authors of this chapter (Apps & Christie, 2018) carried out a study aimed at better understanding the role of parents and the interactions and communications between young people and their parents in cases where the young people were considering their post-18 futures and the parents had not been to university. We found that decisions about post-18 choices were made in the context of the family, and parents were important to this even where students felt their parents were not able to relate specifically to information about higher education or when parents described themselves as 'baffled' by higher education information and application processes. Parents adopted the roles such as collaborators, time keepers, sounding boards and providers of emotional support. Raising the educational aspirations of both young people and their parents has been considered as a route into improving educational outcomes in those from disadvantaged backgrounds (Strand, 2007; Goodman & Greg, 2010; e.g. Castro et al., 2015). However, this study found no lack of aspiration towards higher education amongst the young people and parents we spoke to, although we found there to be a more dynamic view of the role of the young person in progression to higher education than is sometimes apparent in the research literature on parental engagement in general (Wikeley & Apps, 2015), with young people often leading decisions and the application process or in a more collaborative role with parents.

## 5 New research direction: school newsletters

We often – implicitly or explicitly – think of parental engagement in terms of the face-to-face contact between school staff and parents or other family members. Yet, in terms of reach and frequency, written messages between school and home are the more common form of communication. Weekly or termly newsletters, school-home diaries and other records, forms, progress reports, signs around the school, website information and texts convey a wide variety of information to parents but have relatively rarely been the focus of parental engagement research or guides for schools on 'best practice' in work with parents.

We undertook research in this area to consider, linguistically, the information contained in UK primary school newsletters (Apps et al., in progress). School newsletters present an opportunity to provide the same information to all parents and to support learning in the home, but the ability to do this rests on communication in newsletters being accessible to all parents, including those with English as an additional language, parents with a learning disability and others who may have lower levels of English language literacy. We analysed a random sample of 36 newsletters from state primary schools, accessed from websites, across the nine regions of England. We used four quantitative readability formulae to explore the average reading age required to understand the newsletters and assessed the use of text features known to enhance comprehension, such as bolding, bullet points and pictures.

The newsletters we sampled required an average reading age of 12–13 or 13–15 (depending on the readability measure used). They used a range of text features but the most common was underlining, which has been associated with reducing rather than enhancing readability (Obendorf & Weinreich, 2003). The readability findings suggest that newsletters were readable to a wide audience but not a universal one, potentially excluding readers with English as an additional language and lower levels of literacy. This tells us something important about the ways in which channels for parental engagement are not made fully equitable to the diverse range of parents in the UK's schools and how parental engagement may be conceived in relatively limited ways.

## 6 Conclusion

The political spotlight in the UK has never shone brighter on parental involvement in education. Despite divergence in systems and approach between the four nations, there is a commonality in political discourse of a notion of the parent who is heard and empowered with a responsibility to be involved in family learning. Many would argue, however, that in reality parents have become burdened by expectations for involvement that favour the majority middle-classes and pathologise and disempower groups whose cultural beliefs and ways of being do not match that of the educational system in which they and their children must function. In a society that is more diverse than ever before, and amidst significant social and ethnic inequalities, many parents are left unable to participate in a system where inclusion should be a priority but is not.

We caution against a blanket acceptance of the value of parental involvement in children's outcomes. Like Gorard and See (2013), we advocate for investment in high-quality research that can elicit strong evidence for which types of parental involvement under what conditions results in positive outcomes for children and young people. Most emphatically, however, we call for investment in critical and creative research that acknowledges and celebrates the increasing diversity of classrooms and that aims to support the effective engagement of *all* parents. Schools and colleges in the UK are facing their greatest ever challenge in the diversification of their parental engagement work in order to meet the needs of an ever-widening range of cultural, faith and ethnic groups. They require evidence-based strategies in order to be able to meet this challenge effectively. We hope, therefore, that a combination of quality, criticality and inclusiveness in research will inform policy and practice in such a way to finally have a reductive impact on the dire educational inequalities that persist.

## References

Apps, J. and Christie, S.L. (2018) First in family to attend university: Understanding and enabling the parent-child support relationship. *International Journal About Parents in Education* (IJAPE), 10(1), 59-69.

Castro, M., Exposito-Casas, E., Lopez-Martin, E. and Lizasoain, L. (2015) Parental involvement on student academic achievement: A meta-analysis. *Education Research Review*, 14, 33-46.

Christie, S.L. and Szorenyi, A. (2015) Theorizing the relationship between UK schools and migrant parents of Eastern European origin: the parents' perspective. *The International Journal about Parents in Education*, 9(1), 145-156.

The Citizen's Charter (1991) Available at: https://publications.parliament.uk/pa/cm200708/cmselect/cmpubadm/411/41105.htm (accessed 1 Oct. 2017).

Clegg, N., Allen, R., Fernandez, S., Freedman, S. and Kinnock, S. (2016) *Commission on Inequality in Education*. London: Social Market Foundation.

Crozier, G. (2000) *Parents and Schools: Partners or Protagonists?* Stoke-on-Trent: Trentham Books.

Crozier, G. (2001) Excluded parents: The deracialization of parental involvement. *Race Ethnicity and Education*, 4(4), 329-341.

Crozier, G. and Davies, J. (2007) Hard-to-reach parents or hard-to-reach schools? A discussion of home-school relations, with particular reference to Bangladeshi and Pakistani parents. *British Educational Research Journal*, 33(3), 295-313.

Crozier, G. and Reay, D. (2005) *Activating Participation: Parents and Teachers Working Towards Partnership*. Stoke on Trent: Trentham Books.

Department for Children, Schools and Families (DCSF) (2008) *Aspiration and Attainment Amongst Young People in Deprived Communities*. Analysis and discussion paper, December. London: The Cabinet Office, Social Exclusion Task Force.

Department for Education (2017) *Special Education Needs in England: January 2017*. Available at: www.gov.uk/government/statistics/special-educational-needs-in-england-january-2017 (accessed 1 Apr. 2018).

Desforges C. and Abouchaar, A. (2003) *The Impact of Parental Involvement, Parental Support and Family Education on Pupil Achievement and Adjustment: A Literature Review*. London: DfES Research Report 433.

Education Endowment Foundation (EEF) (2015) *Parental involvement-teaching and learning toolkit*. Available at: https://v1.educationendowmentfoundation.org.uk/uploads/pdf/Teaching_and_Learning_Toolkit_(July_12).pdf (accessed 20 Oct. 2017).

Education Scotland (2017) Available at: https://education.gov.scot/ (accessed 20 Oct. 2017).
Education Training Inspectorate in Northern Ireland (2017) Available at: www.etini.gov.uk/ (accessed 20 Oct. 2017).
Estyn (2017) Available at: www.estyn.gov.wales (accessed 20 Oct. 2017).
Furlong, J. and Lunt, I. (2016) Education in a Federal UK. *Oxford Review of Education*, 42(3), 249–252.
Goodman, A. and Greg, P. (2010) *Poorer Children's Educational Attainment: How Important are Attitudes and Behaviour?* York: Joseph Rowntree Foundation.
Goodall, J. and Vorhaus, J., with Carpentieri, J., Brooks, G., Akerman, A. and Harris, A. (2011) Review of Best Practice in Parental Engagement. London: DfE.
Gorard, S. and See, B.H. (2013) *Do Parental Involvement Interventions Increase Attainment? A Review of the Evidence*. Project Report. London: Nuffield Foundation.
Government of the United Kingdom (2015) Available at: www.gov.uk/eu-eea (accessed 28 Mar. 2015).
Government of the United Kingdom (2017) Available at www.gov.uk (accessed 25 Oct. 2017).
Hinsliff, G. (2016) Parents in pyjamas: Why the headteacher should stick to her guns. *The Guardian*, 29th January. Available at: www.theguardian.com/commentisfree/2016/jan/29/pyjamas-dressing-for-school-parents-children-headteacher-is-right (accessed 20 Oct. 2017).
HMSO (1975) *A Language for Life 1975 (The Bullock Report)*. London: Her Majesty's Stationery Office.
HMSO (1985) *White Paper: Better Schools*. London: Her Majesty's Stationery Office.
HMSO (1988) *Education Reform Act 1988*. Available at: www.legislation.gov.uk/ukpga/1988/40/pdfs/ukpga_19880040_en.pdf (accessed 17 Oct. 2017).
HMSO (1997) *White Paper: Excellence in Schools*. London: Her Majesty's Stationery Office.
Independent Schools Council (2016) *2016/17 Key figures*. London: Independent Schools Council Constituent Associations. Available at: www.isc.co.uk/media/3783/isc-key-figures-2016-17.pdf (accessed 1 Apr. 2018).
Jerrim, J. and Vignoles, A. (2012) *University Access for Socio-Economically Disadvantaged Children: A Comparison Across English Speaking Countries*. London: Institute of Education.
Kintrea, K., St Clair, R. and Houston, M. (2011) *The Influence of Parents, Places and Poverty on Educational Attitudes and Aspirations*. York: The Joseph Rowntree Foundation.
Machin, S., McNally, S. and Wyness, G. (2013a) *Education in a Devolved Scotland*. Report to the ESRC. London: LSE.
Machin, S., McNally, S. and Wyness, G. (2013b) Educational attainment across the UK nations: Performance, inequality and evidence. *Educational Research*, 55(2), 139–164.
Melhuish, E.C., Sylva, K., Sammons, P., Siraj-Blatchford, I., Taggart, B. and Phan, M. (2008) Effects of the home learning environment and preschool center experience upon literacy and numeracy development in early primary school. *Journal of Social Issues*, 64, 157–188.
Northern Ireland Assembly (2017) Available at: www.niassembly.gov.uk/ (accessed 20 Oct. 2017).
NPFS National Parents Forum of Scotland (2017) *Review of the impact of the Scottish schools (parental involvement) act 2006*. Available at: www.npfs.org.uk/wp-content/uploads/2017/05/Final-E-versionpdf.pdf (accessed 20 Oct. 2017).
Obendorf, H. and Weinreich, H. (2003) *Comparing link marker visualization techniques: Changes in reading behavior*. Proceedings of the 12th International Conference on the

World Wide Web (2003): 736–745. Available at: www.researchgate.net/publication/ 221024011_Comparing_link_marker_visualization_techniques_-_Changes_in_reading_ behavior (accessed 4 Apr. 2018).

Office for Standards in Education (Ofsted) (1994) *Reporting Pupils' Achievements*. London: HMSO.

Office for Standards in Education (Ofsted) (1995) *Guidance on the Inspection of Nursery and Primary Schools*. London: HMSO.

Ough, T. (2016) School grades its parents on their support of children's education. *The Telegraph;* 3rd December. Available at: www.telegraph.co.uk/education/2016/12/ 02/school-grades-parents-support-childrens-education/ (accessed 20 Oct. 2017).

Passey, R., Morris, M. and Waldman, J. (2009) *Evaluation of the Impact of Aimhigher and Widening Participation Outreach Programmes on Learner Attainment and Progression: Iinterim Report*. Slough: NFER.

Power, S. (2016) The politics of education and the misrecognition of Wales. *Oxford Review of Education*, 42(3), 285–298.

PTA UK (2017) Available at: www.pta.org.uk/blog/6789/Parents-in-education— what-can-the-rest-of-the-UK-learn-from-Wales (accessed 20 Oct. 2017).

Reay, D. (2008) Tony Blair, the promotion of the 'active' educational citizen, and middle-class hegemony. *Oxford Review of Education*, 34(6), 639–650.

Richardson, H. (2018) Special needs cash shortfall leaves thousands of pupils unplaced. *BBC News*. Available at: www.bbc.co.uk/news/education-43604865 (accessed 1 Apr. 2018).

Sales, R., Ryan, L., Lopez Rodriguez, M. and D'Angelo, A. (2008) *Polish Pupils in London Schools: Opportunities and Challenges*. Middlesex University Multiverse & Social Policy Research Centre.

Scottish Council of Independent Schools (2016) Available at: www.scis.org.uk/facts-and-figures (accessed 1 Apr. 2018).

The Scottish Schools (Parental Involvement) Act (2006) Available at: www.legislation. gov.uk/asp/2006/8/pdfs/asp_20060008_en.pdf (accessed 20 Oct. 2017).

Strand, S. (2007) *Minority ethnic pupils in the longitudinal study of young people in England* (LSYPE), University of Warwick. DCSF report RR002. Available at: webarchive. nationalarchives.gov.uk/20130401151715/www.education.gov.uk/publications/ eOrderingDownload/DCSF-RR002.pdf (accessed 30 Jun. 2015).

Turner, C. (2017) Pushy parents live vicariously through their children and become obsessed with 'trophy-hunting', deputy head warns. *The Telegraph*, 3rd January. Available at: www.telegraph.co.uk/education/2016/12/23/pushy-parents-live-vicariously-children-become-obsessed-trophy/ (accessed 5 Oct. 2017).

Welsh Government (2015) Available at: http://gov.wales (accessed 1 Apr. 2018).

Wikeley, F. and Apps, J. (2015) Parental involvement: possibilities and tensions. In: Dazzani, M.V., Ristrum, M., Marsico, G. and Bastos, A.C., eds. *Educational Contexts and Borders Tthrough a Cultural Lens*. Basel: Springer International. 311–322.

# 12 United Kingdom

Parental involvement: a feminist critical review from a UK perspective

*Miriam E. David*

## 1 Introduction

This chapter is a review of feminist research on parental and/or family involvement in education, especially in the UK. Using a feminist methodology, the focus is on collaborative research studies that have been concerned with the history, policies and changing practices of education (David, 2015; David, 2016a). Underpinning all these policies and practices has been a commitment to equality of opportunity, but this has to be deconstructed to reveal the hidden gender and sexuality norms.

By education, I refer not only to changing policies and practices with respect to compulsory schooling but also to early childhood or preschool education and lifelong learning, including higher education. The expansion of higher education has also altered the relationships within families, by the introduction of both research and pedagogies about parental involvement in education. There is clear evidence of the transformations of parenting and the development of explicit pedagogies, as well as research, on parental involvement within higher education. Gendered parenting has emerged as an analytical category in the changing contexts of patriarchy, sexism and what now is often called either 'hegemonic' or 'toxic masculinity', and 'everyday sexism or misogyny' (David, 2016b).

By parental involvement, I mean not only the different roles of mothers and fathers within their children's formal schooling but also in the wider processes of bringing up their children in diverse families (from single, lone, divorced or traditional two-parent married couples). Thus, some policy studies focus on what have sometimes been referred to as 'home–school relations' and the wider changing society, including higher education. Here, ideas about higher education institutions being *in loco parentis* have been transformed, as global higher education has expanded and the age of majority and adult responsibility has also changed.

Finally, by feminist, I am explicitly concerned to tease out the differences between notions of male and female, men and women, boys and girls or more broadly concepts of gender, sexual orientation and sexuality. In the 21st century, there has been attention to lesbian, gay, bisexual, transgender, queer and intersexual (LGBTQi) relations in policy and practice. This is by way of understanding the socio-cultural, socio-economic and socio-political contexts of learning to be and becoming the gendered and sexualised adults or parents that we are. These have also altered as notions of gender and sexuality have been legalised (David, 2016a).

Drawing on second-wave feminist theories and methods, whereby personal, sexual and familial experiences are seen as part of micro-political power relations, I consider the 'personal as political' (David, 2003). Historically, power relations were seen as being about the wider economy, political and social systems. As feminist theories developed in the academic world, arts and social science methodologies took on new approaches around standpoint theories (Harding, 2004). As a feminist, I write from my personal standpoint (David, 2016b). My notions of feminism have been transformed by my own learning both within higher education and through the wider socio-political environment and political activities. At heart, feminism is a political movement for socio-economic change: to transform men and women's lives in the direction of greater equality, fairness and social justice. In *A Feminist Manifesto for Education* I noted:

> First I present what is now known about gender and sexual relations through feminist, educational and social research, given the increasingly widespread international public debates about sexual abuse, bullying, harassment and overarching violence against women and girls (VAWG). Second, I draw from this voluminous research and policy-based evidence a series of pointers as to how we could develop a fairer, more equal and gender-conscious education for both boys and girls, including those with diverse sexualities and from ethnic, racialised, classed families. This 'manifesto' would ensure a society that is more socially just, safe and free from violence for both men and women.
>
> (David, 2016a, 1)

Historically speaking, feminists aimed to achieve their goals by considering how societies had been dominated by patriarchy, broadly interpreted as 'the rule of the father', or patriarchal rule, later to be mixed with notions of sexism and ideas about masculinity versus femininity (Morley, 2011). Indeed, in some feminist research, ideas about 'hegemonic' or 'toxic masculinity' have emerged in more recent times, as have ideas about misogyny, depending upon theoretical tendency. This is also because of the growing explicit understanding of the fundamental violence(s) embedded within our socio-economic and socio-political systems around VAWG, and gender-related violence (Mayes, 2017).

Changing the 'patriarchal rules' or how 'misogyny rules' is vital to creating a fairer, more equal and respectful society for both men and women, whatever their social class, ethnic or racial background or diversity, sexuality (LGBTQi) and (dis)abilities. I also take an 'intersectional' approach to the complex questions of parental involvement in education (Hill-Collins, 2000;

Mirza, 2009). This means looking at the ways that gender links with sexuality, social class, ethnicity or race (such as Black, Asian and Minority Ethnic, BAME). At the same time, I try to develop feminist pedagogies by which to counter the current deeply embedded power relations within our socio-economic and political systems, including VAWG. As feminists, we want to lead on the curriculum and pedagogical changes necessary to transform the power relations between men and women, boys and girls and the sexualised and often deformed people that we become, given the nature of globalisation and academic capitalism (Blackmore & Sachs, 2007).

## 2 Background to the socio-political and economic developments 50 years ago

During the 1960s and 1970s, under social democracy, a range of civil and human rights movements began to campaign for legal and policy changes in the direction of socio-economic equality. The women's liberation movement, later to become known as second-wave feminism, was part of a wider growing international movement of women seeking such changes in women's lives, together with other movements for social rights. The movement initially aimed for women's equality or equality between the sexes, in terms of the balance between employment and family life and what was also considered public and private lives. At the time, men had greater access to full-time work, whereas women, especially after marriage, were responsible for housework and bringing up children. This latter included working with schools on a daily basis. Gender equality was an unknown concept although there were many tendencies within this political movement.

Higher Education was expanded as a response to economic growth from the late 1960s (David, 2016b). This meant that there was also a growth of women as undergraduate students, although from a very low base. Initially, women also tended to cluster within teacher education, not always included in higher education but within teacher-training colleges (David, 2016a). As women began to enter the academy, first as students and later as academics, they began to develop the social research on which to base the demands for sex equality. Many have argued that the women's liberation movement emerged from students' movements (David, 2016a, 19–89).

Thus, there was a growing interest in developing new concepts and ideas by which to gather evidence about women's lives, especially as becoming or young mothers, inside and outside families. With the benefit of hindsight, 1970 proved to be a pivotal year for this kind of activist academic work (David, 2016a, 23). Hitherto, of course, there had been international women's movements, feminisms and campaigns about women's suffrage (David, 2016a, 42–84). Some have referred to these, during the 19th and early 20th century, as first-wave feminism, to distinguish the types of campaign and the women involved as, at that stage, there were few such women involved in the academic world, whether or not as feminists (Banks, 1985, 1986).

Many 21st century British policies and practices have seemed ignorant of the wider socio-economic and patriarchal context, even as recently as 50 years ago. To understand better how the idea of 'parents' or families in relation to the ever-changing education 'system' has come about, we need knowledge of educational policy developments, their economic and social contexts, and the voluminous research into mothers' and fathers' involvements and investments in education; how parents' choices, roles and responsibilities are constrained by sexual and social expectations, about who they are and what they should do; and, most importantly, what their sons and daughters should learn to be and do (David, 2014a).

## 3 A feminist analysis of parental involvement in education

My initial feminist study was to use Althusser's (1971) notion of the 'family-education couple' to develop a socialist-feminist analysis of the ways men and women were differently portrayed in legislation, policy and educational practices. 'The family-education couple' was useful to review parental involvement in education and parallel changes in the teaching profession, teasing out the histories of men's and women's roles with respect to education and schooling from the 19th century.

In summary, 150 years ago, there was no education 'system' as we know it today, and women as mothers, wives, daughters and sisters were not educated on a par with men – fathers, husbands, sons and brothers – whatever their social, religious or cultural family backgrounds. Whilst there were 'dame' schools – run by single women or spinsters for young children, equivalent to nurseries and infant schools today – they were not funded by the state. It was only in 1870 that the British state began to make schools available to the masses; when made compulsory, parents still had to pay fees, and as many could not afford this their children did not routinely attend.

Over the next 70 years, compulsory schooling was extended for different classes of family, although boys were afforded better opportunities than girls, in the expectation that they would become family 'breadwinners' and girls would become wives and mothers staying at home to care for the family. Indeed, a 'marriage bar' was imposed so that married women could not routinely work, particularly not as teachers (although this varied across the UK and London was something of an exception).

Towards the end of the Second World War, the framework for post-war education was set through the 1944 Education Act. A commitment was made to equality of educational opportunity, aiming to equalise children with family backgrounds of privilege and poverty or working class (or both). Although differences between boys and girls were not explicit, there were normative expectations that it was mothers' responsibility to make sure children were ready and able to benefit from education. Compulsory education was for all children between the ages of 5 and 15, and it was not until the 1970s that the school leaving age was raised to 16. There was very little state help provided for preschool children, so inevitably mothers had to stay at home.

It was another 30 years before any modest provisions were made for state nursery education for children aged 3 to 5, and it is still the case that they are not funded as generously as compulsory education. In 2016, the UK Government promised to pay for nursery costs for parents who worked more than 16 hours each, but this virtuous aim has not yet been realised. At this stage, the Government is committed to a mix of private and public resources.

It was not until the 1960s that women teachers got equal pay on a par with men, given the on-going assumptions that men were the breadwinners and women the stay-at-home mothers; other workers (in the UK) did not get equal pay until after the 1975 Equal Pay Act. This remains to be fully realised through the revised Equalities Act 2010. For 44 years there was a bipartisan political consensus on equality of opportunity, but the Education Reform Act (ERA) (1988) transformed this to markets and parental choice in education (David, 2014a).

From this brief historical synopsis, one can note that, until the 1960s, the concept of 'parental involvement in education' or 'home–school relations' (often used interchangeably) in the UK was obscured and appeared ungendered. Teaching was considered like other professions, and signs such as 'no parent beyond the school gate' were common occurrences in state (primary) schools. The British state did not pay very much attention to the differential roles that mothers and fathers played in their children's schooling and education at home.

However, an uncritical notion of mothers' involvement in bringing up children rather than involvement in both childcare and employment was at the root of this. Indeed, government social and educational policies laid the emphasis on women's economic dependence on men, or rather on husbands once married, and especially after having children (Land, 1976). It was in the late 1960s and 1970s that critical feminist studies of policies began to emerge, providing the basis for campaigns about changes to childcare and educational practices in the UK. Ann Oakley (1974a, 1974b) was one of the first to write a feminist critique of women and housework, although she did not explore childcare or childrearing.

## 4 Feminist research studies on mothers, parents and education from the 1980s

As I developed my academic feminist persona, I considered how parents might be involved in creating early childcare programmes for preschool children and for working mothers, especially. There was very little preschool provision for children aged 2 to 5: what was available tended to be for poor families, where mothers needed to work and/or their children were at risk. This was enshrined in the UK Nurseries and Childminders Act of 1948. Denise Riley wrote of the origins of this system in the Second World War (Riley, 1983).

Parents were not expected to be involved in this professional work of childcare provision and preschool education. The majority of mothers, however, were expected to bring their children up in the privacy of their own homes: childcare was seen as a private familial responsibility. Mothers, moreover, were routinely expected not be involved with paid employment. Indeed, far less than 10 percent of mothers with preschool children worked full-time.

Since the late 1970s, this proportion has slowly been transformed and the vast majority of mothers of preschool children are now involved in the labour market on a full- or part-time basis. This maternal employment has become the norm of necessity, given changes in the labour market and the economy towards neoliberalism and increasing rates of divorce or single parenthood. Nevertheless, there remains very patchy state or public provision for 3–5 year-olds, in a mix of nurseries and nursery schools. Nursery schools or classes are free but only for school hours, i.e. 9 am to 3.30 pm, rather than the hours of the working day. All provision for children under age 3 remains essentially private, despite the development of Sure Start schemes under New Labour in the early 21st century, for babies and toddlers. These have since been cut back by a Coalition then a Tory Government from 2010.

An important example of a shift in practice was the founding of the Pre-schools Playgroup Association (PPA), as a middle-class voluntary response to looking after preschool children in the late 1960s. This has subsequently become the basis for much private provision today, based as it is on voluntary 'parental involvement'. What is remarkable is that Caroline New and I used the conventional term 'parental involvement' and did not recognise its gendered nature, although we did immediately note that we meant maternal rather than paternal involvement (New & David, 1985, 120–121). We also considered a series of innovative projects to deal with preschool education and childcare, some of which involved fathers in their creation and establishment (ibid., 239–355). We also reviewed the notion of parenting and focused especially on what we called 'the changing rule of fathers' (ibid., 197–211).

Changing expectations for mothers to invest in their children's education were explored against a backdrop of changing state policies and educational practices, from the rise of the then so-called New Right (David, 1993). Phil Brown's concept of 'parentocracy' was an imaginative way to think about the rise of the notion of parents as a category in policy and practice (Brown, 1990). He also commented upon the shifts in official policies around that notion where a child's education is increasingly dependent upon the wealth and wishes of parents, rather than the ability and efforts of pupils, through educational privatisation under the slogans of 'parental choice', 'educational standards' and the 'free market' (ibid., 60–67, cited in David, 1993, 54).

Whilst Brown's comments are eerily prescient today, around 25 years on, what is notably absent from his essay is any reference to the changing gender expectations and gender norms embedded within the changing socio-economic and political situations:

> Despite their importance, feminist and critical perspectives remain marginal to our understanding of right-wing approaches to social and educational reforms [...] parents and education are indeed central issues on the public agenda, both in concert and in tandem. Given the ways in which the social sciences have developed and been incorporated into the public policy arena, these two will remain partial questions until such time as gender is also included explicitly on the agenda.
>
> (David, 1993, 221)

In a series of research studies, we began to explore the realities of mothering and schooling and the experiences of different groups of mothers in relation to education. Ros Edwards (1993) had presented her thesis on mature women students at university who were also mothers of school-age children. It was a very creative study, and led us to a rethink of our analytical framing of mothers' involvement in their children's education. Edwards became a key figure in sociological research on families and especially fathers' involvement in children's education (see for example Edwards, 2017). It also influenced work on the transformations of HE students from a young, usually 18-year-old (white male and middle-class) student to a more diverse population that would include mature women students, often mothers, and from diverse social-economic backgrounds (Crozier, 2015; Moreau, 2016; West & Lewis, 2018). Parental involvement in HE has thus become an important topic of study.

Jane Ribbens also explored mothers and childrearing in her doctoral thesis (Ribbens, 1994). She, too, has become a key figure in feminist sociology, especially around meanings of family life (see for example Ribbens McCarthy, Doolittle & Sclater, 2012). Together, we presented a sociological framework for the case studies that showed the constraints on mothers' other work, given their responsibilities for bringing up children. We looked at how women were mediators with schools, and how the boundaries between maternal authority and home–school relations were policed and maintained. We also explored the oft-hidden relations about women, mothers and post-school education. We looked at adult education policies and women, and the boundaries between ways of knowing in higher education or the university and 'the university of life'. We concluded that:

> given that we are all feminists, professionals, academics and mothers who are in mid-career, we have concentrated our attention on these issues of family-education relations. [...] We wish to concur and argue for the

view that *home* (sic) may be as subversive or as questioning of public knowledge and public agendas as public feminist activities. [...] Rearing children and constructing the understanding and knowledge on which we all come to 'know' the world is as importantly done by mothers in circumstances of their own choosing as it is done by constricting, controlling and confining public agendas which do not acknowledge these issues.

(ibid., 222–223)

Ribbens and Edwards (2009) went on to develop feminist methodologies on the family and diverse forms of education and policies, most notably *Feminist Dilemmas In Qualitative Research: Public Knowledge And Private Lives*. Edwards (2017) has undertaken a range of comparative socio-psychological studies, most recently of fathers from diverse racial backgrounds (Ribbens McCarthy, Edawrds & Gillies, 2002). This body of work has focussed on sociological understandings of family life, including step-parenting and other forms of guardianship.

Jane Ribbens and I also collaborated with Anne West to write about our study of how mothers chose secondary schools for their children (David, West & Ribbens, 2018). In this mixed methods study, we showed how it was the mothers who did the legwork of looking at appropriate schools, with fathers merely ratifying the decisions. As we argued:

We found that parents (or rather mothers, given that we interviewed predominantly women) do, on the whole, feel that this issue of secondary school choice has a certain salience, although they may see it only as between limited options, rather than being able to make decisive choices.

(ibid., 133)

Moreover, there are three features of schools that, taken together, can be positively identified as being the reasons for opting for a particular school – what we have called the three Ps [rather than the 3Rs] – the academic results or *performance;* the atmosphere/ethos or *pleasant feel* and the school's location or *proximity to home*. However, we do not wish to argue that any one of these three features/factors taken on its own is the *main* reason for choice, but these three best approximate the *amalgam* of factors that parents presented as reasons or factors associated with their "choice" for opting for particular schools.

(ibid., 136)

Finally, we recognised that

the differences between families, in those who find it hard to give it consideration and those who would not abrogate the responsibility, has more to do with the ways in which they are now positioned with respect to the educational marketplace than with their own wishes and desires. Diversity and choice in education has indeed created and exacerbated social and family diversity.

(ibid., 145–146)

Anne West has done comparative work on markets in childcare, and on 'helicopter parenting', both with Jane Lewis (Lewis & West, 2017; West & Lewis, 2018). Diane Reay published her thesis that took these former studies to a more critical and analytical stage (Reay, 1998). Reay has also been incredibly productive in this area, especially with Gill Crozier (2015) and most recently, she has been intrigued by her own working class background to consider how inequalities are maintained and reproduced (Reay, 2017).

With Diane Reay and Stephen Ball (2005), we aimed to show that the welcome expansion of higher education

has been accompanied by a deepening of educational and social stratification and the emergence of new forms of inequality. We have found that young and mature, male and female students confront very different degrees of choice and these are significantly shaped by their social class.

(Reay, David & Ball, 2005, vii–viii)

We considered parents' changing role in university choice, arguing that

many [students] [...] had reached the stage of separating out from their family of origin. [...] This appears to impact on how *they feel about the involvement of parents*, (my emphasis) which is often read as an intrusion rather than support. [...] They talk about anxious mothers, proud fathers, parents who are diffident and ill-informed in relation to education, and those who are confident and well-informed. [...] Sometimes there are glitches and ruptures.

(ibid., 69–71)

This has been extended into the notion of helicopter parenting (West & Lewis, 2018). Finally, with Amy Stambach, I reviewed a range of studies linking feminist theories with educational policies, especially considering 'how gender has been "involved" in family school choice debates' (Stambach & David, 2005). We concluded that this study

may not bring us any closer to breaking free of gender structures that constitute and construct our social lives, but it would at any rate enable more mothers, as parents and educators, to work collectively in the arena of education, contributing, in their myriad ways, to the development of future generations.

(ibid., 1653)

United Kingdom 171

## 5 Developing a critique of pedagogies of gender & sexualities

This research trajectory has led into thinking about how to develop future generations of parents through a pedagogical approach. With Pam Alldred, I explored how schools and parents today think about healthy sexual relationships and where they should be taught, either at home or at school, for boys and girls to learn to be the mothers and fathers of the future (Alldred & David, 2007). We explored young people's attitudes to sex and relationships education (SRE), as well as how teachers and other professionals approach teaching about these intimate social and sexual relations, and notions of future parenting as mothers or fathers.

> We found that such teachers feel inadequate to the question, especially without training and advice. And yet they are still not trained specifically to teach or deal with issues around gender relations [...] or bullying, sexual harassment and other forms of GRV [gender-related violence]. Moreover, there is nothing in the formal school curriculum or in the governance of schools that attends to questions of sexual consent.
> (David, 2016a, 35)

> Together with Pam Alldred and Barbara Biglia, we also developed a European Union (EU) funded study in the Daphne programme about how to train educational practitioners and professionals to challenge GRV for children and young people across six countries.
> (ibid., 36–37)

> This was part of a broader EU recognition of the problems of VAWG [violence against women and girls], through the Daphne programmes instigated in 1997 as a result of the murders of young schoolgirls in Belgium. The EU aimed to train education professionals. Ours was a successful bid in Daphne III in 2013 [...] Each of the four partner countries designed and delivered new training for practitioners [...] that is, through improved knowledge and understanding youth practitioners would be better able to, first, identify and challenge sexist, sexualising, homophobic or controlling language and behaviour, and, second, support children and young people (CYP), and know when and how to refer to the most appropriate services.
> (ibid., 36–37)

I contextualised this study with recent work on gender equality in education, reflecting on feminists' work in developing studies on parental involvement (ibid.). In the first part of the book I therefore presented

> the history of feminist scholarship on gender and education and, separately, that of work on campaigning for socio-political and legal changes in the position of women and girls. I also consider international debates from the UN and its educational arm UNESCO about how to effect

neoliberal change around gender equality in education. And I look at feminist campaigns for transformations in socio-political and economic contexts, especially across Europe.

(ibid., 15)

From the European study, I concluded that the underlying gender norms affect parental education and involvement in schools. Everyday (parental) practices are shaped by and, in turn, reproduce these structures reinforcing gender inequality, while at the same time emphasizing there is always the potential to unsettle these structures, especially through sensitive education (ibid., 157). These studies led me to consider what should be included in *a feminist manifesto* from an educational viewpoint, enhancing both paternal and maternal involvements. I argue that

> gender equality cannot have been achieved, if VAWG [violence against women and girls] and GRV [gender-related violence] remain unresolved questions. What kind of equality have we achieved if women and girls, along with young boys, remain subject to sexual abuse and harassment, bullying, rape and violence? […] Any programme of change would need to tackle these […] through a *systematic form of lifelong learning, through families, communities, schools* and higher education. *A radically new social philosophy or sociological approach is needed towards what it means to be fully human*, regardless of one's gender or sexuality.

(ibid., 158–160)

My final point is that

> we need to transform the way misogyny rules to ensure that women and girls are afforded dignity and respect in all aspects of their/our lives. A proper education about respect and dignity in appropriate relationships between men and women must surely be the best place to start.

(ibid., 180)

## 6 Conclusions

In this short chapter, it is difficult to do justice to the depth and range of studies on education policies and parental involvement in the UK alone. Whilst the British policy context has moved from a social democratic to a neoliberal one, making responsibilities ever more individualistic rather than collective, there are important studies providing critical perspectives on this ever-changing situation. Feminist studies of parental involvements in education have been incredibly generative of a range of sociological and psychosocial theories about meanings of family and family life, as well as specific focuses on particular parents including Black, Asian and Minority Ethnic parents (BAME), Lesbian, Gay, Bisexual, Transgender, Queer and intersexual (LGBTQi) and diverse sexualities, fathers and different cultures and changing socio-economic and political contexts. These changes also allow for different gender identities to emerge, including transitioning, and for this to become a topic of consideration in schools and higher education. More individualistic notions of responsibilities amongst students, academics and administrators have become the norm in neoliberalism. This is in a situation of 'academic capitalism' whereby academic institutions are inevitably intertwined with the advanced or global economies of which they are increasingly and inevitably a part (Slaughter & Rhodes, 2004).

All of these studies are now reflexive, considering the changing world of which we are now inevitably a part, and how we can use our knowledge and understandings to try to transform policies and practices in the direction of social and gender equalities and justice, despite the continuing context of VAWG and GRV. The implications of this are that knowledge is distorted and deformed and, until it is transformed, we will not have gender equalities in education or family lives let alone adequate and consensual parental involvements.

## References

Alldred, P. and David, M. (2007) *Get Real About Sex. The Politics and Practice of Sex Education*. London: McGrawHill: Open University Press.

Althusser, L. (1971) Ideology and ideological state apparatuses. In: Althusser, L., ed. *Lenin and Philosophy and Other Essays*. London: New Left Books 13.

Banks, O. (1985) *The Biographical Dictionary of British Feminists. Vol 1: 1800-1930*. New York: New York University Press.

Banks, O. (1986) *Becoming A Feminist. The Social Origins of First Wave Feminism*. Brighton: Wheatsheaf Books.

Blackmore, J. and Sachs, J. (2007) *Performing and Reforming Leaders: Gender, Educational Restructuring, and Organizational Change*. Albany: State University of New York Press.

Brown, P. (1990) The third wave: Education and the ideology of parentocracy. *British Journal of the Sociology of Education*, 11(1), 65–85.

Crozier, G. (2015) Middle class privilege and education. *British Journal of Sociology of Education*, 36(7), 1115–1123.

David, M.E. (1993) *Parents, Gender & Educational Reform*. Cambridge: Polity Press.

David, M.E. (2003) *Personal and Political: Feminisms, Sociology and Family Lives*. London: Trentham Books.

David, M.E. (2014) Preface to parents. In: McQueen, H., ed. *Roles, Rights, and Responsibilities in UK Education: Tensions and Inequalities*. London: Palgrave Macmillan. 79–81.

David, M.E. (2016a) *A Feminist Manifesto for Education*. Cambridge: Polity Press.

David, M.E. (2016b) *Reclaiming Feminism: Challenging Everyday Misogyny*. Bristol: Policy Press.

David, M.E., West, A. and Ribbens, R. (2018/1994) *Mother's Intuition? Choosing Secondary Schools*. London: Routledge Revival series.

Education Reform Act 1988, c.40 Available at: https://www.legislation.gov.uk/ukpga/1988/40/contents (accessed 01 Jul. 2017).

Edwards, R. (1993) *Mature Women Students: Separating Or Connecting Family and Education*. London: Taylor & Francis.

Edwards, R. (2017) Partnered fathers bringing up their mixed-/multi- race children: An exploratory comparison of racial projects in Britain and New Zealand. *Identities: Global Studies in Culture and Power*, 24(2), 177–197.

Harding, S.G. (2004) *The Feminist Standpoint Theory Reader: Intellectual and Political Controversies*. London: Routledge.

Hill-Collins, P. (2000/1990) *Black Feminist Thought: Knowledge, Consciousness and the Politics of Empowerment*. London: Routledge.

Land, H. (1976) Women: Supporters or Supported? In: Barker, D.L. and Allen, S., eds. *Sexual Divisions and Society: Process and Change*. London: Tavistock. 118–133.

Lewis, J. and West, A. (2017) "Learning from others": English proposals for early years' education and care reform and policy transfer from FRANCE and the Netherlands, 2010-2015. *Social Policy and Administration*, 52(3), 677–689.

Mayes, E. (2017) Review symposium: Violence, liberations, ambivalences: Miriam David's 'a feminist manifesto for education'. *British Journal of the Sociology of Education*, 38(7), 1066–1080.

Mirza, H.S. (2009) *How Black Women Succeed and Fail*. London: Routledge.

Moreau, M.-P. (2016) Regulating the student body/ies: University policies and student parents. *British Educational Research Journal*, 41(3), 505–519.

Morley, L. (2011) Misogyny posing as measurement: Disrupting the feminisation crisis discourse. *Contemporary Social Science*, special issue: Challenge, change or crisis in global higher education, 6(2), 223–237.

New, C. and David, M. (1985) *For the Children's Sake: Making Childcare More than Women's Business*. Harmondsworth: Penguin.

Oakley, A. (1974a) *The Sociology of Housework*. London: Martin Robertson.

Oakley, A. (1974b) *Housewife*. Harmondsworth: Penguin.

Reay, D. (1998) *Class Work: Mothers' Involvement in Children's Schooling*. London: University College Press.

Reay, D. (2017) *Miseducation: Inequality, Education and the Working Classes*. Bristol: Policy Press.

Reay, D., David, M. and Ball, S.J. (2005) *Degrees of Choice: Social Class, Race and Gender in Higher Education*. London: Trentham Books.

Ribbens, J. (1994) *Mothers and Their Children: A Feminist Sociology of Childrearing*. London: Sage.

Ribbens, J. and Edwards, R., eds. (2009) *Feminist Dilemmas in Qualitative Research: Public Knowledge and Private Lives*. London: Sage.

Ribbens McCarthy, J., Doolittle, M. and Sclater, S.D. (2012) *Understanding Family Meanings: A Reflective Text*. Bristol: Policy Press.

Ribbens McCarthy, J., Edwards, R. and Gillies, V. (2002) *Making Families: Moral Tales of Parenting and Step- Parenting*. Durham: Sociology Press.

Riley, D. (1983) *War in the Nursery: Theories of Mother and Child*. London: Virago.

Slaughter, S. and Rhodes, G. (2004) *Academic Capitalism and the New Economy: Markets, State and Higher Education*. Baltimore, MD and London: John Hopkins University Press.

Stambach, A. and David, M. (2005) Feminist theory and educational policy: How gender has been "involved" in family school choice debates. *Journal of Women in Culture & Society*, 30(2), 1633–1659.

West, A. and Lewis, J. (2018) *'Helicopter Parenting' and 'Boomerang Children': How Parents Support and Relate to Their Student and Co-Resident Graduate Children*. London: Routledge.

# 13 Home-based parental involvement and parental perception of schools
## A cross-country analysis[1]

*Paulína Koršňáková and Miroslav Štefánik*

## 1 Introduction

The degree to which parents are involved in the education of their children varies widely, governed by different customs and rules across European countries. Eurydice (1997) provided the first comparative overview on the diversity of national situations and the convergence found in Europe on this subject, as well as detail on the initiatives and measures taken to involve parents in compulsory education matters and the powers that are given to parents in the various participatory bodies. How do these realities impact the school attainment of students across European countries? The experiences of many of these countries are represented in other chapters of this book, but in this chapter, we aim to identify, describe and analyse the impact of parental involvement on student outcomes in mathematics in relation to other factors that are known and supposed to influence students' achievement. To accomplish this, we exploited the context questionnaires framework (Mullis & Martin, 2013) used in the International Association for the Evaluation of Educational Achievement's Trends in International Mathematics and Science Study (TIMSS; for details see www.iea.nl/timss), and the resulting survey response data from the TIMSS *Home Questionnaire: Early Learning Survey* (TIMSS & PIRLS International Study Center, 2014) collected in 2015. TIMSS collects data at both 4th and 8th grade. Here, we explored the differing associations between parental involvement and student outcomes only at 4th grade. We focused on European countries where comparable TIMSS 2015 data on parents' support for and attitudes towards mathematics and science, and their engagement with their child's school and perceptions of school performance, were available for at least 50 percent of students. There were 18 such countries: Bulgaria, Croatia, Cyprus, Czech Republic, Denmark, Finland, France, Germany, Hungary, Ireland, Italy, Lithuania, Poland, Portugal, Slovak Republic, Slovenia, Spain and Sweden.

## 2 Literature review

### 2a Comparative research

The way in which parental involvement is conceptualised and the body of contemporary research into the topic often differ substantially in approaches, methods and perspectives. Nonetheless, parental support is reported to have strong influence on children's educational outcomes (Mullis & Martin, 2013). Parental involvement has been positively linked to academic success and students' general enjoyment of school, and their behaviour, attendance and attitudes towards learning by Borgonovi and Montt (2012), who explored the OECD PISA 2009 data in relation to reading.

International large-scale assessments of education provide rich comparative data. Such assessments focus on student achievement by administering objective tests to a sample of students who have been selected as representative of national populations, but they also collect diverse background information about the contextual factors that may affect learning. The contexts covered by the IEA's TIMSS framework (Mullis & Martin, 2013) range from the national and community contexts, home contexts, and school and classroom contexts, to student characteristics and attitudes towards learning. Context questionnaires grounded in this analytical framework are administered to school principals, teachers, students, and, in some cases, the parents of participating students.

> Because the primary purpose of the context questionnaires is to identify factors that may contribute to differences in achievement within and between countries, the framework focuses on topics in educational research found to be related to achievement across a variety of settings and contexts.
> (Hooper, 2016, 2.5)

This approach resulted in a variety of scales and variables available in the TIMSS 2015 data that were suitable either for measuring of parental involvement or as a control variable.

### 2b Measuring parental involvement

Recognising that parents, guardians or other caregivers and the general home environment may influence children's success in school, and in order to better understand the effects of the home environment, TIMSS 2015 was designed to gather data on four distinct areas, which are outlined in the context questionnaires framework (Mullis & Martin, 2013): (1) home resources for learning; (2) early literacy, numeracy, and science activities; (3) language(s) spoken in the home; and (4) parental educational expectations and academic socialisation.

'Home resources for learning' encompasses essential socioeconomic characteristics of the parents, such as their education level and occupation (serving as proxy variables for the cultural capital of students), together with 'home supports for learning', with an emphasis on educational activities.

According to Punter et al. (2016), within the general framework of parental involvement, helping with homework and early learning activities are aspects of home-based parental involvement. While socioeconomic characteristics are not malleable, 'parental involvement is seen as one of the most malleable factors of the student's home situation, which makes it a relevant subject for schools, educational policies, and research' (Punter, Glas & Meelissen, 2016, ix). Punter et al. (2016, xi) aimed to 'establish whether there were any cultural differences in the measurement of parental involvement' in the data collected by the IEA's 2011 Progress in Reading Literacy Study (PIRLS). Their analyses showed that the reliability of indicators related to early literacy activities and help with homework met the minimum standard for a survey of 0.70 within all countries and seemed 'to work identically in a large number of countries and cultures'. Since the TIMSS 2015 home questionnaire (TIMSS & PIRLS International Study Center, 2014; Punter et al., 2016, 91) was based on home questionnaire used in PIRLS 2011, we found these results encouraging.

TIMSS 2015 collected data about homework from responses to the following questions from the home questionnaire (TIMSS & PIRLS International Study Center, 2014): 'Approximately, how often does your child do homework?' and 'How often do you or someone else in your home do the following things?', where the child is asked to report about their homework or parental help with homework.

Working with PIRLS 2011 data, Punter et al. (2016) found that parental involvement in early literacy activities with their child had a small, but positive influence on student achievement. Borgonovi and Montt (2012, 19) pointed out that the

> activities that treat letters and words in isolation (e.g., playing with alphabet toys or writing words) are not consistently associated with students' reading enjoyment; these activities may help children recognize and understand those specific words and letters, but may not convey the importance of words or of the oral and written language.

Howie and Chamberlain (2017, 6) undertook a PIRLS 2011 follow up study and found that the language of instruction had a considerable effect: 'students who frequently spoke the test (equal to the instruction) language at home scored higher on average than students who sometimes or never did'. Language(s) spoken in the home can influence learning mathematics and science in school, because students that learn the concepts and content of the mathematics and science curricula through a second or third language may achieve lower results. In previous research, belonging to a language group has not generally been considered as an aspect of parental involvement, and thus in our analyses we only controlled for this additional factor in the full model.

The TIMSS 2015 contextual framework (Mullis & Martin, 2013, 67) that shaped the TIMSS home questionnaire focused on parents' educational expectations and academic socialisation. Here, academic socialisation is seen as 'the process of stressing the importance of education, and includes parents and children talking about the value of education, discussing future educational and occupational expectations for the child, and helping children draw links between schoolwork and its real-world applications' (Hill & Tyson, 2009; Taylor, Clayton & Rowley, 2004). This is well aligned with the notion that academic socialisation is supposed to be subject-specific (Hong et al., 2010). Parents pass on the values and opinions that they have about education to their children (see for example, Alexander, Entwisle & Olson, 2007; Green et al., 2007; Bowles, Gintis & Groves, 2009).

Borgonovi and Montt (2012, 19) distinguished between academically and non-academically oriented parental involvement: 'Parents who talk to their children about school and discuss how they are doing in school not only supervise their children's school lives, but also signal the importance of succeeding in school'.

Cabus and Ariës (2014) focused on parental involvement in the education of their children by focusing on its effects on student achievement in compulsory education. They defined parental involvement as 'parents who create a school supportive home climate by (1) actively involving in homework or study, and (2) elementary communication on education with the child' (Cabus & Ariës, 2014, 21), observing 'that academic performance is rooted in a school-supportive home climate' (ibid., 22).

## 3 Data, variables and estimation

TIMSS considers the processes and outcomes of education and draws on the notion of 'opportunity to learn' in order to understand the linkages between what policy requires, what is taught in schools, and what students learn. It has a strong empirical basis, and relies mainly on cross-sectional and longitudinal non-experimental designs, with data collection through sample survey methods.

### 3a Description of available data

The target population of TIMSS 2015 is 4th graders or, more accurately, 'all students enrolled in the grade that represents four years of schooling counting from the first year of ISCED Level 1, providing the mean age at the time of testing is at least 9.5 years'. TIMSS employs a two-stage random sample design, with a sample of schools drawn as a first stage and one or more intact classes of students selected from each of the sampled schools as a second stage. 'Intact classes of students are sampled rather than individuals from across the grade level or of a certain age because TIMSS pays particular attention to students' curricular and instructional experiences, and these typically are organised on a classroom basis' (LaRoche, Joncas & Foy, 2016, 3.1). Each education system participating in TIMSS defines its own national target population, determines the sample size and stratification plan, and applies the TIMSS sampling methods in order to achieve a nationally representative sample of schools and students. The resulting sample usually comprises around 4,500 students in just over 150 schools per country. When sampling has been completed and all data collected, the population coverage and school and student participation rates are documented, and appropriate sampling weights constructed for use in analysing and reporting the results. Here, the major focus at the system level is on the average student outcome in mathematics and, as a starting point, we used the TIMSS 2015 data to establish the landscape of average achievement in mathematics across Europe (Figure 13.1).

The TIMSS home questionnaire (TIMSS & PIRLS International Study Center, 2014) was completed by fourth grade students' parents, guardians or caregivers (throughout this chapter we refer to these respondents as 'parents', and indicate the number of responses used in our models). It was only introduced in the 2015 cycle of TIMSS as an addition to the questionnaires routinely given at the 4th grade to students, teachers, school principals, and curriculum specialists in the previous cycles of TIMSS. It is important to stress that this study was not a study of parents. Parents that responded to the TIMSS 2015 home questionnaire were the parents of randomly sampled students attending the 4th grade of their schooling in 2015. Low response rates prevented us from including parental data from Norway and the Netherlands.

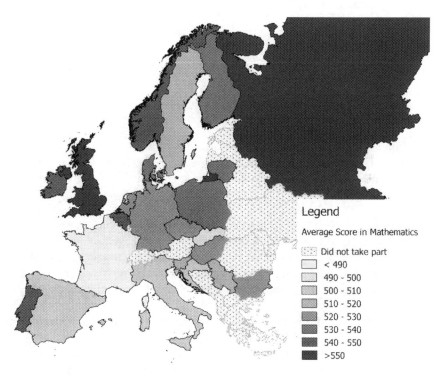

*Figure 13.1* Average student outcome in mathematics for European countries that participated in TIMSS 2015

Source: Authors' calculations using TIMSS 2015 data.

Note: UK based on the average for England and Northern Ireland; BE based on the figure for the Flemish part.

The TIMSS home questionnaire asked questions about preparations for primary schooling, including preschool attendance and literacy and numeracy-oriented activities undertaken in the home before the child began school. In addition to these early learning experiences, a brief evaluation of school readiness, and overview of the learning activities in and outside the school, parents provided their views on the quality of the school. Parents also shared their reading practices, provided their opinions on the value of education and the role of mathematics and science, answered questions about home resources, and provided information about their highest level of education and employment status.

Many of the TIMSS 2015 context questionnaire items were developed to be combined into scales measuring a single underlying latent construct. For reporting, the scales were constructed using item response theory (IRT) scaling methods. The procedures for constructing, interpreting, and validating scales based on responses to the student, teacher, school, and home questionnaires are provided in *Methods and Procedures in TIMSS 2015* (Martin, Mullis & Hooper, 2016). We used these ready-made scales and also created additional indicators of parental involvement based on our own analyses of the TIMSS responses.

All the TIMSS 2015 reference materials and reports prepared by the TIMSS & PIRLS International Study Center at Boston College are freely available at https://timssandpirls.bc.edu/timss2015/and the TIMSS data may be downloaded from the IEA's Data Repository at www.iea.nl/data.

### 3b Variables referring to parental involvement

The TIMSS 2015 Assessment Framework (Mullis & Martin, 2013) identified the main factors influencing the average student outcome in mathematics. Out of these, we selected six main explanatory variables to represent parental involvement:

(1) The TIMSS 'home resources for learning' (HRL) scale based on students' and parents' responses concerning the availability of five resources: books (student's response); children's books (parents' responses); home study support (Internet connection, own room); highest level of education; and highest level of occupation of either parent (Martin, Mullis & Hooper, 2016, 15.33).
(2) The 'help with homework' scale constructed as the sum of self-reported assessments: asking + helping + reviewing homework by parents, weighted by the actual frequency of receiving homework.
(3) In order to analyse more general supervision signalling the importance of school attendance, we used student responses to the question: 'About how often are you absent from school?' from the TIMSS 2015 student questionnaire (Foy, 2017), and created a review of 'school attendance'.
(4) The TIMSS 'early literacy and numeracy activities' before beginning primary school (ELN) scale based on parents' reported frequency of doing

16 activities covering various early literacy, numeracy, and science-related tasks (Martin, Mullis, Hooper, 2016, 15.28).
(5) The 'parental attitude towards mathematics and science' scale, a new scale developed and included in TIMSS 2015, designed to assess parents' attitudes towards science, technology, engineering and mathematics (STEM) fields (Martin, Mullis, Hooper, 2016, 15–48). We used this scale as a proxy of 'parental educational expectations and (the subject-specific) academic socialisation'.
(6) The 'parents' perceptions of school performance' (PSP) scale, based on parents' responses to eight statements seeking parents' opinions about the safety of the school environment, the care provided to their child, and the opportunities available for school-based parental involvement. For the last two categories, parents were invited to express their satisfaction on a Likert scale in response to the following statements: 'My child's school does a good job including me in my child's education', and 'My child's school does a good job informing me of his/her progress'.

Education happens in complex contexts, and we have already indicated that other factors may have an impact on student achievement in addition to the variables we selected to model parental involvement (for example, the variable language spoken at home). The IEA's TIMSS framework (Mullis & Martin, 2013) elaborates on previous research, and we used this resource to create a list of additional variables available in the TIMSS 2015 database that represent factors at a school level (school location; emphasis on academic success; composition by student socioeconomic background; safe, orderly, and disciplined; and instruction affected by mathematics resources shortages) and student level (gender; language spoken at home; immigrant background; preschool attendance; student's sense of school belonging; and student bullying). This enabled us to control for the context beyond the factor of parental involvement.

### 3c Estimation strategy

Our aim was to identify and present those aspects of parental involvement that relate to the student outcome in mathematics. Where TIMSS 2015 data from the home questionnaire early learning survey were available, we explored how these associations differed among the European countries.

To explore their associations with the student outcome in mathematics, we estimated a linear regression model. Student outcome in mathematics was used as the dependent variable, with the six variables referring to parental involvement introduced previously used as independent variables, without further controlling variables. The further factors we identified as influencing the student outcome in mathematics were used in our full model as additional control variables.

We assumed that, where the coefficients estimated in the parental involvement model lose their statistical significance in the full variant of the model, the association is driven by some further context relation, potentially linked to one of the additional variables. However, when we compared the results from the two models to identify any changes, we found nothing of significance.[2] In the following section, we only report the coefficients related to the parental involvement variables estimated under the full model (these are not sensitive to adding further controlling variables).

## 4 Results

We used a linear regression model to estimate the association between the student outcome in mathematics and six selected variables of parental involvement (the PI variables). In estimating this association, we control for further characteristics of wider school, classroom and home context of pupils, as identified in the theoretical framework behind the design of the TIMSS questionnaires (Mullis & Martin, 2013). We estimated the regression coefficients, after controlling for further context variables, for each of the six PI variables to establish their association with the student outcome in mathematics. We identified no significant change in the direction, significance or the magnitude of the estimated coefficients following the inclusion of the additional control variables.

Most 'home resources for learning' were reported by parents, but the number of books in the home and information on home study supports were derived from responses to the student questionnaire. The *TIMSS 2015 International Results in Mathematics* (Mullis et al., 2016, Exhibit 4.1) provided an overview of student home resources across Europe. In Sweden, Denmark, Finland and Ireland, at least one-third of students belonged to the category 'many resources' (reporting they had more than 100 books in the home and both of the home study supports, and with parents reporting that they had more than 25 children's books in the home, that at least one parent had finished university, and that at least one parent had a professional occupation, on average); the percentage of the students with 'few resources' was negligible (< 2 percent) in these countries. Conversely, in Bulgaria, 20 percent of the student population belonged to the 'few resources' category (students reporting that they had 25 or fewer books in the home and neither of the home study supports, and parents reporting that they had ten or fewer children's books in the home, that neither parent had gone beyond upper-secondary education, and that neither parent was a small business owner or had a clerical or professional occupation, on average). In Slovak Republic, Hungary, Italy and Portugal, 7–8 percent of the student population had 'few resources'. The majority of European students belonged to the 'some resources' category. However, the achievement gap among these three categories (few, some and many resources) can equal one or two years schooling. For example, in Hungary, the difference among the 24 percent of students from the 'many resources' category and the 69 percent of students from the 'some resources' category was 68 score points, and the gap between the 'many resources' students and the 7 percent of students with 'few resources' was 109 score points. It is important to note here that 75 score points is equivalent to an entire proficiency benchmark, the low benchmark being 400 score points, the intermediate 475 score points, the high 550 score points, and the advanced benchmark being 625 score points.

In contrast to the intercountry inequalities in home resources observable on detailed results (reported in the TIMSS almanacs available for download from IEA Data Repository at www.iea.nl), our estimates show fairly homogenous evidence (Table 13.1, first column). The association between home resources of students and their student outcomes in mathematics is positive and statistically significant in all of the countries. Students from more well-off households have higher scores in mathematics. This association was confirmed separately in every country included in the analysis.

*Table 13.1* Estimated regression coefficients for the six main parental involvement variables after controlling for the influence of the additional variables

| Country | Home resources for learning | Help with homework | School attendance | Early literacy and numeracy activities | Parental attitude towards mathematics and science | Parents' perceptions of school performance | Adjusted R-Squared |
|---|---|---|---|---|---|---|---|
| Bulgaria | 11.97*** | -5.49*** | 21.51*** | 2.2 | 1.06 | 1.62 | 0.22 |
| Croatia | 13.62*** | -9.53*** | 15.58*** | 4.44*** | 1.41 | 0.31 | 0.26 |
| Cyprus | 13.6*** | -7.75*** | 23.81*** | 3.34*** | -0.12 | 1.09 | 0.19 |
| Czech Republic | 18.72*** | -5.24*** | 11*** | 1.94** | 1.17 | -0.16 | 0.26 |
| Denmark | 11.64*** | -8.3*** | 10.87** | 3.71** | 1.67 | 2.27* | 0.19 |
| Finland | 10.63*** | -11.63*** | 8.99*** | 4.01*** | 3.79*** | -0.06 | 0.21 |
| France | 15.56*** | -4.54*** | 16.1*** | 2.03* | 1.71* | 0.61 | 0.26 |
| Germany | 14.36*** | -7.38*** | 6.7 | 1.03 | 0.73 | 2.18* | 0.27 |
| Hungary | 19.15*** | -4.84*** | 23.72*** | 2.93*** | 1.55 | 0.27 | 0.39 |
| Ireland | 14.29*** | -5.99*** | 13.91*** | 1.09 | 2.35 | 2.16 | 0.28 |
| Italy | 12.61*** | -5.19*** | 17.74*** | 2.48** | 1.03 | 0.68 | 0.2 |
| Lithuania | 15.69*** | -8.05*** | 6.92 | 1.22 | 2.27** | 2.03* | 0.28 |
| Poland | 15.83*** | -7.11*** | 22.15*** | 1.96** | 2.77*** | 0.37 | 0.24 |
| Portugal | 13.04*** | -3.95*** | 25.01*** | 1.65 | -0.08 | 3.13*** | 0.22 |
| Slovak Republic | 17.2*** | -5.94*** | 15.43*** | 0.8 | 0.47 | 0.79 | 0.31 |
| Slovenia | 14.89*** | -8.93*** | 13.38*** | 2.94** | 1.83* | 0.79 | 0.25 |
| Spain | 10.48*** | -5.29*** | 15.99*** | 3.25*** | 2.04* | 0.52 | 0.22 |
| Sweden | 13.47*** | -6.22*** | 9.89** | 3.21*** | 0.83 | 1.4 | 0.24 |

Notes: Results for Poland based on the PI model without additional control variables (see Appendix). Regression coefficients are statistically significant to *p<0.05; **p<0.01; ***p<0.001.

Our model found that help with homework, as reported by parents, had a negative association with student outcomes, and this was also the case after controlling for socioeconomic background and other factors. This finding (Table 13.1, second column) is in agreement with the results of Punter et al. (2016), although their research was based on the PIRLS 2011 data and investigated homework activities and their relationship to reading achievement. Note that in Punter et al.'s (2016) exhaustive review of the literature on the effect of homework on learning achievement, they mentioned multiple studies that reported the positive effects of homework, as did Cabus and Ariës (2014). In this context, a cross-country comparison showing a homogeneous direction in the association may be considered surprising. Ho and Willms (1996) noted that parents tend to help low-achieving children, who need help the most; children who succeed in school generally do not need their parents' help with homework. Similar findings were confirmed by the PISA 2009 data and reported by Borgonovi and Montt (2012).

We consider that the view on the role of homework may be distorted by various factors that are governed by educational policy (with regard to assigning homework) and the differing reactions of parents to homework. While our model's result implies that parents help with homework more frequently if their child has poor achievement, and that parents of the high achievers are less involved in helping with homework, we found that the situation was not always so straightforward (Figure 13.2). While in some countries the majority of parents reported that their child was doing homework every day and these children generally had the highest achievement (for example in Bulgaria or Poland), in other countries (for example Denmark and Sweden) the students with the lowest achievement were those that did homework every day. In Denmark, where almost 8 percent of parents reported that their children did no homework at all, the children that did no homework achieved similar results to those that did homework once or twice a week. There were some countries where the children from the 'never do homework' category were the lowest achievers: namely, Finland, Germany, Lithuania, Portugal and the Slovak Republic. Our index dealt with these international differences in the frequency of homework assignment by weighting the declared frequency of helping with homework by the frequency of assigning homework.

Another contradictory pattern emerged regarding the reported frequency of parental checks on homework. Almost 77 percent of parents in Bulgaria and more than 92 percent of parents in the Slovak Republic reported asking their children if they had done their homework; these children achieved the highest average score. In the Slovak Republic, the frequency of asking was directly related to achievement; if parents asked less, student achievement was lower. In Croatia and Slovenia, 4 percent of parents reportedly never asked their children if they had done their homework, and yet the children from this group were achieving the highest scores in all categories. The data indicate that some parents do not follow up on their children's homework because it is not necessary, while others may lack interest. An uncontrolled

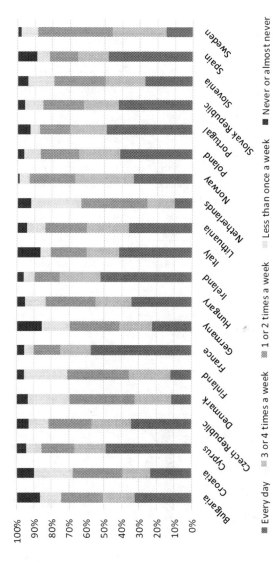

*Figure 13.2* Parents response to the TIMSS question: 'How often do you or someone else in your home help your child with homework?'
Source: Authors' calculations using TIMSS 2015 data.

correlation between parental help with homework and the student outcome in mathematics is thus probably unhelpful, and including additional PI variables, such as school attendance, provides a more informative picture.

We established the average attendance of students from all European countries that participated in TIMSS 2015 (Table 13.1, third column). Among the parental involvement variables, school attendance demonstrated a very strong association with student achievement in mathematics. This pattern was observable across all countries, with the exception of Germany and Lithuania. The less frequently a student is absent from classes, the better their outcomes. This is true in 16 out of the 18 investigated countries. As shown in Figure 13.3 the Slovak Republic showed the lowest level of never or almost never absent students (41 percent), which was unexpected because in that country an absence of more than three days should be confirmed by a doctor and specific social payments are linked to a child's school attendance.

Early numeracy and literacy activities performed with children of preschool age also showed a statistically significant and positive association with student achievement in mathematics (Table 13.1, fourth column). This association was observable in 12 out of the 18 investigated countries. The TIMSS 2015 international results in mathematics used parents' questionnaire responses to determine early literacy, numeracy and science activities before beginning primary school (Mullis et al., 2016, Exhibit 4.6). The students considered to be 'often

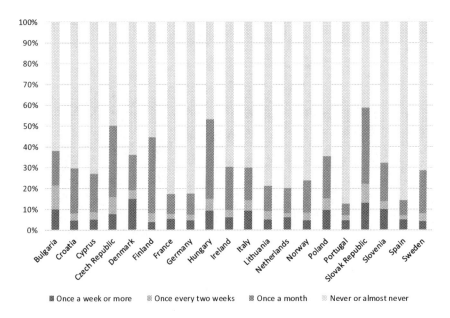

Figure 13.3 4th Grade student response to the TIMSS question: 'About how often are you absent from school?'

Source: Authors' calculations using TIMSS 2015 data.

engaged' in early learning activities were those whose parents reported 'often' doing 8 of 16 activities with them and 'sometimes' doing the other 8, on average. Out of 18 investigated European countries, all but Bulgaria reported that less than 2 percent of students had parents who reported 'never or almost never' doing 8 of the 16 activities with them and 'sometimes' doing the other eight, on average; however, 11 percent of students fell into this category in Bulgaria.

Parental attitudes towards mathematics and science showed a positive association with the mathematics achievement in only six out of the 18 European countries (Table 13.3, fifth column). The transference of attitudes towards mathematics from parents to their children is an important aspect of parental involvement. However, the association between parental attitudes and the student outcome in mathematics appears to be positive, but not universally valid across European countries. Moreover, parental attitudes towards mathematics and science seem to depend heavily on national contexts. This can be observed in a relatively higher variance in the median values of the index at the country level.

As part of TIMSS 2015, parents reported their perceptions of school performance (Mullis et al., 2016, Exhibit 6.1). Here, we observed that European parents were mostly happy with the schools (for example, Ireland), or that there was no clear link between their level of satisfaction and the mathematics achievement of their children (for example, in Bulgaria or Spain). However, some countries had a high percentage of dissatisfied parents: 12 percent of parents in the Czech Republic, Denmark and Germany were less than satisfied with the school. Parental dissatisfaction was not linked to lower student achievement.

In our model, the link between parents' perceptions of school performance and their children's score in mathematics was statistically significant only in a few European countries (four out of the 18 countries in our model, Table 13.1, sixth column). This association also varied within European school systems.

## 5 Conclusions

Using the analytical framework of the TIMSS 2015 study and the data generated by the study, we selected six variables to represent parental involvement and used them in a linear regression model. Furthermore, we included some additional variables to control for factors beyond parental involvement. According to Livingston (2012), significance levels provide some assurance that an observed association is not just a result of sampling variability. From this perspective, we confirmed an internationally observable association between two out of the six parental involvement variables: 'home resources for learning' and 'help with homework'. The additional two parental involvement variables 'school attendance' and 'early literacy and numeracy activities' did not prove to be observable across Europe at the significant level. However, they did remain positive. 'Parental attitudes towards mathematics' and 'parental perceptions of school performance' proved to gain less significance overall, and, in addition the associations varied in their direction. In some countries, these factors were also more likely to be moderated by other factors beyond parental involvement.

We found that there was a positive association between student outcomes and three of the parental involvement variables: 'home resources for learning' (which is at least partially malleable, for example, the number of books for children in the household), 'early literacy and numeracy activities' (malleable), and 'school attendance' (malleable). There was a negative association with 'help with homework'; however, comparing the absolute size effects, we assumed that there were instances when parents were not supporting their children's homework by helping. A new scale could be created, based on Cabus and Ariës's (2014) view that supportive parental involvement or home climate is created by 'elementary communication on education with the child'. Such communication on education could be seen as an explicit questioning (parents asking, children responding), but also as children's implicit observation of parents' habits (such as their assessment of their parents' reading habits, as collected by the TIMSS home questionnaire) and parents' attitudes towards education in general.

We analysed available comparable data from 18 European countries to determine the context and situation, looking especially at countries like the Slovak Republic where parental involvement has not received much research attention.

TIMSS 2015 provided useful data on (mostly) home-based parental involvement, and its analytical framework enabled us to model parental involvement. Our parental involvement model also included data reported by students. The model included additional data from the home and schools questionnaires, reflecting the complex situation within the field of education, where, according to UNESCO's Global Education Monitoring Report (UNESCO, 2017, 16), 'Individuals cannot be held accountable for an outcome that also depends on the actions of others. Everyone has a role to play in improving education'. The challenge for parents seems to be to facilitate their children's engagement with their school and education.

## Notes

1 This work was supported by the Slovak Research and Development Agency under projects: APVV-14-0324 and VEGA 2/0182/17.
2 A more technical description of the estimation strategy as well as the extended results for both variants of the model can be found online at: http://ekonom.sav.sk/uploads/work/TIMSS2015_estimation_results.htm

## References

Alexander, K.L., Entwisle, D.R. and Olson, L.S. (2007) Lasting consequences of the summer learning gap. *American Sociological Review*, 72(2), 167–180. DOI:10.1177/000312240707200202

Borgonovi, F. and Montt, G. (2012) *Parental involvement in selected PISA countries and economies, OECD Education Working Papers, No. 73*. OECD Publishing, Paris. http://dx.doi.org/10.1787/5k990rk0jsjj-en

Bowles, S., Gintis, H. and Groves, M.O. (2009) *Unequal Chances: Family Background and Economic Success*. Princeton, NJ: Russel Sage Foundation, Princeton University Press.

Cabus, S.J. and Ariës, R.J. (2014) *What Do Parents Teach their Children? On Birth Order and Performance Differences in Dutch Compulsory Education*. TIER Working Paper Series TIER WP 14/25. Amsterdam/Maastricht/Groningen, the Netherlands: TIER. Available at: www.tierweb.nl/tier/working-paper/all-working-papers.html.

Eurydice (1997) *The Role of Parents in the Education Systems of the European Union*. Brussels, Belgium: Eurydice European Unit. Available at: https://eric.ed.gov/?id=ED426950.

Foy, P. (2017) *TIMSS 2015 User Guide for the International Database*. Chestnut Hill, MA: TIMSS & PIRLS International Study Center, Boston College. Available at: http://timssandpirls.bc.edu/timss2015/international-database/downloads/T15_UserGuide.pdf.

Green, C.L., Walker, J.M.T., Hoover-Dempsey, K.V. and Sandler, H.M. (2007) Parents' motivations for involvement in children's education: An empirical test of a theoretical model of parental involvement. *Journal of Educational Psychology*, 99(3), 532–544.

Hill, N.E. and Tyson, D.F. (2009) Parental involvement in middle school: A meta-analytic assessment of the strategies that promote achievement. *Developmental Psychology*, 45(3), 740–763.

Ho, E. and Willms, J.D. (1996) Effects of parental involvement on eighth-grade achievement. *Sociology of Education*, 69(2), 126–141.

Hong, S., Yoo, S., You, S. and Wu, C.-C. (2010) The reciprocal relationship between parental involvement and mathematics achievement: Autoregressive cross–lagged modeling. *Journal of Experimental Education*, 78, 419–439.

Hooper, M. (2016) Developing the TIMSS 2015 context questionnaires. In: Martin, M.O., Mullis, I.V.S. and Hooper, M., eds. *Methods and Procedures in TIMSS 2015*. Available at: Boston College, TIMSS & PIRLS International Study Center website: http://timss.bc.edu/publications/timss/2015-methods/chapter-2.html. 2.1-2.8.

Howie, S. and Chamberlain, M. (2017, May) *Reading Performance in Post-Colonial Contexts and the Effect of Instruction in a Second Language* (Policy Brief No. 14). Amsterdam, the Netherlands: IEA

LaRoche, S., Joncas, M. and Foy, P. (2016) Sample design in TIMSS 2015. In: Martin, M.O., Mullis, I.V.S. and Hooper, M., eds. *Methods and Procedures in TIMSS 2015*. Available at: Boston College, TIMSS & PIRLS International Study Center website: http://timss.bc.edu/publications/timss/2015-methods/chapter-3.html. 3.1-3.37.

Livingston, S.A. (2012) *How to write an effective research report*. ETS Report RM-12-05. Princeton, NJ: ETS. Available at: www.ets.org/research/policy_research_reports/publications/report/2012/jefb.

Martin, M.O., Mullis, I.V.S. and Hooper, M., eds. (2016) *Methods and Procedures in TIMSS 2015*. Available at: Boston College, TIMSS & PIRLS International Study Center website: http://timssandpirls.bc.edu/publications/timss/2015-methods.html.

Mullis, I.V.S., Martin, M.O., Foy, P. and Hooper, M. (2016) *TIMSS 2015 International Results in Mathematics*. Chestnut Hill, MA: TIMSS & PIRLS International Study Center, Boston College. Available at: http://timssandpirls.bc.edu/timss2015/international-results.

Punter, R.A., Glas, C.A.W. and Meelissen, M.R.M. (2016) *Psychometric Framework for Modeling Parental Involvement and Reading Literacy*. IEA Research for Education, Volume 1. Cham, Switzerland: Springer. DOI: 10.1007/978-3-319-28064-6.

Taylor, L.C., Clayton, J.D. and Rowley, S.J. (2004) Academic socialization: Understanding parental influences on children's school–related development in the early years. *Review of General Psychology*, 8(3), 163–178.

TIMSS & PIRLS International Study Center (2014) *Home Questionnaire: Early Learning Survey*. Chestnut Hill, MA: Boston College. Available at: https://timssandpirls.bc.edu/timss2015/questionnaires/downloads/T15-_HQ_4.pdf.

UNESCO (2017) *Global Education Monitoring report 2017/2018. Accountability in education: Meeting Our Commitments*. Available at: http://unesdoc.unesco.org/images/0025/002593/259338e.pdf.

# 14 Parental involvement across European education systems
## A critical conclusion

*Delma Byrne and Angelika Paseka*

**Introduction**

In this final chapter of the volume, we look back across the country case studies and bring out some key features of their findings when taken together. As highlighted in the introductory chapter, the point of departure for the majority of the case studies was a common template, used by country experts to produce in-depth country reports for eleven countries. This common approach, applied across very different institutional settings, provides a unique opportunity to evaluate and cast new light on the following research questions:

(1) To what extent is the national background of parental involvement (legislation, national policy, rights and duties of parents) comparable across education systems?
(2) To what extent is current policy and practice pertaining to parental involvement inclusive of a diverse range of parents and students across education systems?
(3) What are the commonalities and differences in the research base and theoretical framing of parental involvement across education systems?
(4) What are the key policy challenges pertaining to parental involvement?

The common template allows for comparison between countries, but also gave country experts the scope to present new research findings on parental involvement that are pertinent to the current discussion on parental involvement in their country contexts. In this chapter, we seek to look back across the country case studies and bring out some key features of their findings when taken together, and relate these findings to the broader institutional characteristics of each country context (political context, extent of economic inequality, degree of equity in the education system, and the role of the state in family matters).

In this concluding chapter, the first and central point we wish to emphasise is the richness of the country case studies and chapters themselves. Clearly, there are varied country experiences of the development of parental involvement, highlighting the importance of the national context in trying to explain them. Here, we stand back and look across the eleven countries covered and can draw out some striking features, beginning with the national policy development of parental involvement and then turning to a focus on the existing research conducted in this area, policy and practice regrading inclusion, and finally, key policy challenges facing parental involvement in Europe.

**Question 1: To what extent is the national background of parental involvement (legislation, national policy, rights and duties of parents) comparable across education systems?**

The legislative basis for parental involvement in education can be conceptualised through both the individual rights of parents and the collective rights of parents. Given the dearth of comparative research on parental involvement across European countries, an exploration of the similarities and differences in the national background of parental involvement (legislation, national policy, rights and duties of parents) is especially significant.

We begin with a review of the legislated obligations of parents. For the majority of countries in this volume, parental duties and obligations with regard to the education of their children first appeared as a statutory provision in constitutional legislation (Switzerland in 1907, the Netherlands in 1917, Ireland in 1937, Germany in 1949, Portugal in 1976, Slovenia in 1991). In other instances, the duties and obligations of parents with regard to the education of their children first appeared in a diverse range of legislative documents, including those pertaining to child protection (Norway 1981, England and Wales in 1989, Iceland in 1992, Northern Ireland in 1995), education policy such as Education Acts (Scotland in 1980, Wales in 1996) and specific legislation relating to parents (the Parent Code in Sweden in 1949). Beyond the legislation, common across the country case studies was the use of curriculum documents (local or national) to highlight the importance of parental involvement, cooperation, or collaboration between parents and teachers/schools.

Here, we define individual rights in relation to legislation regarding (1) the freedom of school choice for parents, and (2) parental rights to information about the educational progress of their child. While each of the case studies in this volume has enacted legislation to encourage a flow of information regarding student progress between parents and the school, we make a distinction between legislation that offers parents this right and that which places the onus on the school to provide information to parents. This distinction is important, as it separates the legislated right of parents from the (legislated or not) obligations of schools.

In terms of accessing (typically publicly funded) schools, a number of countries in the volume share a constitutional basis for freedom of school choice (Ireland, the Netherlands, Slovenia) while it has become a more recent legislative development in other contexts (England and Wales since 1988; the voucher system in Sweden since 1991; Northern Ireland since

1997; Iceland since 2008; Portugal since 2012). However, as identified in many country chapters, the legislative basis for freedom of school choice is constrained by geographical offerings as well as processes of social and cultural reproduction and through the use of selective admission policies. In three country contexts there is no freedom of school choice as admission is regulated by catchment areas (Cyprus, Norway, Switzerland), while in Germany freedom of school choice varies across states.

As indicated above, individual rights can be further defined in relation to parent rights to information about the educational progress of their child. Only in a minority of county contexts is the right for individual parents to receive information on student progress legislated for (England and Wales since 2002, Iceland since 2008, Portugal since 2018). In other institutional contexts, parents do not have an individual right to receive information, but schools are obliged to inform and consult parents (Sweden, Ireland, Switzerland). In Scotland and Germany (although it varies across *Länder*), both parental rights to information and school obligations to inform and consult parents are legislated for.

Taking these aspects of individual rights together, we conceptualise the individual rights that each country contexts offers to parents. Through this comparative lens, parents in Portugal, Iceland, the Netherlands, England and Wales have achieved what we term 'extensive' rights for individual parents in the education field, with both freedom of school choice and a legislated right to receive information. In contrast, some muncipalities of Switzerland and Cyprus, parents neither have freedom of school choice nor a legislated right to receive information, representing countries with 'limited' parental rights. In between there are the systems where parents have freedom of school choice (in theory) but parent rights are limited to receiving information (Ireland, Slovenia, Sweden). In these contexts, while freedom of choice exists, the onus is on schools to provide information to parents, as opposed to a parent's rights to receive information. Finally, there is Norway, where individual parents do not have a right to freedom of school choice but have a legislated right to receive information.

In terms of *collective* rights, each of the country case studies in this volume have explicit public policies and legislation in terms of parent representation, and have experienced an expansion of the collective rights of parents. This includes the collective rights of parents to (1) organise themselves through the establishment of parent associations/councils, and/or (2) to be represented on school boards or equivalent, as well as (3) to have influence on schooling matters at local and/or national levels. The chapters show that the legislative process to establish parent associations/councils began earlier in the decentralised systems of Switzerland and Germany, but also Norway. Later developments occurred in the 1970s in Iceland, Ireland and Portugal, the 1980s in the UK, the Netherlands, and the 1990s in Cyprus, Slovakia and Sweden.

Yet in terms of collective rights, clear differences emerge across countries. Firstly, there is variation in the extent to which parents have a right to organise themselves through the establishment of parent associations/councils. More often, the obligation is on schools to establish parent councils or associations, than for parents to have a right to do so. In other contexts, parent representation varies across municipalities (Norway and Switzerland) where some municipalities have a school board for each individual school while others do not, in what OECD term as a 'democratic gap' (OECD, 2006). There are also some subtle differences across countries. For example, in Ireland membership to the parents' association is free of charge and must be open to all parents in the school, while in Cyprus individual parents must pay to participate. Secondly, while there is less variation in the extent to which parent representatives have a right to sit on a school board or equivalent, not all countries allow parents the same level of influence in decision-making. Increasingly, representatives of parents have a right to be involved in the workings of the school, but this is more advanced in some countries than others. Increasingly, there is an obligation on the government to consult with parent associations on education policy, while in others parent representative bodies have no formal influence at national level (Iceland).

## Question 2: To what extent is current policy and practice pertaining to parental involvement inclusive of a diverse range of parents and students?

A review across our country case studies shows the gradual promotion of parental involvement by government and policymakers across each of the eleven countries under investigation. In this section, we map the policy construction – past and present – of the meaning of parental involvement across the case study sites, and the drivers of such legislation. Here, we are interested in the extent to which current policy and practice is inclusive of parental diversity.

Our review suggests that an education policy focus on parents was driven by societal changes more broadly. Other than the constitutional positioning of parents in relation to the education of their children, prior to the 1960s few countries acknowledged the role of parents. For the most part (with some exceptions), as a result of the 1960s movement and the demand for greater democratisation in society the rights of parents with regard to the education of their children were expanded in many countries in the 1970s and 1980s (see also Crozier, 2018). While the opportunities for parents to become involved in school affairs were enlarged through participation in school boards and committees, and even enlarged by processes of decentralisation, for the most part a recognition of parental diversity and intersectionality had not yet emerged.

By the 1980s and 1990s (and later in Iceland), policy in many countries had placed more onus on schools to facilitate and to be accountable to parents. By now a rhetoric of 'shared responsibility' or 'cooperation between parents and schools' became dominant, as well as the concept of 'parent power'. This period also saw an increase in the marketisation of schools, leading to enhancing competition between schools. The underlying idea was to improve school-quality and to raise the choice of parents by emphasising and expanding their rights with regard to the education of their children.

An (un)intended effect of increasing parental rights, particularly around school choice, was that schools became more interested in attracting the type of parents and children who would help to raise the achievement levels of their school: typically middle-class parents and majority ethnic parents. Thus, the meaning of parental involvement that was encouraged by policy and legislation in this heightened context sought, on the one hand, to encourage schools to be more open to parents, while, on the other hand, to use parental involvement as a way to improve school effectiveness and the achievement levels of schools (rather than make schools more democratic). Emphasis was placed on parents to engage in home-based and child-centred parental involvement activities to improve the educational attainment of children, but also to improve the positioning of schools. When the large-scale assessments began in the 1990s and the first results were published, highlighting a strong correlation between children's social background and their achievement results, a new perspective was established: not schools, but parents were made increasingly accountable for such results.

While the policy intent of parental involvement in many of the case studies was to promote equality of opportunity, drawing largely from the work of Epstein (1995), it was around this time that strong critiques of policy promoting parental involvement began to emerge, particularly in contexts where the individual rights of parents were extensive. As indicated by Christie and Apps in this volume, the discourse of 'parent power' in the UK served as an effective mask for increasing shifts in responsibilities away from schools and towards parents (Reay, 2008), bringing on the intensification of parenting (Gillies, 2012) through raised expectations of parents and schools. Here, high expectations towards 'good parenting' is accompanied by a homogenisation of parents by assuming that all parents, irrespective of their resources, are able to support and promote their children in an effective way through the recommended home-based and child-centred parental involvement approaches (Ostner, Betz & Honig, 2017). As indicated by Byrne in this volume, this reinforces the classed-dimension of parental involvement. Furthermore, as indicated by David in this volume, the policy construction of parental involvement then and now continues to reproduce dominant gender, majority ethnic, racialised and sexuality norms (see also Goldberg et al., 2017).

From the mid-1990s, our country case studies indicate that processes of individualisation have intensified, whereby government intervention in parental involvement has grown, specifically targeted at parents whose children are at greater risk of underachievement in the education system. Such approaches are especially evident in, but not confined to, countries where social class or migrant educational inequalities are pronounced (see OECD, 2018). While the type of parental involvement that parents are encouraged to aspire to mirrors that of middle-class parenting, interventionist policies and programmes are increasingly orientated towards working class, migrant, refugee and minority ethnic parents. This approach has been criticised for unequally positioning parents in education discourses, widening inequalities in the UK context (see Christie and App in this volume) and not recognising the varied ways in which parents support the education of their children.

Our review of each of the case studies reveals both commonalities and differences in the inclusion of a diverse body of parents. It also highlights that state intervention in the family is increasingly considered as a solution for improving educational attainment, and for achieving greater equity. For example, more recently, the OECD (2018) recommends that schools encourage parent–teacher communication and parental engagement for improving equity in education and social mobility. As shown in the country case studies, parents are increasingly being held responsible for educational disadvantage, where policy looks to engage parents in individual-led strategies to improve student educational outcomes. This emergent process appears to occur across country contexts irrespective of whether societal norms position children's well-being as a public responsibility. That is, parental involvement in schooling draws our attention to the tensions and paradoxes along a continuum of familialism (family responsibility) and de-familialism (public and state responsibility).

## Question 3: What are the commonalities and differences in the research base and theoretical framing of parental involvement across education systems?

Within this volume, the country case studies document considerable variety in the existing research base and theoretical framing of parental involvement. Among our case studies, with regard to the *amount* and *tradition* of research in this area, we can distinguish between four groups of countries along a continuum of parental involvement as a research field that is 'established' or 'in its infancy'. Countries that have an established research field include the UK and Germany, both in terms of the volume of existing research and the use of a range theoretical approaches. Countries that represent a research field in its infancy include Iceland and Slovenia, as, in both, research on parents, parental rights and parental involvement have emerged more recently. In between, we find Switzerland, Ireland, Sweden and the Netherlands, in which a relatively established and differentiated body of research exists, and finally Cyprus, Portugal and Norway, where the field is beyond its infancy, and a small group of researchers are pushing forward research in this area.

Further examination of existing research across our case study sites reveals three main *research fields* on parental involvement: (1) research that highlights the heterogeneity of parents and social inequality; (2) research about the political discourse that parental involvement is embedded within; and (3) research about different forms and types of parental involvement.

In contrast to a normative construction of parents, a considerable body of research exists that highlights the heterogeneity and diversity of parents, and processes of social inequality. This body of research draws from a variety of empirical approaches. Quantitative research emphasises parental diversity and processes of social inequality by looking for statistical correlations between educational assessments and the characteristics (education level, social or migrant background) and attitudes of parents towards school or attitudes towards the development of their children (often using large-scale datasets). Qualitative research focuses on processes of social inequality in the perceptions of teachers and parents towards each other. In some studies, the production of inequality is the focus of the research by taking a closer look at forms of parental involvement, how schools and parents communicate with each other (e.g. parent–teacher conferences, school policy). From this research, typically two groups of parents are constructed: privileged and non-privileged parents, mostly along the criteria of social class and ethnic background, with much less attention being paid to gender dynamics.

Research about the political discourse analyses the way that parents are addressed in educational policy. Analysts use a large variety of documents: government policy documents as well as policy and practice documents relating to the work of schools, local communities and parental associations. As highlighted above, research in this area shows that in most countries a shift in the roles and responsibilities of parents and schools took place at the end of the 20th century, driven by wider societal changes and hand-in-hand with the rise of international large-scale assessments, the hype about rankings, test scores and student accountability, as well as the discourse about economic competitiveness, school efficiency and learning results.

Methodologically, research on parental involvement adopts a range of epistemologies (post-positivism, interpretivism) and methods: questionnaires for parents, students and teachers, but also interviews and observations. Across Europe, research results confirm that all parents irrespective of their social, cultural or specific context want the best for their children. That is, child-centred and home-based parental involvement in supporting the learning processes of children seems to be taken for granted by most parents. Research on parental participation in school-based involvement shows ambivalent results. Some studies find that middle-class parents have a greater propensity to engage in school-based forms of parental involvement, in formal committees and on school boards, while others do not. Within this body of literature, there is considerable emphasis placed on the effect of parental involvement (particularly school-based and child-centred) on academic achievement.

Looking across the new research on parental involvement that is presented in this volume, a number of new perspectives on parental involvement have emerged. Firstly, teachers are the focus of two chapters, highlighting the *implicit knowledge* of teachers about parents and how teachers construct parents (Cyprus), and the construction of parents in teacher education (Norway). Secondly, new processes of inequality within *schools* are highlighted: their role in defining parental involvement as well as their role in facilitating or preventing opportunities for parents to become involved (Germany, Iceland, Ireland, Portugal, United Kingdom). A third focus looks at the wider *context* within which parental involvement is embedded: not only is it driven by marketisation, privatisation and (global) competition in the education system, but also by political changes and the tax system (Portugal, Slovenia, Sweden).

While existing research addresses many aspects of parental involvement, some *blind spots* exist, both empirically and theoretically. From an *empirical* viewpoint, these include (1) studies of parental involvement beyond primary level as the majority of studies are carried out in primary schools, and parental involvement in secondary schools and beyond is much less frequently analysed, (2) the perception of children and young people towards the involvement of parents in their education, as children and young people are seldom the focus of research, (3) research on the experiences of minority ethnic parents with the education system are still in their infancy across a number of country contexts, and (4) research which seeks to get beyond normative forms and types of parental involvement.

A review of existing research across the case study sites reveals a number of blind spots in terms of *research designs*. That is, the field of parental involvement draws largely from case study and cross-sectional designs as opposed to longitudinal or ethnographic designs. Few studies adopt a mixed methods design, drawing on a range of methods. Furthermore, while targeted interventions seek to increase parental involvement especially for 'hard-to-reach' parents, evaluations of such programmes are limited.

Looking to the *theoretical approaches* within which parental involvement is framed, the field draws from a range of schools of thought and intellectual movements to include functionalism, (post)structuralism, (de)constructivism, yet work from Feminism, Black Studies or Asian Studies is less represented across country case studies. The field of parental involvement research draws largely from sociological and psychological disciplinary frameworks. Among these the work of Joyce L. Epstein (a sociologist) and Kathleen Hoover-Dempsey (a psychologist) have been particularly influential since the mid-1990s in defining and theorising the concept of parental involvement (Epstein, 1995; Hoover-Dempsey & Sandler, 1995, 1997). These works are frequently the theoretical orientation for educators who seek to develop school-based interventions designed to enhance parental involvement. While highly influential as theoretical tools, the studies have also been critisised as being highly normative in their call for shared responsibility between school and families as desirable and worthwhile, and for a normative stance on the construct of parent. Academic work, which adopts a more critical perspective on the concept of parental involvement has frequently been guided by the analytic work of Bourdieu (social reproduction and capitals), Boudon (rational choice theory) and Foucault (power relations). Yet what is missing from this body of theoretical work are approaches that combine activities at the meso level (schools) with the micro level (concrete interactions between parents and teachers) and the macro level, looking at dominant norms in which the actions of schools and the interactions of the involved actors are embedded. For combining the micro-meso-macro levels, complex theories such as Giddens' Theory of Structuration (1984, 2009) (see the example of new research in Chapter 7:

Portugal), could be used, also taking into account the practical knowledge that refers to the underlying assumptions used by the actors (Bohnsack, 2014).

## Question 4: What are the policy challenges pertaining to parental involvement?

Across our case study sites, the meaning of parental involvement has taken on considerable significance, and we are struck by the many challenges for policy and practice. Firstly, a review of current policy and practice with regard to parental involvement for all parents reveals a number of pitfalls. On the one hand, school programmes aimed at enhancing parental involvement that are orientated towards *all* parents run the risk that well-informed middle-class parents are more likely to participate and profit from such initiatives. As a result, parental involvement represents an axis of enhanced social inequality. On the other hand, interventions that are for targeted specifically for underrepresented parents run the risk that these parents are labelled as clients and their situation is judged as precarious. As a result, those parents might refuse to take part in such initiatives and are constructed as 'bad parents'. To find a way out of this dilemma, new paths and policy solutions seem necessary. Initiatives seem to be required that seek to redress the issue of power relationships and power imbalances between parents and teachers/schools, and address parents as experts with specialised knowledge of their children. In cooperation with parents, participatory approaches appear to have some potential for empowering parents without constructing them as deficient, by asking them for their ideas and wishes and by uncovering alternative forms of parental involvement by giving them a voice.

We end this volume with a number of challenges concerning research in the area of parental involvement. Some attention has been given to parental involvement in comparative perspective by Eurydice (1997) and the OECD (2006, 2010, 2012, 2017) largely with the acknowledgement of parental involvement as a key mechanism for improving attainment in education, but less recognition of the role of parental involvement as a mechanism for equity and promoting social mobility. The marginal position of parental involvement is also reflected in the lack of European Commission funding for European or international scientific collaboration. Our study shows that there is a need for researchers in Europe to collaborate and get beyond normative constructions of the ways in which parents are involved in the education lives of their children. This volume also clearly points to the need for more comparative research on the drivers of education and social policy that shape the interactions of families with the education system, and how schools recontextualise governmental policies in their efforts to reach all parents.

## References

Bohnsack, R. (2014) Documentary method. In: Flick, U., ed. *The SAGE Handbook of Qualitative Data Analysis*. London: Sage. 217–233.
Crozier, G. (2018) Editorial. *International Journal about Parents in Education*, 10(1), I-II.

Epstein, J.L. (1995) School/family/community partnerships: Caring for the children we share. *Phi Delta Kappan*, 76(9), 701–712.

Eurydice (1997) *The Role of Parents in the Education Systems of the European Union*. Brussels: European Unit of Eurydice.

Giddens, A. (1984/2009) *The Constitution of Society: Outline of a Theory of Structuration*. Cambridge, UK: Polity Press.

Gillies, V. (2012) Family policy and the politics of parenting: From function to competence. In: Richter, M. and Andresen, S., eds. *The Politicization of Parenthood*. London: Springer. 13–26.

Goldberg, A.E., Black, K.A., Manley, M.H. and Frost. R. (2017) 'We told them that we are both really involved parents': Sexual minority and heterosexual adoptive parents' engagement in school communities. *Gender and Education*, 29(5), 614–631.

Hoover-Dempsey, K.V. and Sandler, H.M. (1995) Parental involvement in children's education: Why does it make a difference? *Teachers College Record*, 97(2), 310–331.

Hoover-Dempsey, K.V. and Sandler, H.M. (1997) Why do parents become involved in their children's education? *Review of Educational Research*, 67(3), 3–42.

OECD (2006) Parent and community 'voice' in schools. In: OECD *Demand-Sensitive Schooling? Evidence and Issues*. Paris: OECD. 83–102.

OECD (2010) Special section: School choice, parent voice. In: OECD *Education at A Glance: OECD Indicators 2010*. Paris: OECD. 81–88.

OECD (2012) *Parental Involvement in Selected PISA Countries and Economies*. Paris: OECD.

OECD (2017) *School Choice and School Vouchers: An OECD Perspective*. Paris: OECD.

OECD (2018) *Equity in Education: Breaking down Barriers to Social Mobility*. Paris: OECD.

Ostner, I., Betz, T. and Honig, M.-S. (2017) Introduction: Parenting practices and parenting support in recent debates and policies. *Journal of Family Research*, 11, 5–19.

Reay, D. (2008) Tony Blair, the promotion of the 'active' educational citizen, and middle-class hegemony. *Oxford Review of Education*, 34(6), 639–650.

# Index

*Note*: Boldface page numbers refer to tables and italic page numbers refer to figures.

Abouchaar, A. 155
academic achievement of students, parental involvement and 69–70
*Action Plan for Education* (2016–19) 53
adult education 168; Iceland 37; Slovenia 105
Alldred, P. 171
Allmendinger, J. 105
*All Our Children* 51
ALSPAC *see* Avon Longitudinal Study of Parents and Children (ALSPAC)
Althusser, L. 165
Archer, M. 97–9
Ariès, R.J. 178, 184, 188
Artelt, C. 28
Avon Longitudinal Study of Parents and Children (ALSPAC) 156

Bakker, J. 70
Ball, St. 170
BAME *see* Black, Asian and Minority Ethnic parents (BAME)
*Better schools: A White Paper* 152
Betz, T. 24
Biglia, B. 171
Black, Asian and Minority Ethnic parents (BAME) 164, 172
Blair, T. 152
Board of Management 50, 52, 55
Borgonovi, F. 176–8, 184
Boudon, R. 139, 140, 145, 198
Bourdieu, P. 17, 24, 55, 69, 138, 198; habitus theory 138; social capital theory 59, 69; symbolic capital 24
Brown, Ph. 167, 168

Cabus, S.J. 178, 188
caregivers 66, 135, 176, 179
Chamberlain, M. 177
Chartier, M. 137
child-centred parental involvement 56, 138, 139, 195
Commissioner for the Protection of Children's Rights Laws of 2007 10
compulsory schools 162; Germany 24–5; Iceland 36–7, 41–5; Norway 77; Sweden 122; United Kingdom 162, 165–6
Côté, J. 109
Creaven, A.M. 54, 60
Crozier, G. 155, 156
cultural capital 14, 17, 69, 93, 110, 111
Cyprus, parental involvement in 3, 4, 10–13; District Parents' Associations (DPAs) 11–12; education system in 8–9; events in school 12–13; Greek-Cypriot education system 8, 12; national legislative and regulative context 10–13; new research perspectives 15–17; Pancyprian Confederations of Parents' Associations 11, 12; parents' associations 11–12; parents' weekly visiting period 12; primary schools 15; relationship between teachers and parents 16–17; research on parental involvement 13–15; school–family relationships 10–13, 17–18; teachers' conceptions of families 15–17; terminology 10; Turkish-Cypriots 8

202  Index

Davies, J. 156
de-familialism 3, 4, 196
Deluze 55
Desforges, C. 155
de Wit, C. 66
Driessen, G. 70

early childhood care and education (ECCE) system 49, 91
ECCE system *see* early childhood care and education (ECCE) system
ECER *see* European Conference on Educational Research (ECER)
educational inequality, parental involvement and 68–9
Educational Project 94
Education Commission 9
Education Endowment Foundation (EEF) 155
Education Reform Act (ERA) 150, 152, 166
education system 1; Cyprus 8–9; European 2; Germany 21–2; Iceland 36–7, 45–6; Ireland 49–50; Netherlands 64–6; Norway 77–8; Portugal 90–1; Slovenia 105; Sweden 120–1; Switzerland 133–4; United Kingdom 149–51
Education Training Inspectorate 152
Edwards, R. 168, 169
EEF *see* Education Endowment Foundation (EEF)
EERA *see* European Educational Research Association (EERA)
Effective Provision of Pre-school Education (EPPE) 154–5
Effects of Tracking (WiSel) 140
Eilbracht, L. 87
Eivers, E. 54, 55, 60
empirical discourse, parental involvement in Germany 27–9; communication between school and parents 28; evaluation of programmes and projects 28; home–school relationships 27; learning results effects on pupils 28; parents expectations 27
EPPE *see* Effective Provision of Pre-school Education (EPPE)
Epstein, J. L. 195, 198; model of overlapping spheres 26; theory 67
ERA *see* Education Reform Act (ERA)
European Commission 199

European Conference on Educational Research (ECER) 5, 6
European Educational Research Association (EERA) 5
European education systems, parental involvement 191, 197–8; blind spots 198; collective rights of parents 193–4; commonalities and differences across education system 196–9; education policy 194–5; government policy documents 197; individualisation processes 195; individual rights, relation to legislation 192–3; legislative basis 192; national background 192–4; parental rights 195; parent power 195; parent–teacher communication 196; policy challenges 199; practice pertaining to 194–6; qualitative research 197; quantitative research 196–7; research designs 198; research fields 196; research questions 191; rights to information about educational progress 193; school-based involvement 197; school choice for parents 192–3; theoretical approaches 198–9 *see also individual countries*
European Parents' Association (EPA) 12
Eurydice 175, 199
Everaert, H. 70

familialisation 3, 4, 24, 107, 116, 16
family involvement 17, 18, 162; in schools 10, 15; in university undergraduate programmes 15
family literacy, parenting and 51
family–school relationships 14, 17, 18, 133
feminist perspective, parental involvement and 7 *see also* United Kingdom, parental involvement in
Foucault, M. 24, 55, 198

Georgiou, S.N. 11
Germany, parental involvement in 3, 22–6, 33; activities *30, 31*; *Basic Law (Grundgesetz)* 23; changing rhetoric 23–4; communication between school and parents 28; compulsory school education 24–5; cooperation between parents and school 23; *Decision of the Federal Constitutional Court* (1972) 23; different ways of treating parents 24–6; educational partnership *(Erziehungs- und*

*Bildungspartnerschaft)* 23, 24; empirical discourse 27–9; evaluation of programmes and projects 28; further research 29–32; good and bad parents 26, 32; *gymnasium* 22; home-based parental involvement 29; home–school relationships 27, 32; JAKO-O 2014 survey 21, 27, 29–30; *Länder* 22, 23, 33; latent class analysis 30–1; learning results effects on pupils 28; national legislative and regulative context 23; normative discourse 26; parents expectations 27; research on parental involvement 26–9; school-based parental involvement 29–32; school system in 21–2; stages of change 24–6; The Standing Conference of the Ministers of Education and Cultural Affairs of the Länder 21–2; terminology 22–3; Vodafone-Stiftung, ed. 26, 27; working with parents *(Elternarbeit)* 23–4
Giddens, A. 97–9, 198; theory of structuration 97, 198
Gill, T. 115
GOETE (Governance of Educational Trajectories in Europe) 104–5, 108, 109
Goodman, A. 156, 157
Gorard, S. 158
Green, T.L. 73
Greg, P. 156, 157
GRV *see* Violence

Hall, K. 55
Ho, E. 184
home-based childcare 126–8
home-based parental involvement 7, 29, 138, 175; at age 17 55–60; in child schooling 110; comparative research 175–6; cultural capital 59; data and measures 56; description of available data 178–80; estimation strategy 181–2; frequency of 57; individualism and competitiveness 112; measuring parental involvement 176–8; multilevel random intercept model of **58–9**; parenthood, overprotecting 110–14, **111**; physical access to school 60; primary schools 59–60; results 57, 182–7; variables referring to 180–1
home–school collaboration 121–2
home–school cooperation, in Norway 78, 82; background 83; findings 84–6;

formal fora for 80–1; in national education policies 87; practice teaching 85; professionalism 86; in programmes and course plans 85–6; study 84; teacher education 83–4, 86, 87; teachers' insecurities 87
homework support, in Sweden 124–9; facilitate student learning 128; first reform period 126–7; home-based childcare 127; homework and parental involvement 125; out-of-home supplementary education 128–9; parents as providers 126–7; parents as unreliable providers of 127–9; responsible consumers to unreliable providers of 125–9; second reform period 127–9; in Swedish national curricula 124; tax deductions for 124–6
Hoover-Dempsey, K. 70, 198
Howie, S. 177
Hujala, E. 70
human capital theory 138

Iceland, home–school cooperation in 3, 36; adult education 37; characteristics of 42–3; Compulsory School Act 37, 39–40; compulsory schools 36–7, 41–2; educational equity in 45; educational system 36–7, 45–6; *General Data Protection Regulation and the extensive use of school information systems* 40; higher education 37; home–school relationship, 38, 40–3 Icelandic National Curriculum Guide for Compulsory Schools General Section 39; informal parental involvement 54; National Curriculum Guide for Compulsory Schools 37; national legislative and regulative context 39–40; parental involvement 37–40; *parental involvement in compulsory schools in Iceland* project 41–2; parental participation 38; Parents Council 39, 40; parents' education and marital status matters 44–5; *The Parents Paper* 39; parent–teacher relationship 44; policymakers in 37; research on 40–1; pre-primary *(leikskóli)* education 36; School Council 39–40; secondary education 37; special schools 37; Statistics Iceland 37; supervisory teachers 38, 43–4; teenagers' opinions

## 204  Index

on parents' participation 43–4; terminology 38–9
individualisation 24, 104, 108, 112, 116
International Association for the Evaluation of Educational Achievement (IEA) 1, 7, 175
Ireland, parental involvement in 3, 49; accountability discourse 53; Catholic schools 51; Constitution of Ireland 51; Department of Education 53; Department of Education and Skills (DES) 50, 53; Educate Together 52; Education Act (1988) 50, 52; education system 49–50; equity 3; formal parental involvement 54; Gaelscoil (Irish medium schools) 52; Guardianship of Children Acts (1964 to 1997) 50; home-based parental involvement at age 17 55–60; Irish Free State 51; national legislative and regulation context 50–1; parent as choosers and consumers 51–2; parenting and family literacy 51; partnerships and charters 52–3; research on 53–5; social inequality 61; terminology 50

kindergartens: Germany 22; Netherlands 65, 69; Norway 77, 78; Slovenia 107; Switzerland 133, 134, 137
Kintrea, K. 157
Kirkhaug, B. 83
Kristoffersson, M. 40
Krumm, V. 140

Lareau, A. 68
Lesbian, Gay, Bisexual, Transgender, Queer and intersexual (LGBTQi) 162–3, 172
Livingston, S.A. 187
Lusse, M. 71

McCoy, S. 51
McElvany, N. 28
Ministry of Education 79, 91, 93
Ministry of Education and Culture 9, 12
Ministry of Education and Research 78, 84
Montt, G. 176–8
morphogenetic cycle 97
Munn, P. 14

National Curriculum: Iceland 39; Norway 78; United Kingdom 150
national legislative and regulative context: Cyprus 10–13; Germany 23; Iceland 39–40; Ireland 50–1; Netherlands 66–8; Norway 79–80; Portugal 92–5; Slovenia 106–7; Sweden 121–2; Switzerland 135–6; United Kingdom 151–4
National Parenting Strategy 153
National Parents' Committee for Primary and Secondary Education 79
National Parents Council 54
Netherlands, parental involvement in 3, 64, 74–5; academic achievement of students 69–70; alternative ways of involvement 72; bridges between families and schools 67; dark side of 68–9; Dutch Education Council 67–8; Dutch Education Research Council 69; Dutch Inspectorate of Education 68; Dutch government 74; early tracking system 65–6; *educatief partnerschap* 66; educational inequality 67, 68–9; education system 64–5, 73; freedom of education 64–5, 73; Islamic schools 65; middle-class normativity 71–2; national legislative and policy context 66–8; new directions 73; research on 69–72; school choice 65; teacher attitudes towards parents 70; teacher education and school reform 70–1; teacher professionalism 72; terminology 66; uninvolved parents, exclusion of 72
non-privileged parents 25, 27–9
non-public-government-funded schools, in Netherlands 66–7
normative discourse, parental involvement in Germany 26
Norway, parental involvement in 3, 77; communication between home and school 82, 83; Coordinating Committee *(SU Samarbeidsutvalget)* 81; Education Act 77, 79, 80, 86; education system 77–8; home–school cooperation 78, 80–1, 83–6; National Council for Teacher Education 84; National Framework Plan for Teacher Education 84; National Guidelines for Teacher Education 84, 85; national legislative and regulative context 79–80; parent cooperation 79–80; parent representatives 80–1; Parents Working Committee *(FAU Foreldrerådets: arbeidsutvalg)* 81;

Post-Graduate Certificate of Education (PGCE) 84; practice teaching 85; relationship between teachers and parents 82–3; research on 82–3; teacher education 83–4; terminology 78–9; university colleges 84

Oakley, A. 166
Office of The Ombudsman for Children 38–9
Ofsted (the Office for Standards in Education, Children's Services and Skills) 152
Organisation for Economic Co-operation and Development (OECD) 1, 3, 4, 196, 199

parental effects on achievement, in lower secondary education 140–6; data and method 140–1; findings 141–5; gain in achievement **142**, 143; independent variables 141; multinomial regression of school track assignment **144**; Nagelkerke model fit 143; parental SES 140
parental involvement 1; in European countries 2; from feminist perspective 7; national background of 3, 4; pedagogical justification for 4; policy challenges 4; research on 2; school's perspective on 15; and social inequality 14–15 *see also individual countries*
Parental Involvement in Schools in Different National Contexts: Future Challenges for Practice and Research 5
parental socio-emotional support 69
parenthood, overprotecting 109–15; data and methodology 109–10; home-based involvement 110–14, **111**; school-based involvement 114–15
parenting 13, 15, 67, 87, 152–3, 171, 195; child-rearing to 24; family literacy and 51; gendered 162; helicopter parenting 170; notion of 167; over-parenting 108, 116
parentocracy 167
parent organisations 40
parents: as accountable 53; as actors 21, 25, 26; as choosers 51–2; as clients 25, 26, 199; as consumers 25, 51–2, 126–7, 130, 152; Cypriot, attitudes 14; involvement in schools 13–14; as learners 51, 53; as opponents 25; as partners 21, 49, 52–3, 67, 71, 86, 87; as primary caregivers 135; relationship between teachers and 16–17; as stakeholders 96; as supporters 25, 86; teacher attitudes towards 70; tensions between schools and 72; typologies of 70
*Parents and Teachers: Power and Participation* (Vincent) 155
*Parents as Partners in Education* 53
parents' association (PA) 14, 52, 54–5; in Ireland 52, 54–5; at national level 12; in Portugal *93*, 93–4, 97; at regional level 11–12; at school level 11
*Parents' Charter* 152
Parent–Student Charters 53
Parent-Teacher Association (PTA) 26
participation 81, 122; family involvement and 90–101; formal 92, 99, 100; informal 92, 99; parental 4, 6, 23, 25, 38, 69, 78, 81, 106, 135, 152, 197; parents' councils 106–7; in school 10, 13, 68; school councils 106, 107; teenagers' opinions on parents' 43–4
partnership 4, 14, 82, 101, 106,153, 154; charters and 52–3; educational 23, 24; home–school 26; for parents 53; school–family 66, 71, 72, 73, 96–100
Payet, J.-P. 137
pedagogy and pupil related skills 85–6
PGCE *see* Post-Graduate Certificate of Education (PGCE)
Phtiaka, H. 14
PIRLS *see* Progress in Reading Literacy Study (PIRLS)
Plowden report 152
Portugal, family involvement in 3, 4, 90; decentralisation process 90; early childhood care and education system 91; education system 90–1; families choosing school 93; guardian 91, 92; legislative discourse 100–1; 2005 modernisation project 91; research on 95–6; school–family relationship 91–100; school principals 101
power, concept of 24
PPA *see* Preschools Playgroup Association (PPA)
Preschools Playgroup Association (PPA) 167
Primary and Lower Secondary Education Act of 1969 79

primary schools 59, 180, 186, 198; Cyprus 9, 12, 15; Germany 22, Iceland 49–50, 53;Ireland 49–51, 54, 55, 59; Netherlands 64, 65, 66, 68; Portugal 91; Sweden 120, 123, 128; Switzerland 133, 136, 137, 140; United Kingdom 149, 150, 152, 156–8, 166
private schools: Germany 22, 23, 25; Netherlands 65; Norway 78; Portugal 91, 93; Slovenia 105; Switzerland 134
privileged parents 28, 29
professional education and training course (PET) 134
Progress in Reading Literacy Study (PIRLS) 60, 177, 180, 184
Punter, R.A. 176, 177, 184

rational choice theory 138
Reay, D. 152, 153, 170
research, parental involvement: Cyprus 13–15; Germany 26–32; Iceland 40–1; Ireland 53–5; Netherlands 69–72; Norway 82–3; Portugal 95–6; Slovenia 107–9; Sweden 122–4; Switzerland 136–40; United Kingdom 154–7
research questions 4–5; diverse education systems 6; empirical discourse 6; key challenges 5–6; language 6; policy discourse 6; research fields 6; terminology 5
Ribbens, J. 168–9
Riley, D. 167

Sales, R. 156
school-based parental involvement 29; empirical results for 29–32; parenthood, overprotecting **114**, 114–15
School Board 39
school-centred parental involvement 138
school–family–community partnerships 66
school–family partnerships 66, 73; teacher competences for 71
school–family relationship 10, 17–18, 90–100; Administrative Council 94; Class Councils 94–5, 98, 100; context and research questions 96–8; familiar involvement 100; families as partners and stakeholders 100; family representatives 99; formal participation 99, 100; formal relationships 11–12; General Council 94, 98, 99; influences on 97; informal relationships 12–13;

involvement 92; legislative change in 92–5; main results 98–100; methodology and data collection 98; morphogenetic cycle 97; parental freedom of school choice 95; parents' associations 11–12, *93*, 93–4, 97; parents' weekly visiting period 12; Pedagogical Council 94; reasons for promoting 95; research on 95–6, 101; responsibilities of families 94; scholarly involvement 99–100; socioeconomic background on 95–6; between teachers and families 92; terminology 91–2; theory of structuration 97
school newsletters 157–8
Schwanenberg, J. 27
secondary schools: Germany 22; Iceland 37; Ireland 50; Netherlands 65, 66; Norway 77–8
second-wave feminism 165 see B.H. 158
SEN see special educational needs (SEN)
Simão, V. 92
single-sex schooling 52
Slovenia, parental involvement in 3, 4, 104–5; education system 105; familialisation 116; GOETE (Governance of Educational Trajectories in Europe) 104–5; identity capital 109; individualism and competitiveness 112; intra-class differentiation 109; national legislative and regulative context 106–7; overprotecting parenthood 109–15; parental cooperation with school 106–7; parental good intentions 113–14; parents' councils 106–7; politicisation of parenthood 116; relationship between parents/guardians and school 106, 108; research on 107–9; school councils 107; socialisation patterns 108; social-liberal policy 108; *sodelovanje* 106; terminology 106
Smit, F. 70
Smyth, E. 51
social inequality, parental involvement: Cyprus 14–15; Switzerland 138–9
special educational needs (SEN) 53
special schools 9, 22, 37, 50
Stambach, A. 170
state schools 9, 12, 22, 91–3, 95, 100, 105, 134

Sweden, parental involvement in 3, 120–1, 129–30; Budget Bill 128; Centre for Mathematics 127; Education Act 122; education system 120–1; Foundation for Homework Support 128; home-school collaboration 121–2; homework support 124–9; middle-class parents' involvement 124; National Agency for Education 120–2; national legislative and regulative context 121–2; non-profit organisations 130; parental involvement in schools 123; parents' choice of schools 123; parent–teacher–student conference 122, 123, 129; research on 122–4; Parliamentary Tax Committee 127; Proposition (2006/07:94) 126; Swedish Education Act 122, 124; Swedish National Agency for Education 122; terminology 121

Switzerland, parental involvement in 3, 133, 145; cantonal law 135, 136; child-centred parental involvement 138; cooperation between parents and teachers 135–7, 145; education, counselling and support for parents 139; education system 133–4; effects of family on student motivation 138; empirical research 136–7; home-based parental involvement 138; municipal school authority 136; national legislative and regulative context 135–6; parental effects on achievement 140–6; school and family, functional aspects of 137; school career decision-making 136; school career, effects of family on 138–9; school-centred parental involvement 138; social inequality 138–9; Swiss Civil Code 135; teachers for collaboration with parents 139–40; terminology 134–5

teachers: attitudes towards parents 70; conceptions of families and parents 15–16; education and school reform 70–1; education in Norway 83–4, 86, 87; professionalism 72; relationship between parents and 16–17

*Teaching and learning in Icelandic compulsory schools* project 41

teenagers, on parental involvement 43–4

Thatcher, M. 152

Thijs, J. 87

TIMSS *see* Trends in International Mathematics and Science Study (TIMSS)

*TIMSS 2015 International Results in Mathematics* 182

Tóth, I.G. 3

Trends in International Mathematics and Science Study (TIMSS) 60, 175–7; academic socialisation 177–8; analytical framework of 187; assessment framework 180–1; average student outcome in mathematics *179*; context questionnaire 180; description of available data 178; design of 176; early literacy and numeracy activities 180–1; estimation strategy 181–2; framework 176, 177; help with homework scale 180; home-based parental involvement 188; home questionnaire 179, 180, 188; home resources for learning 176, 180, 182, **183**, 188; homework on learning achievement 184; IEA's 176, 181; parental attitude towards mathematics and science 181, 187; parental checks on homework 184–5; perceptions of school performance scale 181; question, parents response to 185; school attendance 180, 186; student outcome in mathematics 181

Tyrell, H. 25

UNESCO's Global Education Monitoring Report 188

United Kingdom, parental involvement in 3, 149, 159, 162; Brexit referendum 156; Bullock Report 152; childcare programmes for preschool children 166–7; Childminders Act of 1948 167; children with special needs 151; compulsory schooling 162, 165; Daphne programmes 171; Education Act (1944) 165; Education Endowment Foundation 155; *The Education Reform Act* 152; Education Scotland 152; education systems in 149–51; Effective Provision of Pre-school Education 154–5; Equalities Act (2010) 166; Equal Pay Act (1975) 166; *Excellence in Schools* 153; feminist analysis of 162–6, 172; *Feminist Dilemmas In Qualitative Research; Public Knowledge And Private Lives* 169; *A Feminist Manifesto for Education* 163; first-wave feminism 164–5; gender equality 164; gender norms 172; gender-related violence 171; General Certificates of Secondary Education 150, 156; higher education 157, 164, 170; independent ('fee-paying') education 151; LGBTQi relations 162–3; misogyny rules 163–4; national legislative and regulative context 151–4; National Parent Forum of Scotland 153; New Right 167; 'one-size fits all' approach 155; parental influence on educational outcomes 156; parenting 152–3; parentocracy 167; parent-teacher contact 151–2; pedagogies of gender & sexualities 171–2; realities of mothering and schooling 168; research on 154–7; *Rewriting the Future* 154; school newsletters 157–8; Scotland, non-statutory curriculum 150; Scottish Schools (Parental Involvement) Act 153; secondary school choice 169–70; sex and relationships education 171; social inequalities 154; socio-political and economic developments 164–5; standardised assessment tests 150; terminology 151; UK National Curriculum 150; UK Nurseries 167; Wales, standardised assessment tests 150

Vandenbroeck, M. 24
van der Wolf, K 70
VAWG *see* violence against women and girls (VAWG)
VET school 134
Vincent, C. 155, 156
Violence (GRV) 171–3
violence against women and girls (VAWG) 163, 164, 171, 173
Vygotsky, and socio-cultural theories 55

West, A. 169, 170
Westergård, E. 82
White Paper (1995) 105
Willms, J.D. 184
Wippermann, K. 27
working with parents *(Elternarbeit)* 23–4, 68

Printed in the United States
By Bookmasters